THE HISTORY OF THE

IRISH

BRIGADE

A COLLECTION OF HISTORICAL ESSAYS

69th New York

Edited by
Pia Seija Seagrave, Ph.D.

Copyright 1997

Published & Distributed by
Sergeant Kirkland's Museum
and Historical Society, Inc.
912 Lafayette Blvd., Fredericksburg, Virginia 22401-5617
Tel. (540) 899-5565; Fax: (540) 899-7643
E-mail: Civil-War@msn.com

Manufactured in the USA
The paper in this book meets the guidelines for permanence and
durability of the Committee on Production Guidelines for Book
Longevity of the Council on Library Resources, Inc.

Library of Congress Cataloging-in-Publication Data

The History of the Irish Brigade: A Collection of Historical Essays /
Edited by Pia Seija Seagrave, Ph.D., Compiled and Introduction by
Phillip T. Tucker, Ph.D.
      p.   cm.
      Includes bibliographical references and index.
      ISBN 1-887901-03-5 (sc : alk. paper)
1. United States. Army of the Potomac. Irish Brigade. 2. United States–
History--Civil War, 1861-1865 – Participation, Irish American. 3. Irish
Americans – History--19th Century. 4. United States – History – Civil
War, 1861-1865 – Campaigns. I.
E493 . 5 . I683   1997
980 . 03' 1--dc2O   95-45872
                                          CIP

Revised Edition

1 2 3 4 5 6 7 8 9 10

Cover illustration courtesy of Donna J. Neary, entitled *Do Your Duty, Boys --* Brigadier General Thomas Francis Meagher and the 69th New York Regiment in Fredericksburg, December 13, 1862. The first rays of light filter through the early morning fog, revealing ranks of men in blue drawn up along Water Street near the Fredericksburg city wharf. Columns of smoke rise from the burning town, and the rumble of cannons from the heights west of the city combines with the crash of shells to mark the dawn of a day of battle. It is December 13, 1862, and the soldiers of the Army of the Potomac's famed Irish Brigade ready themselves to storm the Confederate entrenchments on Marye's Heights. Lacking their war-torn Irish banners sent home for replacement, the men placed sprigs of boxwood in their caps to mark them with the green badge of Erin. Riding down the line of the 69th New York is their commander, the former Irish revolutionary Brigadier General Thomas Francis Meagher, "Meagher of the Sword," accompanied by Division Commander Winfield Scott Hancock. Cheer after cheer echoes through the streets, "...each man...aware of the great and terrible work before him."

HERITAGE STUDIO FINE ART GALLERY, 606 Caroline Street, Fredericksburg, VA 22401, (540) 374-1872, 669-1070.

This book is dedicated to
those who were
on the field
at
Fredericksburg
December 13, 1862

Mr. Joseph G. Bilby, in his *Remember Fontenoy! The 69th New York and the Irish Brigade in the Civil War*, writes, "Some of the Irish wounded received succor from Sergeant Richard Kirkland of the 2nd South Carolina (C.S.A.), who crawled out between the lines on the afternoon of December 14, 1862, with water for those Yankees who still survived." (Photo - Sergeant Kirkland's Museum and Historical Society)

Captain David Power Conyngham, Irish Brigade staff officer. (Courtesy Library of Congress)

CONTENTS

Editor's Remarks   IX

Introduction
Celtic Warriors in Blue   1
By Phillip T. Tucker, Ph.D.

CORCORAN AND
THE IRISH LEGION

Chapter I
**Colonel Michael Corcoran,
Fighting Irishman of
the Irish Brigade**   13
By Phyllis Lane

Chapter II
**The "Fighting" Sixty-Ninth
New York State Militia
at Bull Run**   35
By Christopher-Michael Garcia

THE IRISH BRIGADE

Chapter III
**Sprig of Green:
The Union Irish Brigade** 59
By Kevin E. O'Brien

Chapter IV
**The Irish Brigade
in the Wheatfield**   95
By Kevin E. O'Brien

Chapter V
**Colonel Richard Byrnes
Irish Brigade Leader**   119
By Barry L. Spink

Chapter VI
**Weapons of
the Irish Brigade**   177
By Joseph G. Bilby

Chapter VII
**The Green Flags
of the Irish Brigade**   183
By Barney Kelly

Contributors' Biographies 211

Bibliography   213

Index   215

Editor's Remarks

This second edition of *The History of the Irish Brigade* has several changes in it. There are grammatical corrections as well as substantial content rearrangement. For example, those chapters having to do with Corcoran and the Irish Legion are now arranged in the beginning of the book while those chapters concerning the various formations of the Irish Brigade comprise the latter portion of the essay selections. Additionally, the introduction has been tightened, editorially, and the whole of the book, including dust jacket and lay-out design, has been re-configured.

It is our hope that these emendations will improve the overall quality and visual appeal of this title, and that our readers will further enjoy the fascinating tale of the men, mission, and history of this famous unit, the Irish Brigade.

Pia Seija Seagrave, Ph.D.
Editor

Five Irish Brigade soldiers, including Catholic chaplains James Dillon (*seated, center*) and William Corby (*seated, right*), rest at a Virginia campsite in 1862. Many of the fighting Irishmen would die for a country that they had not yet had time enough to know.

Introduction

CELTIC WARRIORS IN BLUE

by Phillip Thomas Tucker, Ph.D.

The most colorful, uniquely ethnic, and culturally distinct combat brigade of the Civil War was the famous Irish Brigade. In fact, no brigade in the Civil War was more distinguished by its ethnic character and quality than the hard-fighting Irish Brigade of the Army of the Potomac. This crack brigade of Irish immigrants and Irish-Americans was also unique because the command was, seemingly, always hurled into the hottest part of the fray. Repeatedly, the elite Irish regiments of the Irish Brigade played key roles during some of the most decisive battles of the war, spearheading attacks and covering the retreats of the Army of the Potomac. These Catholics and Protestants, mostly common laborers, who hailed primarily from the large cities of the northeast, compiled one of the most impressive combat records of the Civil War.

In total, more than 4,000 Irish Brigade soldiers became casualties while fighting under the green flags of Erin. Taking unprecedented losses, even by the unprecedented standards of the Civil War, these young Irish soldiers fought and died to the jaunty Irish tune of *Garry Owen*, while struggling in the tradition of those inspirational Irish nationalists, patriots, and revolutionaries of Ireland's past conflicts against oppressors and invaders.

By any measure, no ethnic unit in the long history of America's wars has received more recognition than the Irish Brigade; the Celtic warriors in blue were a formidable fighting machine. Under the green flags of Ireland, made at Tiffany's in New York City and which were distinguished by gold Irish harps and such Gaelic fighting mottoes as "Who Never retreat from the clash of spears," the Irish Brigade achieved glory on battlefields across the South.

Based upon time-honored themes of Irish history, tradition, and culture, these symbolic battle flags were constant reminders to the Irish Brigade's soldiers that the "...green flag, with its ancient harp, its burst of sunlight, and its motto ... in the old Irish tongue, recalls, through the long lapse of many centuries, the period when Ireland was a nation, and conveys more eloquently than by words how that nationality was lost through the practical working of that doctrine of secession for which the rebellious States of the South have taken up arms." These Irish soldiers also maintained a unique distinctiveness, which separated them from their Army of the Potomac comrades via their "Irish cheer," memorable St. Patrick's Day festivities, the brass and silver emblems of the shamrocks and harps of Ireland, which were proudly worn on uniforms and hats.

Despite engaging in almost every major campaign of "Mr. Lincoln's Army" in the eastern theater, most of the Irish Brigade's legendary reputation for superior battlefield performances was earned primarily within only a three-month period. During the nightmarish fighting at Antietam, Maryland, on September 17, 1862, for instance, two New York regiments of the Irish Brigade lost more than sixty percent of their strength during the assaults at the Bloody Lane. Less than three months later, the slaughter continued as the Irish Brigade hurled itself into the terrible battle wall at Fredericksburg, Virginia.

By the third bloody summer of the war, the Irish Brigade added to its distinguished legacy by struggling furiously in "the Wheatfield," near Gettysburg. During, the following year, the Irish Brigade struck the Confederate forces at the Bloody Angle in Spotsylvania, Virginia, while fighting and dying in the mud, and rain.

The special calling and strange destiny of the hard-fighting Celtic soldiers of the Irish Brigade seemed to repeatedly draw this most colorful combat unit of the Civil War into the vortex of the fiercest battles in the East like a magnet. Year after year, the Irish Brigade's casualties were excessively high, matching the severity of battlefield challenges across three states.

The sacrifices made by the Irish on the battlefields of Virginia, Maryland, and Pennsylvania were not in vain. In many ways, the Irish Brigade soldiers in their core units -- the 63rd, 69th, 88th New York; 29th and, eventually the 28th Massachusetts; and the 116th Pennsylvania Volunteer Infantries -- died so that Irish immigrants and Irish-Americans would be more readily accepted by Americans.

More than for the abstract principles of saving the Union, these Celtic soldiers were fighting, most of all, for their own futures and for an

America which did not segregate, persecute, and discriminate against Irish people and their Catholicism, culture, and distinctive Celtic heritage, as did the hated English in the old country. By the time of the Civil War, their adopted nation in the New World had not fulfilled its promises to the Irish people in the North; the Irish bluecoats were determined to force America to live up to its promises of equality for all people by proving their worth on the battlefield. Consequently, the Green Isle soldiers of the Irish Brigade were fighting not one but two wars, struggling on two fronts -- the battlefield and the home front -- to a degree unlike any other troops of the Civil War.

The Sons of Erin of General Thomas Francis Meagher's Irish Brigade were given an opportunity to prove their worth at an early date. The Celts' baptism under fire began with the 69th New York State Militia, which fought with distinction during the battle of First Bull Run, July, 1861, at Manassas, Virginia. Sustaining very heavy losses and Colonel Corcoran's capture, the 69th was mustered out of service. This unit never again served during the Civil War; however, it remains an active unit to this date. Many of its original members later joined the 69th New York Volunteer Infantry upon its formation thus imparting the heritage of the previous militia, and helping to form a foundation for the establishment of the "Irish Brigade." By the following summer, the tradition of hard fighting had continued for Irish Brigade members, during the blood-bath of the Seven Days, and at Fair Oaks, Gaines' Mill, Savage Station, and Malvern Hill, Virginia. The Irish Brigade's fighting prowess and superior performances on battlefields across Virginia became legendary before the end of 1862. The demands of these battlefield challenges transformed the Celtic command into an elite unit at an early date. This early reputation for reliability and hard fighting capabilities resulted in the Irish Brigade's being used continuously by the Army of the Potomac's commanders for the greatest battles in the bloody years ahead.

Year after year, the Irish were repeatedly employed in leading roles in both offensive and defensive operations for the Army of the Potomac. One role of the Irish Brigade was to cover the army's withdrawal after the slaughter at Malvern Hill. There, on July 1, 1862, the Irishmen in blue battled the Louisiana Irishmen in gray during their own, personal, fratricidal conflict on Virginia soil. That was the forgotten Civil War, and a constant source of grief among the Irish on both sides.

Brigadier General Thomas Francis Meagher regarded his New York "Irish Brigade" as a symbol of Irish glory rather than as a unit of the U.S. Army. On July 1, 1867, during a drunken spree near Fort Benton, Montana, he is presumed to have fallen from the deck of a steamboat into the Missouri River under rather mysterious circumstances and was drowned. His body was never recovered. (Sergeant Kirkland's Museum and Historical Society)

The Irish Brigade's supreme moment came on a cold day at Fredericksburg, Virginia; no member of the hard-fighting unit would ever forget December 13, 1862, when the folly of "attack and die" tactics was again demonstrated as 1,300 Irishmen gallantly charged across the open fields before the high ground overlooking the town. Charging forward with precision and the green battle-flag of the 28th Massachusetts waving under the pale sky, the Irish warriors surged across the killing fields before the imposing Marye's Heights. The sons of Erin attacked, while wearing green sprigs of boxwood in their blue kepis; the Irishmen were coming straight at the Confederates.

In the words of an awed Midwestern Yankee, the Celtic warriors charged up the slopes "...in glorious style, their green sunbursts waving. Every man had a sprig of green in his cap, and a half-laughing, half-murderous look in his eye" during the suicidal assault against the impregnable Marye's Heights. In yet another gallant, but futile, effort, the Irish Brigade lost more than forty percent of its strength during the butchery before the terrible stone wall of Fredericksburg. The spirited attack and sad decimation of the Irish Brigade reportedly caused General Robert E. Lee to exclaim, "Never were men so brave." An Irish Brigade officer penned a gloomy letter about the slaughter at Fredericksburg, writing "...as for the Brigade, may the Lord pity and protect the widows and orphans of nearly all those belonging to it!"

Nearly five hundred and fifty Irishmen fell during the charge at Fredericksburg. Some Emerald Islanders reached the wall of death in the futile bid against the position on high ground. The victorious Confederates could readily identify those bluecoats who had fallen nearest to the stone wall, from the sprigs of boxwood in their caps.

On battlefields across the South, the mere sight of the flapping battle-flags of the Irish Brigade at the head of the charge was enough to cause some of the Confederacy's best troops to lament, "Here comes that damned green flag again." The fighting prowess of the Irish Brigade was reported to have caused Stonewall Jackson to curse out loud for, perhaps, the only time during the war. According to legend, Jackson paid an ultimate compliment by calling the Irish regiments "that damn Brigade." While before the assembled ranks of the Irish Brigade, President Abraham Lincoln proclaimed, with emotion, "God Bless the Irish Flag!"

Strong and unbending faith in Catholicism was a key factor in partly explaining the superior battlefield performances of the Irish Brigade. The best-known example of the importance of religious faith to fortify the resolve of Irish Brigade troops was Father William Corby, the chaplain of the 88th New York Infantry, while on the bloody field of Gettysburg. Standing atop a boulder, overlooking the bowed heads of hundreds of Irish warriors in blue, and the Irish flags of green, the young Order of the Holy Cross priest gave the absolution in Latin to the silent and kneeling soldiers, both Protestant and Catholic. While under fire and immediately before marching into the raging storm of Gettysburg, the Irish Brigade's members were spiritually prepared by Chaplain Corby to face the challenge at the Wheatfield. During this memorable absolution under fire, the inspiring words of the esteemed chaplain helped to reconfirm the common soldiers' faith in God, themselves, and the future destiny of the Irish people in America. Father Corby, bearded and in a long, black, ceremonial robe at Gettysburg, later explained the important role that religion played in terms of motivating the Celtic soldiery, when writing about how the Irish Brigade consisted of "…a body of about 4,000 Catholic men marching -- most of them -- to death, but also to the glory of their Church and country."

The stories of distinctive Irish units in armies around the world have been well-known throughout the annals of military history. As expatriate fighters, with unmatched fighting spirit and prowess, the Irish compiled legendary combat records around the world. For these expatriates, foreign service offered escape from the oppression, poverty, and humiliation of British rule in Ireland. Regardless of which country and leader they served, what these Irish units had in common was a mutual struggle for freedom and liberty, which was identical to Ireland's historic struggle against British domination. This was especially true throughout the nineteenth century as the Irish participation in various conflicts grew with the rise of revolutionary and nationalist movements around the world, beginning with the American Revolution.

The contribution of the Irish to American independence was important. It began when a patriotic Irishman was killed during the Boston Massacre, setting the stage for a sizable Irish contribution to the war effort. Three Ireland-born delegates signed the Declaration of Independence in Philadelphia, Pennsylvania, in 1776. Without exaggeration, General Sir Henry Clinton lamented, to his superiors in London, in 1778 how "…the emigrants from Ireland are in general to be looked upon as our most serious antagonists." The number of Irish who fought in George Washington's Continental army was in the thousands. In fact, the Continental Line -- the backbone of Washington's revolutionary army -- was described as "the Line of Ireland." The French army, which laid siege to British-held Savannah, Georgia, in 1779, contained an Irish Brigade. In addition, hundreds of Irishmen fought in the colonial navy under John Paul Jones and other naval commanders.

In France, during 1803, Napoleon Bonaparte ordered the formation of an Irish Legion. During an impressive ceremony, Napoleon presented the green flag of Ireland to his Irish Legion in preparation for the invasion of Ireland in conjunction with his invasion of England. Throughout Napoleon's army, Irish soldiers won a reputation for superior discipline and fighting qualities.

Thousands of freedom-loving Irishmen also flocked to the armies of Generals Jose de San Martin and Simon Bolivar, who had fought wars of liberation in order to overthrow the oppressive rule of Spain and Portugal in South America. With obvious pride and a clear understanding of this historical tradition of fighting against foreign domination and oppression, Father William Corby explained, in his *Memoirs of Chaplain Life*, "...no wonder the Irish soldier is so renowned, since he springs from a fearless race, whose valor has been tested in a war that was incessant for three hundred years, with the Danes and Normans, followed by contests, more or less fierce, for centuries, with England."

The real significance of the story of the Irish Brigade is much more than that of the narrowly-focused military role, which has been emphasized and popularized by generations of historians. Ironically, the dramatic battlefield roles and achievements of the hard-fighting Irish have only served to obscure the real meaning behind the struggles of the famous Irish Brigade, which lies forgotten under the glorified and romanticized shroud of these well-publicized accomplishments and sacrifices. For generations, historians have focused their attention almost exclusively on the military aspects of the Irish Brigade, while overlooking the larger implications of the importance and the real meaning of its fighting and sacrifice at Malvern Hill, Antietam, Fredericksburg, Gettysburg, Spotsylvania, and at other battlefields across the South. Most of all, the significance of the Irish Brigade can best be understood in the overall context of the story of America and the struggle of the ethnic immigrant to fulfill its elusive dream and promise.

Thomas Waterman Wood's *Return of the Flags of the Irish Brigade*. This engraving of the original oil painting, held by the West Point Museum, shows the bullet-riddled Irish colors as they were returned to New York City at the close of the war. (Sergeant Kirkland's Museum and Historical Society.)

What the hard-fighting soldiers of the Irish Brigade demonstrated to the nation was that the immigrant -- despite prejudice and against hostility and ignorance towards him -- could, eventually, earn a measure of equality in American society as promised by the United States' Constitution. Hundreds of Irishmen dying on the battlefields of the South proved to an unconvinced and racist America, that Irish immigrants and Irish-Americans were worthy of respect, equality, and citizenship.

Indeed, the Irish immigrants in blue uniforms were motivated by the hope that America was where their dreams would become reality as promised by their vision of America. Earning equality on the battlefield would then open the doors to greater equality and acceptance on the home front. Hence, the Celts of the Irish Brigade were fighting for more than high bounties, personal glory, or the abolishment of slavery. Most of all, these men were struggling for their own futures and for relief for the oppressed people of both Ireland and America. In addition, the Irish also viewed this struggle in ideological terms. One member of General Meagher's staff, David Power Conyngham, wrote, "...the Irish felt that not only was the safety of the great Republic, the home of their exiled race, at stake, but, also, that the great principles of democracy were at issue with the aristocratic doctrines of monarchism. Should the latter prevail, there was no longer any hope for the struggling nationalists of the Old World."

In many ways, these Celts of the Irish Brigade were also fighting for the equality of other oppressed people in America, regardless of religion or ethnicity. Ironically, in the world's greatest democracy, this egalitarian concept had been fiercely resisted by the antebellum, Nativist movement of a hostile, Protestant America. Therefore, the Irish Brigade's struggle was also on behalf of other immigrants as well. Thousands of Germans, Poles, French, Swedes, Hungarians, Italians, and other immigrants in the ranks of the Army of the Potomac intently watched the progress of the Celts of the Irish Brigade. These foreign warriors in blue knew that the success of the Irish Brigade was closely linked with their own struggle for equality in America. If the Irish could win respect and equality both on the battlefield and at home, then so could they. These bluecoat soldiers believed that superior battlefield accomplishments would help to improve the lives of ethnic people in cities across the Northeast. Clearly, much was at stake in regard to the performance of the Irish Brigade from 1862-65. Hence, the Irish Brigade was an "experiment" in terms of the immigrant warrior's ability to successfully rise to challenges on the battlefield, and served as a test case for the qualification of equality.

Clearly, the soldiers of the Irish Brigade were fighting for much more than themselves. Some sons of Erin were struggling primarily for Ireland. This fact represents yet another forgotten aspect of the story of the Irish Brigade's struggle because these men were, in part, fighting for a land thousands of miles from America. The officer corps of the Irish Brigade contained several of the core leaders and many followers of the Fenian Movement. The Fenians' goal was the liberation of Ireland by forcefully breaking British shackles.

Because so many of the Celtic soldiers of the Irish Brigade were illiterate immigrants from the Emerald Isle, relatively few letters or diaries were written during the war, and even fewer have survived today. In addition, few books and memoirs by Irish Brigade members were published after the war. Consequently, much of the historical record of the Irish Brigade has not been based upon primary source material, leaving a gap in Civil War historiography. Often, what little has been published on the Irish Brigade by historians, popular writers, and academic presses has been mostly glorified, romanticized, and embellished. As a result, a romantic lore and mythology has continued to wrap a shroud around the men and history of the Irish Brigade, obscuring the real significance, role, and meaning of the Irish Brigade's struggle and its proper place in history. No brigade in the annals of Civil War historiography has been more fabled than the Irish Brigade, resulting in more fiction than fact.

Despite its distinguished history and today's soaring interest in the Civil War , the Irish Brigade has garnered relatively little accurate recognition from historians. The Irish Brigade's struggle on a multi-front war and other aspects of its history have remained one of the forgotten chapters of the Civil War. This is especially ironic since the Irish Brigade was, perhaps, the most colorful, popular, and recognizable unit of the Civil War. Indeed, the full significance of the Irish Brigade's role in the conflict continues to be ignored and overlooked by many of today's most respected Civil War historians.

Because the Irish Brigade is yet somewhat of an enigma and a mystery to the American public, this work has been dedicated to presenting a comprehensive and analytical look at its story, including analyses of the battles, leaders, weapons, motivations, and personal struggles of the Irish. This close look at the men, missions, and history of the Irish Brigade has not been based upon out dated, romanticized, or inaccurate secondary source material, but upon extensive modern research of primary source material by leading Irish Brigade scholars and experts. In using this modern approach, the roles, accomplishments, and significance of the Irish

Brigade and of the Celtic warriors in blue have been explored and analyzed more thoroughly, in more detail, and to a greater extent than ever before.

Most importantly, another purpose of this study has been to shed new light on previously unexplored aspects of the Irish Brigade in the hope of breaking down the many, time-worn, negative stereotypes of Irish soldiery and character. These stereotypes, which helped fuel the anti-Catholic, anti-immigrant, and anti-Irish movements of the 1850s, have generalized the Irish as irresponsible, drunk, immoral, criminal, etc., ideas that served as excuses to justify their status as second-class citizens. Unfortunately, some of these generalized views of the Irish character persist to this day. Because these degrading stereotypes continue to thrive, a central objective of the work has been to expose these myths by proving that the Celtic warriors of the Irish Brigade consisted primarily of a moral, spiritual, and determined soldiery who were not unlike fellow Americans. The noble efforts, accomplishments, and sacrifices of the Irish Brigade's soldiers to prove this undeniable reality to America explains why they fought so hard and valiantly on battlefields across the South.

THE IRISH LEGION

MICHAEL CORCORAN
THE SOUL OF THE
69TH New York State Militia

Thomas Francis Meagher said it just right, as usual, when he thanked Heaven that there were men like Michael Corcoran who would assert their independence, stand erect and intractable in their integrity, and do and say what they believe is right even though they stand alone. General Meagher was referring to Corcoran's principled conduct during the Prince of Wales affair, one of many events that revealed and proved his character. Honorable as a man, fearless in adversity, steady under fire, Mchael Corcoran begot the soul of the 69th New York State Militia, which mustered out at New York City on August 3, 1861.

Chapter I

Colonel Michael Corcoran Fighting Irishman

by Phyllis Lane

Three passions sparked Michael Corcoran's life during his pre-war years as an immigrant New Yorker: politics, the 69th New York State Militia, and the liberation of Ireland. When war finally broke out in 1861, volunteers, North and South, rallied to serve their country in the best way they could. Corcoran's military genes prevailed and the events that followed brought him renown as an immigrant patriot.

Those genes came from Ireland, at least as far back as his mother's ancestor Patrick Sarsfield, the Earl of Lucan.[1] A brigadier general in the army of King James II, he was the most beloved Irish leader of his day.[2] Corcoran's father, too, was an officer in the British army, serving in the West Indies during the early part of the nineteenth century.

Michael Corcoran was born to Mary McDonagh and Thomas Corcoran in 1827 at Carrowkeel, the McDonagh family estate in Sligo. He attended a local school, one of the early national schools that provided a small, but growing, number of Irish children with a surprisingly sophisticated English education.[3] Being a British subject, Corcoran took an oath to uphold the Crown in Ireland when he received an appointment to the revenue police in early 1846.[4] That specialized, quasi-military, police force was charged with hunting and arresting outlaw distillers.[5] It was violent

---

[1] Habitually asserted but as yet unproved, this genealogical claim might, indeed, be true. Ongoing research continues to uncover convincing evidence.

[2] Piers Wauchope, *Patrick Sarsfield and the Williamite War* (Dublin: Irish Academic Press, 1992), 1.

[3] *The Irish-American* [New York] 22 June 1861: 1; Samuel Lewis, *Topographical Dictionary of Ireland* vol. 1 (1837; Baltimore: Genealogical Publishing Co., Inc., 1984) 599; Donald H. Akenson, *The Irish Education Experiment* (London: Routledge & Kegan Paul, 1970) 227-239. Corcoran completed his schooling at age 18, *New York Herald*, Dec. 24, 1863: 8.

[4] Terence O'Rorke, *The History of Sligo: Town and County* Vol. 2 (Dublin, [1890?]) 532-533.

[5] Robert B. McDowell, *The Irish Administration 1801-1914* (London: Routledge & Kegan Paul, 1964) 138-139.

work; these moonshiners were gangs of hard men, armed and murderously protective of their still operations. Deadly resistance to arrest was returned in kind.

Corcoran was stationed at Creeslough in Donegal.[6] He carried out his law enforcement duties while England benignly neglected the effects of a persistent potato blight in Ireland. He watched his countrymen eat their livestock and seed potatoes when their larders were empty, then go hungry because they had nothing more to eat or to plant; they became impoverished because they had nothing to sell, and, finally -- malnourished, weak and unable to work – they were homeless. He saw infectious diseases kill the starving who had no means to immigrate, spotting the hilly coastal landscape with skeletal corpses and desolate survivors. Famine began to slash the population.

For two years, Private First Class Corcoran did his job, kept his eyes open, and felt growing revulsion. That feeling swelled and festered until it burst open one night in 1848, transformed into tangible outrage.

Michael Corcoran joined the Ribbonmen, a loose-knit society of rural guerrillas that had existed in Ireland since the previous century.[7] This covert brotherhood of night riders harassed ruthless landlords and their agents, and self-serving scab tenants. Organized into small, anonymous circles, phantom men slipped through the darkness to burn barns and haystacks, to hamstring cattle, to shoot out windows -- and worse.

Those were attention-getting acts of protest against a disdainful government, demonstrations of sympathy for compatriots, and terrorist signs of smoldering nationalism. If arrested, Queen's Men who were also Ribbonmen would not be indulged with second chances. Corcoran led a double life for about a year before he came under suspicion, which prompted his sorrowful and permanent exit from Ireland.[8]

Michael Corcoran landed in New York City on a rainy October day in 1849, just another famine immigrant.[9] He was homesick and his pockets were empty, but, nonetheless, he was energized by heartfelt gratitude for the opportunity to improve his position in life, as well as by contempt

---

[6] Revenue Police in Ireland records, London, Public Record Office reference CUST 111/9 f87.
[7] *The Irish-American*, Jan. 2, 1864: 2; John O'Leary, *Recollections of Fenians and Fenianism* vol. 1 (London, 1896) 112.
[8] Revenue Police, London PRO ref. CUST 111/10 f64. This record states that Corcoran was "relinquished"; the term may also mean "resigned" or "terminated."
[9] Passenger Lists of Ships Arriving at New York, NY, reel *ZI 131, Oct. 1849: 1369 (microfilm, New York Public Library).

for the British government.[10] A born go-getter, he quickly found both a room and a job at Hibernian House, a tavern across the street from [Old] St. Patrick's Cathedral.[11]

It turned out to be a classic example of making the most out of something least: being a clerk in a bar in a slum. Corcoran, who wrote a fine hand and could keep the books, helped the proprietor, John Heaney, with the bar in the front room but, mostly, worked in the function room in the back.[12]

Hibernian Hall saw a lot of action. Ex-officer Corcoran began by keeping order at the dances, and by bouncing rowdies. As Mr. Heaney came to know and rely upon him, Corcoran scheduled and prepared for community meetings, planned and hosted club banquets, and supervised the room -- a Democratic district polling place -- on election day. Evidently, the regulars and other patrons of the establishment also thought well of Corcoran, because the opportunities he had so yearned for walked in through the door at 42 Prince Street.

People looked up to him (and not only because he was six feet, two inches tall and a sinewy 180 pounds) because Michael Corcoran was, at all times, a self-assured but modest young gentleman, calm and courteous, kind and dignified.[13] He was conscientious about details and efficient in his own work and life, and had a ready helping hand and encouraging words for others in theirs.[14] Somehow, it seems more complementary than contradictory that this same young man had once worked by day, taking part in official missions of arrest and execution, and then sped through the night, doing seditious mischief, as necessary. Corcoran had, truthfully, listed himself as a "farmer" when he embarked for America, for he grew up on the family farm. At the Hibernian House, he used his agrarian skills to perceive opportunities and to cultivate those he

---

[10] *New York Herald*, Aug. 23, 1862: 2; Michael Corcoran, *The Captivity of General Corcoran* (Philadelphia, 1862) 22 [2] (microfilm, NYPL). The pagination is frivolous: it begins with page 21, and also skips sequential numbers in three different places.

[11] *The Irish-American*, June 22, 1861: 1.

[12] Federal Population Census, 1850, New York City, Ward 14, ZI-109, reel 225, Aug. 31, 1850: 529 (microfilm, NYPL); *Doqqett's New York City Directory for 1850-1851* (microfilm, NYPL). Corcoran is listed with the Heaneys in the 1850 census, and the Heaneys are listed at 42 Prince Street in this directory. Corcoran was first listed in the 1852-53 directory, recorded as both working in the "ballroom" and living at 42 Prince Street.

[13] *The Irish-American*, Jan. 9,1864: 4. Corcoran had blue eyes, light auburn to brown hair, and a pale, clear complexion, (See *New York Herald*, 19 Aug. 1862: 5; *New-York Times*, Aug. 22 1862: 1; *New-York Daily Tribune*,Aug. 22 1862: 8; Aug. 23 1862: 1.)

[14] Michael Cavanagh, *Memoirs of Gen. Thomas Francis Meagher* (Worcester, 1892) 355-357 (from Meagher's eulogy of Corcoran); Alfred Ely, *Journal of Alfred Ely*, ed. Charles Lanman (New York: D. Appleton and Company, 1862) 222.

cherished. His most beloved sprouted first, and was so ordinary that no one could have predicted its celebrated future.

At that time, in the mid-nineteenth century, the American colonists' successful rebellion against Britain was still recent history. Militia readiness laws not only remained in effect but also had been amended after the war with Mexico (1846-1848). To be in compliance with them, groups of immigrants (supposedly citizens) often formed their own companies of "minutemen" because they were generally unwelcome in those of native Americans -- the sons of earlier immigrants of other ethnicity. Obviously, there were advantages to being with one's own kind, notably comradeship, recreation and the opportunity to demonstrate their collective loyalty to America (and perhaps their homeland as well).

Thus, in New York City in 1850, the first regiment of Irish-Americans was mustered into the service of the New York State Militia. Recruiting for another "Irish" regiment began and, by June, 1851, eight new companies had been organized. In August, a unit of thirty more men was added: Company I, the "Irish Rifles," including Private Michael Corcoran, and was captained by a wholesale dealer in groceries and liquors. Finally, in November, this second body of Irish-American New Yorkers was sworn into the state militia as the 69th Regiment, sixty-eight other statewide regiments having already been accepted.[15]

Michael Corcoran's busy life got busier. There was drill practice weekly, on Tuesdays at eight p.m. sharp -- not that he needed practice in the basics of his former profession. Benefit balls and social affairs were held during the winter of 1851-52 to help the men pay for their uniforms, which the state did not issue.[16] Corcoran fit into Company I like a glove; he was soon elected orderly sergeant and then first lieutenant.[17] Late in May, 1852, Thomas Francis Meagher, the dashing and eloquent "Meagher of the Sword," arrived in New York having escaped from exile in Tasmania. The 69th Regiment attended his reception as well as those of other fugitive Irish revolutionaries.

By that time, Corcoran's father had died and his mother had moved to New York. She lived in a room on Mott Street next to the cathedral, around the corner from Hibernian House. A rousing presidential campaign was underway that year and both national and local politics were

---

[15] *The Irish-American*, Aug. 9, 1851: 2; June 22, 1861: 1; Patrick Daniel O'Flaherty, "The History of the Sixty-Ninth Regiment of the New York State Militia 1852-1861," diss., Fordham Univ., 1963, 7.
[16] O'Flaherty 26-27.
[17] *The Irish-American*, June 22, 1861: 1.

hot; so was Hibernian Hall during the primaries and on Election Day in November.

More and more responsibilities descended upon the twenty-five-year-old Corcoran, who just kept reorganizing his schedule without missing a step. He ran the Hibernian House after Mr. Heaney fell ill in 1853, and stayed on as manager after Heaney died the following June.[18] That same month, Corcoran was commissioned captain of the Irish Rifles, now Company A, and Mary McDonagh Corcoran contracted cholera during an epidemic.[19] She died in July.[20] In October, 1854, Michael Corcoran became a naturalized citizen of the United States, abjuring particularly to the Queen of the United Kingdom of Great Britain and Ireland....[21]

Municipal elections were held that autumn; the Tammany Hall Democrats were aggressive, as usual, and successful. The Irish revolutionary movement was taking allegiance root in America, invigorated by power struggles, and attracted Michael Corcoran, a seasoned partisan. As an officer in the 69th, he spent more time supervising drills, organizing company affairs, and attending to paperwork. Somehow, he had also found the time to court and marry Mrs. Heaney's niece, Elizabeth.[22]

These were golden years. Corcoran had a job, a home, a wife, and the freedom to pursue his passions. His enthusiasm for them, and his competence and persistence, brought rewards: swift promotion in the 69th; growing respect and prominence in the cause of Irish liberation; and Tammany Hall proposal and support for his candidacy in district elections.

In light of the virulent anti-immigrant, know-nothing movement, that Tammany connection was noteworthy. It arose from Corcoran's position at 42 Prince Street. He was an able publican, listening to the needs of his regulars, making contacts, finding help for the needy. His widening

---

[18] John Heaney's Will, ms., New York City Municipal Archives, Surrogate's Court (1854) fiber 110, page 323.

[19] New York State, Adjutant General's Office, Annual Report, 1858 [Assem.. no. 184] (Albany, 1859) 152. Michael Corcoran: Capt. DOC 6/20/54, DOR 5/29/52 [54].

[20] Death Records, NYC Municipal Archives (1854) July 5, 1854; Calvary Cemetery, Woodside, NY, ts., burial record and letter to author, July 25, 1979.

[21] Naturalization Record, Court of Common Pleas for the City and County of New York, Federal Archives and Records Center, bundle 131, record 184.

[22] New York State Census of 1855, ms., NYC Municipal Archives, Ward 14, 2nd ed., 1st Div., #s 137, 138; *New York Herald*, Aug. 8, 1863: 8. That she was Mrs. Heaney's niece is inferred from the way Corcoran mentioned certain family members in several of his war-time letters, which were often published in local newspapers. The inferences were reinforced by addresses in the NYC directories, by remarks in some newspaper articles, and by a name in a census and property record. A long, thorough and persistent investigation did not turn up any marriage record.

reputation as a neighborhood leader made him valuable to the local politicos. Tammany was a real, mutual benefit society: it helped Corcoran and his people (with food baskets, buckets of coal, jobs and the like), and Corcoran and the grateful recipients delivered Irish votes.

Everything went smoothly until 1857, when the kinetic prosperity of the previous few years suddenly tripped and an ensuing financial panic caused widespread unemployment, especially in the North. Corcoran was able to keep the Hibernian House open and pay the bills by taking part-time jobs in two other taverns.[23] He also scored with the Irish rebels; as donations to support their Cause dwindled, to their annoyance and hindrance, he pressed even harder for contributions and helped to keep the funds dribbling in.

An outbreak of yellow fever the following summer led to the first activation of the 69th Regiment. People who had become ill were shipped over to the Quarantine Hospital on Staten Island, where the city confined patients who had certain infectious diseases. By September, the neighborhood residents could take no more of the decades-long immigrant pestilence in their midst, so a committee devised a way to end it: they torched the hospital.[24] The governor ordered out a detachment of local state militia. The 69th was not sent over until mid-October after the situation was under control (without injury); its mission was to relieve a unit doing guard duty.

The regiment's debut was soured by the bigoted refusal of a "native" American unit to associate in any way with the rabble Celts.[25] The 69th responded with civility and soldierly comportment and soon won its respect. There were no altercations and the regiment was deactivated after two weeks' reliable service. Company A had performed markedly well and the brigade inspector reported that Captain Corcoran deserved his reputation as "…the very best infantry officer in the Fourth Brigade…"[26]

A brigade inspector's commendation of a keeper of a low groggery meant nothing to uptown notes. They looked down their noses at men like Michael Corcoran, with his brogue and foreign surname. However, in his own circles he was rising like a newfangled gas balloon. In the December ward elections, he won one of the school inspector posts.[27] The following March, in 1859, he was sworn in as the military commander of

[23] *Trow's New York City Directory for the year ending May 1, 1858*, comp. H. Wilson (microfilm, NYPL).

[24] Henry G. Steinmeyer, *Staten Island 1524-1898* (Richmond/own: Staten Island Historical Society, 1950) 54-56.

[25] *New York Leader*, Oct. 30, 1858: 5.

[26] New York State, Adjutant General's Office, Annual Report, 1858 [Assem. no. 184], (Albany, 1859) 40.

[27] Election results, *New-York Times*, Dec. 23, 1858: 6.

the new Fenian organization (the American wing of the nationalist Irish revolutionary movement),[28] and, in August, he was elected colonel of the 69th New York State Militia.[29]

In just ten years Michael Corcoran had come far toward achieving his immigrant dream – to improve his position in life – but, to him, it was more of a foundation to build on. He had already quit one of his part-time jobs and, in June, 1860, could afford to quit the other when he was appointed to a well-paying patronage job in the post office, a Tammany Hall favor.[30]

It was a pivotal political year on several levels. An Illinois lawyer-politician sought the Republican nomination for president. "Let us have the faith that right makes might . . ." he urged when campaigning in New York City, standing firm against both the extension of slavery and the dissolution of the Union.[31] Northern and Southern Democrats could not agree on a candidate and split their party. For the first time, internationally, the Japanese emperor sent an official trade delegation to visit the United States, and a member of the British royal family scheduled a tour of the new, independent republic. The Prince of Wales, Queen Victoria's firstborn, would visit New York City in October.

Bureaucrats, businessmen and fluttering society doyennes planned a spectacular welcome for the nineteen-year-old future monarch, Prince Albert Edward. They would have a royal reception, a big parade with bands and flags, a grand ball, fireworks, and sightseeing around the metropolis. Well-connected, self-important Americans jostled each other for the limited invitations, lusting for the thrill and aggrandizement of being in a sovereign presence.

---

[28] *The Irish-American*, Nov. 29, 1862: 1; Sep. 9, 1862: 2.
[29] New York State, Adjutant General's Office, Annual Report, 1859 [Assem. no. 179], (Albany, 1860) 145. Elected 8/25/59, DOC 8/26/59.
[30] *Official Register of the United States* (Washington, DC, 1862) 467. Several references state that Corcoran worked in the city register's office and in the Custom House. Neither position can be verified. The city register's employee files for that period have been destroyed (personal communication), and Corcoran's name does not appear in the listing of clerks in the city register's office in the so-called *D. T. Valentine's Manual* (actually the Common Council's *Manual of the Corporation of the City of New York*), between 1851 and 1862. Corcoran's name was not found on the Custom House (or city register's office or county clerk's office) appointment lists in the Tammany records of the *Finance Committee of the Democratic Republican General Committee 1859-*(Manuscript Division, NYPL).
[31] The tenth annual National Women's Rights Convention also assembled in the Great Hall at Coooer Institute that year.

Colonel Michael Corcoran, 69th New York State Militia, before the Civil War. (Courtesy of the Massachusetts Commandery Military Order of the Loyal Legion and The U.S. Military History Institute.)

The 69th Regiment met and voted not to be in the parade. It would be a silent protest against England's disregard and exploitation of Ireland; they owed no salute to an heir who would someday be crowned King of England and Ireland.[32] Colonel Corcoran accepted their decision and took the heat for it. He simply declined to promulgate the order to march in the division parade that would pass in review to honor the prince. The notes attacked. Newspapers and magazines vilified him as the worst sort of ungrateful immigrant. Righteous taxpayers insisted upon his removal from the federal payroll. Vindictive chauvinists demanded his arrest and court martial -- and got it.[33]

Throughout the nation, all classes of native and immigrant Irish-Americans cheered and honored Michael Corcoran: from South Carolina, there came a gold-headed palmetto cane; from San Francisco, a one-pound gold medal for the regiment, to be worn by the colonel on public occasions; from fellow New Yorkers, an elegant, gold-ornamented sword.[34] Political backers elected Corcoran to the "imposing" Tammany Hall delegation that would attend the Democratic State Convention in Albany in early 1861.[35] For all of them, he was their voice, their champion, the defender of their heritage. He was also interim chief officer of the Fenians (the chief was in Ireland on Organization business).[36]

The 69th's colonel conducted himself with dignity during the early sessions of the court martial, before he came down with an illness that confined him to bed for several weeks. Then, in the pre-dawn hours of April 12, Charleston cannons began shelling the United States Army unit stationed at Fort Sumter. The new president, Lincoln, ordered the states' militia units to protect Washington. The 69th voted again, this time to help meet New York State's quota for the three months' service; Corcoran's court martial was dismissed. Barely out of a sick bed, he had just three days and three nights to fill and equip his beloved regiment and get it on the transport to Annapolis.

Justifiable or not, the trial that was meant to humiliate Corcoran and to be a stern lesson to all perfidious immigrants fizzled in a flag-waving, huzzahing parade down Broadway. The colonel rode in a carriage because he was too weak to ride his horse at the head of the march. And so, the 69th New York steamed out of New York Harbor on April 23, 1861,

---

[32] *New York Herald*, Oct. 18, 1860: 3.

[33] *Harper's Weekly*, Oct. 20, 1860: 658; *New-York Times* Oct. 23 1860: 4: Cavanach 354.

[34] *The Irish-American*, January 19, 1861: 3; Mar. 16, 1861: 2; Mar. 23, 1861: 3.

[35] Sidney David Brummer, *Political History of New York State During the Period of the Civil War* (New York: Columbia UP, 1911) 114-115.

[36] Cavanagh 370.

just eleven days after the hostilities began.[37] From colonel to private, many of them thought this service would also be good practice for their ultimate quest -- to invade and liberate Ireland.[38]

Intensified basic training occupied the regiment in its quarters at Georgetown College. Captain Thomas Francis Meagher arrived on May 23rd with his brand-new, fancy-dress company of Irish Zouaves, and with Colonel William T. Sherman of the regular United States Army. It was also election day for Virginians, who finally voted to secede from the Union. Colonel Corcoran and the other regimental commanders received orders to be ready to march at a moment's notice. Thirteen thousand Union troops advanced into Virginia in the early hours of May 24th.

The 69th bivouacked along the river bank until mid-day, when they were ordered to occupy Arlington Heights and to build a fort. It took just a week, working day and night, for these Irish laborers to construct Fort Corcoran. The entire ring of fortifications around Washington was finished none too soon. There was a striking force of eight thousand enemy soldiers within marching distance and reinforcements were on the way, all eager to defend their new nation. Sadly, countless Yankee and Confederate soldiers had friends and relations in the opposing army.

The Confederates foresaw a quick victory even though they had enlisted for one year. By early July, the Union volunteers looked forward to release from their obligation within a few weeks. Safely in New York, Horace Greeley's *Tribune* celebrated the Fourth of July by bleating "Forward to Richmond! Forward to Richmond" In truth, the North had no other choice. The regular army was undermanned and many of the earliest volunteers were getting restive, including some in the 69th. No pussy-footer, the colonel called the regiment to attention the next day and laid it out straight: none of them would leave until discharged by the government; furthermore, they were under marching orders; Thomas Francis Meagher was now acting major. And that was that.[39]

The brigade commander, Colonel Sherman, informed Corcoran that they would move out on July 16, and they did, part of a 35,000 man force, 33,000 of whom were green militiamen, one-third of whom had expected to be going home in a few days. Instead, five days later, on the 21st, a sultry Sunday morning, they entered into battle at Manassas, near a creek called Bull Run. By late afternoon, the reinforced Rebels had routed the

---

[37] They were among the first New York regiments to answer the president's call. The very first regiment, the Sixth Massachusetts, had left within twenty-four hours.

[38] Cavanagh 370-71; Charles J. Kickham letter, n.d., quoted in: John Rutherford, *The Secret History of the Fenian Conspiracy*, vol. 1 (London, 1877) 214 (microfiche, NYPL).

[39] *The Irish-American*, July 13, 1861: 2.

Yankees; Colonel Corcoran was wounded and captured during the retreat. The stunned Union survivors straggled back to Washington.

Three days later, exhausted and weakened by his leg injury, Corcoran lay in a Richmond tobacco warehouse and saw to the needs of his men -- those in hospital as well as those present. The prisoners were asked to accept parole, that is, to sign a document promising, on their honor, not to bear arms against the Confederacy if released. Corcoran refused: some did not.[40]

The officers, who were soon separated from the men, formed themselves into the Richmond Prison Association. A New York congressman, captured while looking for his militia constituents on the battlefield, was elected president and Corcoran was elected treasurer. The stated purpose of the group was the "improvement and entertainment of the members;" a Sanitary Committee was formed to regulate and supervise the cleanliness of their surroundings.[41]

Colonel Corcoran also took the position of spokesman. After a man was wounded, he demanded, successfully, that the prison commandant rescind the order to shoot prisoners who looked out of windows, which had no bars. Next, he lodged a complaint against the Richmond postal authorities who kept prisoners' mail in the post office for weeks, and then sometimes charged a postage due fee of up to two dollars .[42]

By early September, the prison authorities had to relieve the crowding, as well as the burden on their commissary, and, therefore, arranged for about half of the captives, including the trouble-makers, to be transferred to South Carolina. Colonel Corcoran was on the list. The train carrying the heavy-hearted citizen-soldiers rattled deeper into Rebellion, puffing into Charleston on September 14th. The next day, they were ferried to Castle Pinckney, a brick and stone fort on an island in the harbor. Corcoran and the other officers in his mess pooled the money they received in the mail to buy necessities for their men as well as themselves. Most of the enlisted men were poor to begin with and neither they nor their families could afford to buy shoes, clothing or blankets -- all essential during the coming winter.

After six weeks of breezy boredom, and Corcoran's thirty-fourth birthday, they were returned to Charleston and confined in the city jail, the only advantage being that it would be warmer than the drafty fort in the wind-blown harbor. Two weeks later, Colonel Corcoran was again

---

[40] *The Irish-American*, Aug. 10, 1861: 5; Oct. 26, 1861: 4.
[41] Ely 32-33, 100; Corcoran 28-29.
[42] Ely 25, 105; Corcoran 27, 29.

asked to accept parole -- instant freedom and a ticket to New York -- and again refused as he had done repeatedly, replying: "I believe that honor and patriotism alike forbid my doing so."[43] He had no way of knowing that it was his last chance.

The next day, a Rebel officer informed Colonel Corcoran, formally, that he had been chosen by lot for execution. He would be hanged as soon as the Confederate government learned that the Yankees had hanged a recently-convicted Southern privateer -- a pirate in the North's eyes. While awaiting his fate, he would be treated as a convicted felon. Thirteen more of the highest-ranking Yankee POWs had also been picked, by lot, to be held as death hostages should the North convict and hang thirteen other captured privateer/pirates. But Corcoran's death was imminent.[44]

Approaching footsteps indicated a summons to the scaffold. On November 19, a Rebel colonel walked up to Corcoran in the day room, refused to let him complete a letter he had been writing, and had him marched off to solitary confinement. The Yankee hostages were to be kept in the cells for condemned prisoners, in the unheated tower of the jail building.

A few days later, Colonel Corcoran awoke with a headache and, during the day, developed chills, fever and a general malaise. It was typhoid fever; he became so ill that the jailers took him out of solitary confinement and permitted two of his men to care for him. By the time Corcoran recovered three weeks later, his weight had dropped significantly.

On December 11, the next plague was fire.[45] Many of the guards ran out to fight the nearby blaze, which was spreading quickly in the wind. Dark smoke and embers swirled through the prison, and it seemed as though felons and POWs alike had been abandoned. Was Michael Corcoran to be roasted instead of hung? Neither, if he could help it. He and his caretakers made a rope out of bedding and let themselves out of a small, unbarred window in the room where he had been recuperating. They were spotted by guards, however, who, fortunately, assumed that their exit was simply an attempt to save themselves from the fire, not the escape it would have been.[46]

Everything in the grimy lockup, including the prisoners, was covered with reeking ashes. The air was thick and oily. Colonel Corcoran was dis-

---

[43] Corcoran 61.

[44] Corcoran 50-52, 72-73; Ely 210-219; New York Herald, Nov. 11, 1861: 5; New York Times, Nov. 15, 1861: 1; Nov. 19, 1861: 1, 4; Nov. 20, 1861: 3.

[45] New-York Times, Dec. 18, 1861: 1, 8.

[46] Corcoran 74 [75]-85; New-York Times, Dec. 24, 1861: 4.

couraged but not defeated, keeping hope alive with his passion for the 69th, and with his dreams of leading them into victorious battle.[47] Nevertheless, he wondered if 1862 would bring his execution as a hostage or exchange as a prisoner of war. On New Year's Eve the command came: he had to be ready to leave at dawn tomorrow, not to death or freedom but to the jail in Columbia, South Carolina.

Corcoran remained in that crowded place for two months, still under the threat of instant hanging. The prisoners received few letters. Then, early in March, the hostages were moved again, this time to the Salisbury prison in North Carolina. Food was scarce; hunger and boredom were plentiful. One day, at the end of March, Colonel Michael Corcoran heard his name called out, not for a trip to the gallows but to Richmond, and to exchange for a Confederate colonel -- and then home.

Corcoran went to Richmond all right, back to the tobacco warehouse and into solitary confinement again. He learned that Union troops were fighting their way up the Virginia Peninsula toward Richmond. There had also been a horrific, bloody clash in Tennessee with thousands of casualties on each side. The colonel heard that friends were trying to get him released and were looking after his loved ones at home, but there was no news about prisoner exchange.[48]

He did learn, early in May, that the governor of New York had appointed him to be one of the harbor masters of New York City; Mrs. Corcoran would receive the emoluments until he returned. Corcoran was politician -- and optimistic -- enough to know that accepting money for work not performed was never a wise move. He respectfully declined the honor and asked that any payments made to his wife be refunded immediately.[49]

By mid-May, the Union navy had steamed up the James River to within eight miles of Richmond before being turned back, but the Union army was still driving closer. The tobacco warehouse prison officials emptied the place quickly by exchanging all the prisoners held there – as for the hostages, they were sent back to Salisbury.

War on the Peninsula raged through June but then died down as it ignited elsewhere in July. During the second week in August, an exhausted Colonel Corcoran and the other hostages were again put on the slow train to Richmond where, on the 14th, the word came: prepare to leave for exchange. They, and some other prisoners, boarded a small

[47] Corcoran 30, 95, 99.
[48] Corcoran 89.
[49] Corcoran 96-97.

steamer for the ride down the James River to an exchange point. In his journal, Michael Corcoran described the moment when he saw his flag for the first time in more than a year: "...as my eyes fell upon its bright stars and stripes, my soul thrilled to its center, and my Irish heart welled up with emotion such as it had never experienced before. And in the wild shout of delight that went up from the prisoners, I joined to the full extent of my voice."[50]

In Washington, D.C., the cachectic and emaciated Colonel Michael Corcoran was cheered, toasted, and exhibited as a hero -- the doomed hostage who had spurned parole. He was offered a book contract;[51] he dined at the White House and the president commissioned him a brigadier general, with rank to date from the Battle of Bull Run.[52] Then Secretary of War, Edwin M. Stanton, offered him a bittersweet choice: the command of an existing but leaderless brigade or the opportunity to recruit and command his own.[53] Neither could possibly include the 69th Regiment, then part of the fighting Irish Brigade, which was led by Brigadier General Thomas Francis Meagher.

There was another choice. Corcoran was so enfeebled that he could have retired honorably, as did many other volunteer officers who had been wounded in -- or were weary of -- action. Yet, he told Stanton that he would be honored to provide the president with a legion of Irish-Americans who would give their lives to help preserve the Union, their adopted country. That decision was not only a response to losing the ardent dream that had sustained him during captivity, it was also breathing, pulsing proof of his gratitude.

Primarily, Michael Corcoran was grateful to be an American, writing in his journal, "God bless America, and ever preserve her the asylum of all the oppressed of the earth, is the sincere prayer of my heart."[54] He referred to the American flag as the "banner of human rights."[55]

---

[50] Corcoran 100.

[51] *New York Herald*, Aug. 19, 1862: 5; *New-York Daily Tribune*, Aug. 22, 1862: 8.

[52] *New York Herald*, Aug. 19, 1862: 5; *The Irish-American*, Aug. 23, 1862: 2.

[53] *The Irish-American*, Aug. 30, 1862: 2.

[54] Corcoran 22 [2].

[55] *New York Herald*, Aug. 19,1862: 5.

Brigadier General Michael Corcoran, shortly after his release from thirteen months in Confederate prisons. (Courtesy of the Massachusetts Commandery Military Order of the Loyal Legion and The U.S. Military History Institute.)

While in Washington, he had learned more about the efforts that had been made to both secure and prevent his release. His insider friends in New York and Boston had mounted and persisted in a "Free Corcoran" campaign, and the House of Representatives had passed two resolutions on his behalf.[56] Even the Tammany Hall Fourth of July "clambake" song featured the refrain "release Mike Corcoran."[57] Also, he was gratified to hear about futile Southern efforts intended to prevent his release. It was rumored that the Confederate authorities had been unwilling to release Colonel Corcoran because of his influence among the many Irish-Americans in the South.[58]

General Corcoran's welcome home to New York City included a Battery Park reception, a hero's parade up Broadway, wining and dining, speeches on the steps of City Hall, honors and presentations, and the native-American benediction of a *New-York Times* editorial proclaiming that he was a "patriot" who..." on all occasions exhibited a devotion to the American government...[59] His personal life, however, briefly shrank back to the little house his wife was renting at 7 Prince Street.

Recruitment for the Irish Legion began the day after his return. The freed hostage sent a telegram to the governor, reporting for duty; he went around the city paying his respects to advocates; he arranged for a trip back to Washington to attend to official business, and planned recruitment and publicity junkets. After returning from Washington, General Corcoran traveled to Boston and Worcester, thanking his supporters and making patriotic speeches along the way; settled some affairs in New York City, then continued on to recruit in Poughkeepsie and Albany. Because time was short, he had to turn down requests for visits and speaking engagements from people in cities all over the Northeast.

Within three weeks after his return from captivity, about 2,500 fighting men had enlisted in Corcoran's Irish Legion and hundreds more

[56] *The Irish-American*, Dec. 7,1861: 2; *Congressional Globe*, 37th Cong., 2d sees., 1862, 1341. The first reference prints a copy of a resolution supposedly passed in the House on Dec. 2, 1861; however that resolution was not printed in the *Congressional Globe*. A nearly identical resolution was recorded in the *Globe* on that date (37th Cong., 2d sees., 1861, 6) for another one of the hostages from New York City. Because it referred to one of the North's prisoners, Slidell, and Corcoran's purported resolution referred to Slidell's associate, Mason, it is likely that the printing of Corcoran's resolution was simply overlooked. The second resolution noted above was first passed, on Mar. 24, 1862, but then held over for debate about the portion directing the Secretary of War to stop all prisoner exchanges until Corcoran was released; apparently Corcoran was exchanged before the debate occurred.
[57] *Tammany Society or Columbian Order -- Annual Celebration at Tammany Hall, July 4, 1862* (New York: Baptist & Taylor, 1862) 19.
[58] *Official Records of the Union and Confederate Armies*, ser. II, vol. 3: 325, 785; vol. 4: 21, 36, 148; *New-York Times*, 30 May 13, 1.
[59] *New-York Times*, Aug. 23, 1862: 4.

awaited state authorization for another regiment. The new legionnaires began their training at an encampment on Staten Island. General Corcoran went back to Albany on brigade business and ongoing recruitment. He returned to New York City on the night boat, docking on the morning of September 19th. The early newspapers clamored in anguish about the carnage in Antietam, Maryland; many thousands of men on each side had been killed or wounded in a battle that had lasted only from daybreak to nightfall. Long casualty lists tolled names from the Irish Brigade. Corcoran set up headquarters at the legion's camp and worked long hours organizing his brigade and supervising the training of his own cannon fodder.

He had no time for Fenian ventures and neatly side-stepped the contentious maneuvering at Tammany Hall. He did not like what he saw there now that he was back in town. Not only had Michael Corcoran's political cronies lobbied for his release, they had managed to get him, in absentia, a seat on the powerful General Committee of the Tammany organization.[60] A surrogate had been sitting in it so Corcoran knew about the prearranged fusion candidate deals.[61] He acted by sending a gracious letter of thanks and resignation, citing the time constraints imposed by his engrossing responsibilities.[62] It was a political decision as well as a patriotic one; this was not the time to make his move.

Politicians of other stripes thought it was. Representatives of three different caucuses asked General Corcoran to be their candidate for Congress. He politely declined.[63] Within a few days, he was bedridden with another high fever. The Irish Legion, under orders to report for duty at Suffolk, Virginia, prepared to relocate. Their commander bought a family cemetery plot and had his mother reburied in it.

The weather turned icy and snowy. Corcoran recovered and was strong enough to lead his troops under fire when they won an engagement at Suffolk, in January, 1863. A couple of months later, he was acting major general there, commanding the First Division of the Seventh Army Corps.[64] Then, in early April, some revolutionaries from the Organization arrived in camp and reminded him of his commitment to liberate Ireland.

---

[60] Tammany Scrapbooks, vol. 1, N. peg.

[61] *New York Herald*, Oct. 14, 1862: 8.

[62] *New-York Times*, Oct. 3, 1862: 1; Oct. 4, 1862: 2. The *Times* article of 3 Oct. also reports that a "large majority" vote declined to accept Corcoran's resignation. Still, no evidence was found showing that Corcoran continued or planned to continue his association with Tammany Hall.

[63] *New York Herald*, Oct. 17, 1862: 8.

[64] *New York Herald*, Apr. 15, 1863: 3.

One of the men headed the Fenians -- he was a good friend of Corcoran's from New York -- and another was a major fund raiser from Ireland.[65] Whether or not they were invited and by whom (many in the legion were Fenians), the timing of their ill-advised visit was grievous.

Late one evening, the fund raiser was presiding over a meeting of the officers when General Corcoran received orders to have his troops under arms by three a.m. He quickly got the Irishman out of the way and set off for the front accompanied by his aides and the other visitor, his chieftain friend from New York.

It was about two a.m., and visibility was about ten yards by the light of the quarter moon. They had ridden just a short way through the wispy nighttime fog when a bearded figure in an officer's uniform suddenly materialized out of the shadows and stepped boldly into the middle of the road. He ordered Corcoran and his party to halt and demanded the countersign but refused to identify himself. General Corcoran gave his own name and rank. He spoke courteously, yet firmly, asking the man several times to stand aside. The man responded with profanities; he sounded drunk. Still ranting, but without warning, he drew his sword, waved it in a threatening manner, and jabbed at Corcoran's horse. The general upholstered his Colt revolver. Again, he asked the man to move out of the way.

"Not for no damned Irish son of a bitch like you or any one else," the man shouted.

Michael Corcoran was about to brush past him when the man raised his sword as though to thrust it again and put his left hand on his belt as though to draw a pistol. Michael Corcoran squeezed the trigger. The aggressor stepped back and cried out, "Shoot again, God damn you" and fell to the ground. The general told someone to look after him and then rode on to the front. Within an hour, as the mobilization was getting underway, he learned that the man was the lieutenant colonel of the Ninth New York, Hawkins' Zouaves, and that he was dead.

Although preoccupied with the enemy offensive, Corcoran reported the incident at once and requested a Court of Inquiry. Three sessions were held in Suffolk a month later, after the Yankees broke the Confederate's siege. General Corcoran was judged censurable for his action; a court-martial was ordered.[66] The Irish Legion stayed in Suffolk until early

[65] O'Leary 212-217; William D'Arcy, *The Fenian Movement in the United States: 1858-1886* (Washington, DC: Catholic UP, 1947) 30-31.
[66] National Archives and Records Service, Records of the Judge Advocate General's Office, Record Group 153, "Michael Corcoran," M 682. The description of Lt. Col. Edgar A. Kimball's shooting was taken exclusively from this Court of Inquiry transcript.

July when they began moving north. News dispatches sketched ghastly scenes of clashing warriors, telling how Union troops repulsed the Rebel invasion of Pennsylvania, at Gettysburg. Within a week, other reports described frenzied, blood-soaked rioting in New York City. The distribution of district draft quotas there seemed to discriminate against underprivileged laborers, many of them Irish-Americans, who took it as the last straw and rampaged for days, completely out of control.

The Irish Legion arrived in Centreville, Virginia on July 22nd; Brigadier General Corcoran would be subordinate to the brigadier general already in command there. Two weeks later, he received a telegram from New York: his wife, Elizabeth, was dead. He went home and buried her.[67]

Three days after returning to camp, Corcoran called upon President Lincoln, and, a week later, sent him a follow-up letter: "...you were kind enough to ask me to suggest some way in which you could relieve me from my present position. . . .[I] respectfully request that I may be ordered to some other command."[68]

September was coming to an end, and there had been no reply from Lincoln. General Corcoran was uneasy; he had fainted a couple of times.[69] So, using common sense and with timeless fortitude, he requested a short leave to consult a physician in New York City. The eminent doctor concluded that Corcoran was suffering from the lingering effects of malnutrition and the bad air during his imprisonment, and was urgently in need of rest. He recommended that the general stay with friends for a few days and try to build up his strength with a diet of oatmeal and barley water.[70] The friends were anxious to help but instead of resting, Corcoran married John Heaney's favorite grandchild, pretty, seventeen-year old Lizzie (Elizabeth) Heaney.[71]

He returned to his legion, now encamped at Fairfax Court House, the division headquarters. General Michael Corcoran was the new division

---

[67] *New York Herald* Aug. 5, 1863: 2; Aug. 6, 1863: 3; Aug. 8, 1863: 8; Calvary Cemetery, burial record.

[68] NARS, JAG records, "Corcoran."

[69] Maria Lydig Daly, *Diary of a Union Lady 1861-1865*, ed. Harold Earl Hammond (New York: Funk & Wagnalls Company, Inc., 1962) 270.

[70] Daly 256.

[71] NARS, Military Service Records, RG 94, "Pension File" for Brigadier General Michael Corcoran, Irish Legion (marriage certificate); *New York Herald*, Oct. 18, 1863: 4 (contradictory wedding report). Her identity is deduced from various records which show that: a) her mother was Mary Heaney; b) Mary Heaney was the widow of John Heaney's eldest son, John, Jr.; c) in his will, John, Sr. left a treasured object to the "eldest daughter of son John." (Lizzie would have been seven years old at the time.) That she was pretty was noted in the article "General Michael Corcoran," by John G. Coyle, in the *Journal of the American Irish Historical Society*, vol. XIII, New York: 1914, 1 91.

commander; the other general had been reassigned.[72] His young bride joined him two weeks later.

For whatever reasons, the most likely being military obligations, Corcoran did not request another leave two weeks after that to attend the first national Fenian convention in Chicago. Even so, he was appointed to the five-man central council that would act as an advisory cabinet to the chief officer, his New York visitor at Suffolk.[73]

In early December, Corcoran heard from Brigadier General Thomas Francis Meagher, who had resigned his command of the famed fighting Irish Brigade. He invited him to Fairfax and, with gentlemanly hospitality, moved out of his own room to give Meagher the best room in the house. Corcoran also invited Mrs. Meagher and Lizzie's mother to the Legion's camp for the Christmas holidays.

On Tuesday morning, December 22, 1863, General Corcoran arose early as usual, but felt ill again. Just before noon, accompanied by an escort party, he and Meagher rode three miles to the Fairfax railroad station. Meagher was going to Washington to fetch his wife and Mrs. Heaney. Corcoran wanted to re-deploy the pickets along the tracks; Mosby and his raiders were in the neighborhood.

Corcoran, an excellent horseman, was galloping ahead of his escorts as they returned to headquarters. Suddenly, he raised one arm as if to stop those behind him but then rode around a bend, out of sight. Spurring their horses in pursuit they found their chief convulsing on the ground, his face purple, and the horse walking quietly nearby. The men commandeered a wagon and hurried the general back to camp where the surgeons bled him and then pronounced him dead of "apoplexy."[74] He was thirty-six years old.

Michael Corcoran's body was embalmed and arrived back in New York City on Christmas morning. All that day and the next, he lay in state in the Governor's Room in City Hall, the usual honor for deceased war heroes. Long lines of mourners paid their respects. Flags flew at half mast. Funeral services took place at St. Patrick's Cathedral, across from 42

[72] NARS, Telegrams Collected by the Office of the Secretary of War (Unbound) 1860-1870, RG 107, M 504, roll 128 (Washington, DC) several communications; New York Herald, Oct. 18, 1863: 1; Oct. 21, 1863: 3; Oct. 22, 1863: 3; New-York Times, Oct. 19, 1863: 4; New-York Daily Tribune, Oct. 19, 1863: 1.
[73] Chicago Tribune, Nov. 3, 1863: 4; Nov. 4, 1863: 4; Nov. 5, 1863: 4; Nov. 6, 1863: 4 (microfilm, Yale Univ. Library).
[74] Corcoran's pension file death report, dated 11 Feb. 1865, lists the cause of death as a "fracture of the base of the skull." This is disputed by Drs. Coyle and Dwyer in Dr. Coyle's JAIHS article. Furthermore, the newspapers' and Mrs. M. L. Daly's Diary descriptions of Corcoran's medical history and final hours indicate that "apoplexy" was the more likely cause. The skull fracture in the line of duty diagnosis perhaps expedited the widow's pension.

Brigadier General Michael Corcoran, shortly before his death, showing strain and fatigue around the eyes. (Courtesy of the Massachusetts Commandery Military Order of the Loyal Legion and The U.S. Military History Institute.)

Prince Street, on Sunday, December 27th. He was interred at Calvary Cemetery that afternoon, with his first wife and his mother.[75]

A memorial service for Brigadier General Corcoran was held a month later, on January 22, 1864, in the Great Hall of Cooper Institute. Thomas Francis Meagher delivered the oration, concluding with these words: "...let him rest in the soil that is sacred to liberty, under the starry arch of the Republic he so nobly served, and within sight of that city which honored him when dead as she honored him when living, and where his name will never sound strange...."[76]

Confederate Fortifications near Manassas Junction

[75] The account of Corcoran's death and funeral is taken from: NARS RG 107, M 504, roll 128; numerous articles in the *New-York Times*, *New York Herald*, *The Irish-American*, and *Alexandria [VA] Gazette*. Burial is documented by Calvary Cemetery.

[76] *New York Herald*, Jan. 23, 1864: 1; *New-York Times*, Jan. 23, 1864: 8; *The Irish-American*, Jan. 30, 1864: 2. The copy in Cavanagh's *Memoirs of T. F. Meagher* 349-361 is the easiest one to read.

Chapter II

THE "FIGHTING" SIXTY-NINTH NEW YORK STATE MILITIA AT BULL RUN

by Christopher-Michael Garcia

At noon on July 21, 1861, Colonel Michael Corcoran and his Irish 69th New York State Militia were sitting in the hot woodlands overlooking Bull Run, where they had been all morning. Meanwhile, the battle of First Manassas was raging across the muddy, little creek called Bull Run. Corcoran's men were hot, tired, and hungry but eager to "see the elephant." These high-spirited Irish soldiers were not content with the situation. After all, if they were not allowed to play a leading role in the battle, how would they prove that their detractors were wrong about the loyalty and character of the Irish? These men now wanted the chance to restore the fair name of the Irish race and the 69th regiment.

Only ten months, earlier Colonel Corcoran had refused to parade his 69th Regiment for the Prince of Wales on October 11, 1860. Citing that he could not, in good conscience, parade before or honor the son of the hated Queen Victoria, whose policies had left Ireland's lands a waste and sent millions of Ireland's sons into exile, Corcoran requested to be excused from the festivities. He was ordered to participate in the parade because it was so unpopular with the many Irish in the First Division of the New York Militia, and it was feared that, if Corcoran was allowed out, all the Irish would do the same. On the appointed day and hour, Michael Corcoran and the 69th Regiment were notably absent. The public outcry against Colonel Corcoran's political statement was so great that following election day, that he was arrested and court martialed for his defiance. To have taken action before election day would have been political suicide in a city where the Irish accounted for over a quarter of the population. Colonel Corcoran's refusal was an affront to the honor of the upper class of New York state. Consequently, the public called for the disbanding of the 69th. The newspaper even demanded that Colonel Corcoran be summarily tried and shot for treason. Clearly, Nativist prejudice and racism still held strong in New York. These Nativist attacks were directed not only against Corcoran and the 69th, but also against the entire Irish community. When, on a Sunday in April, several hundred members of the Regiment, clad in partial military dress, crossed the east river to Brooklyn's "Pigeon Ground" to drill, the people of New York became alarmed.[1] They feared that the Irishmen were attempting to seize Fort Hamilton. However, the drilling was called because the men could not afford to lose time during the week from their jobs to drill.[2]

If Colonel Corcoran's actions put him at odds with the Anglo dominated upper class of New York, who were Protestant, anti-Catholic, and anti-Irish, they endeared him to his fellow Irishmen. To these persecuted, Irish exiles this was another extension of the cause of freedom for the motherland which was languishing under English domination. Consequently, gifts from sympathetic Irishmen poured in from across the country, not only for Corcoran, but also for the 69th. The most prized gift received by the 69th was a Green Flag, emblazoned with a Sunburst and with the words "Presented to the 69th Regiment - In commemoration of October 11, 1860."[3] When war erupted on April 12, the public was unsure of the 69th; and Lieutenant Colonel Robert Nugent made a public statement that any service by the Regiment would only be for the United States.[4] When, on April 19, Corcoran spoke to the men of the Regiment and urged them to volunteer for service, not surprisingly, the charges

[1] *The New York Daily Tribune*, April 15, 1861.

[2] Ibid.

[3] Bernard Kelly, *The Historic Civil War Irish Colors of the 69th Regiment*. Unpublished work in the Regimental Archives.

[4] *The New York Daily Tribune*, April 15, 1861.

Hibernian Hall, Prince St., (Harper's Weekly, 7/29/1871)

against him were dropped.[5] Three days later, the Irishmen in blue prepared to leave for the "seat of War."

On April 23, 1861, at seven in the morning the various companies
assembled at Prince Street outside of Hibernian Hall. There they waited
several hours for their arms to arrive.[6] Corcoran was only allowed to take
one thousand soldiers, although several times that number of Irishmen
were willing to go south with him.

---

[5] *The New York Daily Tribune*, April 20, 1861.
[6] Unnamed Newspaper Clipping, Scrapbook No. 1. Charles P. Daly Papers. Rare Books and Manuscripts
Division, New York Public Library, New York.

One newspaper reporter wrote:

> Men who would have faced a battery with only the charging shout on their lips, wept like children because they could not accompany the Sixty-Ninth - 'The Irish Regiment.'[7]

Finally, at 3:00 p.m., the Irish Regiment formed in Great Jones Street, where they were presented with a silk American flag by Mrs. Maria Lydig Daly, the wife of Judge Charles P. Daly. "Old Glory" would nicely complement the green, Irish battle-flag.

The 69th Regiment wheeled into Broadway and then proceeded to Pier 4 on the Hudson River. Numerous brass bands and Irish societies, as well as the Fenian "Phoenix Zouaves," escorted the 69th. Proceeding the long column of Irishmen was a wagon with a banner reading "Sixty-ninth Remember Fontenoy." A throng of excited civilians, many of whom had turned out at an "early hour," lined Broadway. "Never previously had there been anything like the spirit and enthusiasm of the population on this occasion."[8]

At several times, the procession of Irish soldiers was stopped by large numbers of people who wanted to touch Corcoran's hand.[9] Consequently, the Regiment had "...to force a passage through the enthusiastic multitude."[10] As they neared, the chaos grew. Captain James Butler wrote, "The passage became so severe that many were almost suffocated and were carried away several yards without requiring use of their propellers in their onward march."[11] Finally, at seven in the evening the steamer *James Adger* was loaded with troops and pushed away. The steamboat was crowded, hot, and suffocating. Some men were so exhausted that they rolled themselves up in their blankets to lay down wherever a "...vacant spot was to be met with."[12] Even as the 69th departed New York City for Washington, there was a raging debate of Brotherhood. Corcoran was then the acting head of the Fenian Brotherhood, while John O'Mahony was in Ireland. The heated debate centered upon whether or not they should participate in the war. With Ireland's liberation paramount, Corcoran felt that Irish blood needed to be saved for the impend-

---

[7] Ibid.
[8] Ibid.
[9] Ibid.
[10] Captain James Butler's Diary. Thomas F. Madigan Collection, Rare Books and Manuscripts Division. New York Public Library, New York. Note: The original diary has no page numbers, and so no page numbers will appear in citations of this work. Henceforth it will be referred to as James Butler's Diary.
[11] Ibid.
[12] Ibid.

ing war with England. In a letter to John O'Mahony, for example, he wrote:

> As to your joining us, as you propose, that I must tell you frankly I cannot listen to you for a moment. Irrespective of any other consideration, our Irish cause and organization in America would grievously, if not fatally, suffer by the withdrawal of your immediate services and supervision. It is absolutely necessary that you should remain at your own prescribed post - all the more necessary that others are compelled to be away for a time. That our organization will derive considerable impetus and strength from the military enthusiasm prevailing here at present amongst our race and may, indeed, have favorable opportunities opened out to it by the events that are transpiring, I am strongly impressed if not positively convinced. It is, therefore, most essential that a man like you should remain to enlarge and perfect it.[13]

In view of this letter, apparently Corcoran's primary motivation to serve was not patriotism, but, rather, an attempt to vindicate not only himself, but also the 69th in the wake of the Prince of Wales affair.[14] On the other hand, inspirational leaders, like Thomas Francis Meagher, who would later create and command the legendary Irish Brigade, felt differently. Meagher wrote:

> Another thought focuses itself upon me in connection with the hopes we entertain for Ireland. It is a moral certainty that many of our countrymen who enlist in this struggle for the maintenance of the Union will fall in the contest. But, even so, I hold that if only one in ten of us came back when this war is over, the military experience gained by that one will be of more service in a fight for Ireland's freedom than would that of the entire ten as they are now.[15]

Consequently, Meagher immediately began organizing a company of Zouaves, which would later join the 69th, becoming Company K of the regiment at First Bull Run. Two days later, the 69th arrived at the Naval

---

[13] Michael Cavanagh, *Memoirs of General Thomas Francis Meagher* (Worcester: The Messenger Press., 1892), 359.

[14] Cavanagh, 354. In an oration on January 22, 1864, sponsored by the Fenian Brotherhood, Meagher stated "in what measure did the loyalty of Michael Corcoran and the 69th vindicate itself!" He was referring to the Bull Run campaign, and at least confirms that they did vindicate themselves, and indicates that may have been Corcoran's motive.

[15] Cavanagh, 369.

Yard at Annapolis, and landed amid cheers, after a "pleasant voyage."[16] On April 26, the 69th Regiment was assigned to guard the railroad "...from a point near the Depot in Annapolis to the Junction."[17] The nights were cold and wet, and the men suffered with no shelter from the pouring rain.[18] Due to the hasty departure, the commissariat arrangements of the Regiment were "not in good order."[19] The Irishmen lacked many basic amenities. Consequently, they were forced to use "...whatever containers possible to drink out of as cups were short."[20] Yet, despite the hardships and the tarnishing of some of the war's early romanticism, Corcoran's Irish Militiamen carried out their duties "with a cheerfulness," until relieved by the 5th New York Infantry on May 3, 1861.[21] Probably the most significant part of their task was that they were not yet in Federal Service.

This was in "bright contrast" to another "...state corps whose yet mustered commander refused the duty because they were not into federal service."[22] Corcoran's Celts arrived in Washington at about 6 p.m. and taking quarters on Pennsylvania Avenue, the Regiment moved up north to quarters at Georgetown College, in the Catholic School, no doubt a great comfort to the predominantly Catholic 69th. [23] Georgetown was also pro-Southern in sentiment. On May 9, the soldiers were sworn into Federal service. All but seventeen took the Oath.[24] Those New Yorkers who refused to take the oath were turned out amid "the groans, hisses etc. of their secessionists were not the only ones comrades."[25] Clearly the who had sympathy for States Rights. At the same time, many to secede from the Union and Democrats in New York City wanted become a "Free City."

At Georgetown, the 69th was drilled and trained more than seven hours a day by several regular United States Army officers.[26] Thus the newspaper that had called for Corcoran's execution eight months earlier now changed it's tune, writing; The citizens of the neighborhood speak in

[16] James Butler's Diary.
[17] General Butler to General Scott. *Official Records of the War of the Rebellion.* (U.S. War Department; Washington)J Series IJ Vol. II, No. 2, 605. (Henceforth referred to as OR) All citations from the Official Records in this chapter are from Series I, Vol. II, No. 2.
[18] James Butler's Diary.
[19] Ibid.
[20] Ibid.
[21] Ibid.
[22] *The Irish American* (New York), July 20, 1861.
[23] Ibid.
[24] Ibid.
[25] Ibid.
[26] *Harper's Weekly*, June 1, 1861.

the highest terms of the conduct of the men, and Colonel Corcoran may well be proud of the good name the regiment has earned.[27]

During the initial hours of the Union occupation of Alexandria, Virginia, Colonel Ephraim Elmer Ellsworth's scuffled in the stairwell of the little hotel known as the Marshell House, with its owner, Mr. James T. Jackson, over his display of the *First National Flag*. The result was their deaths on May 21, 1861. The occupying army then began the earnest search for other suspected Confederate sympathizers. A cousin of Mr. Jackson's was quickly "arrested" and locked up in the Sixty-Ninth's guard house.[28] The next day, several more "Rebels" were also rounded up and placed in this guard house.[29]

The newspaper described how "...they were beginning to handle like regulars."[30] On the night of May 23, the 69th regiment was ordered to prepare to march, doing so in utter silence at about one a.m., on May 24. Corcoran's Irishmen crossed the Aqueduct Bridge and began to dig breastworks on Arlington Heights under the direction of Captain Daniel P. Woodbury, of the United States Engineers.[31] Just prior to advancing on the commanding heights of Arlington, which dominated Washington, D.C., Captain Thomas F. Meagher, with three hundred recruits, including Meagher's Irish Zouaves, joined the 69th New York for the duration of the three months' campaign in Virginia, the most powerful southern state. On May 29th, they were inspected by General Irwin McDowell. He noted that the 69th New York was the only Union regiment which was taking the wise precaution of working on the defenses around the Aqueduct Bridge and Ferry, while the other regiments were simply lying idly about.[32]

Colonel Corcoran's Militiamen were making progress in the transformation from green troops to experienced regulars. Captain James Butler noted that visitors to this sector expressed:

> Their astonishment at the rapid progress made by the hardy Sons of Erin who with their boisterous laugh and merry jokes made themselves at home as if they had been enjoying themselves.[33]

[27] Ibid.
[28] Ibid.
[29] Ibid.
[30] Ibid.
[31] Major General Sandford's Report, May 28, 1861. OR II, 39.
[32] McDowell to Assistant Adjutant General Lt. Col. Townsend, May 29, 1861. OR II, 653.
[33] James Butler's Diary.

Quarters of the 69th (Irish) Regiment New York State Militia, at Georgetown College, D.C.

The newly-dug network of fortifications was soon named Fort Corcoran. These defenses were impressive. Fort Corcoran's walls were fourteen feet high and mounted four 68-pounders and twelve 32-pounder guns. The cannon were situated to cover the approaches to the Aqueduct Bridge.[34] Built for a garrison of 3,000 men, Fort Corcoran was considered to be impregnable.[35]

Fort Corcoran was the 69th's first achievement of the campaign. An attraction for Matthew Brady's cameras, Fort Corcoran was 650 feet by 450 feet; it was estimated that it would take 3,000 men one month to complete its works.[36] Corcoran's hearty Irishmen surprised the experts when they completed the main works in one week. On May 29, Corcoran ordered the flagstaff and flag removed from their cantonments at Georgetown, and placed inside Fort Corcoran during a martial ceremony complete with speeches and songs.[37] Two weeks later, a number of heavy guns arrived on June 12, and, upon Colonel Corcoran's request, Father Thomas Mooney, the Regimental Chaplain, blessed one of the guns before a large assemblage of officers and men.[38]

The chance Corcoran's Irish warriors were waiting for appeared to have arrived on the evening of June 3, when Corcoran informed his men that they would be attacked by the Rebels that night.[39] Consequently, the campfires were ordered set one hundred feet before the breastworks, so as to deceive the enemy.[40] However, the prowling Confederates were discovered by patrolling Union cavalry, and they deterred an attack, allowing Corcoran to order his men to get some sleep at 2 a.m., on June 4.[41]

Constant alarms became a part of daily life at Fort Corcoran. When not on alert, the Irishmen advanced beyond their entrenchments and, occasionally, captured prisoners.[42] On June 13, three Companies of the 69th were marched five miles to the Loudon & Hampton Railroad, with reports that the Rebels were going to wreck the railroad.[43] But no Southerners struck. Consequently, they had breakfast and all but sixty soldiers returned to Fort Corcoran.[44] On Sunday, June 16, Corcoran's Irishmen were

---

[34] *The Irish American*, July 13, 1861.
[35] Ibid.
[36] Paul Jones, *The Irish Brigade* (Washington, D.C.; Robert B. Luck. 1969). 73-4.
[37] Butler.
[38] Ibid.
[39] Ibid.
[40] Ibid.
[41] Ibid.
[42] Ibid.
[43] Ibid.
[44] Ibid.

ordered west to Ball's corner to secure the road for a demonstration toward Harpers Ferry. The 69th was relived on June 17, by Brigadier General Schenck's Brigade.[45]

On Monday afternoon, four companies of the regiment were sent back to the railroad as a result of a report that Brigadier Schenck's Ohio troops were being massacred by Rebels.[46] The following morning, General McDowell ordered the remainder of the 69th New York up to Ball's Crossroads, where they linked with the rest of the Regiment.[47] That evening, the entire regiment marched back to Fort Corcoran. June also saw the arrival of a Battery of United States Artillery to service the guns of Fort Corcoran.[48]

The Irish regiment celebrated the Fourth of July by firing the guns of Fort Corcoran for the first time, by having a dress parade, and by the reading of the Declaration of Independence by Captain Meagher during an impressive ceremony.[49] But trouble was brewing just below the surface. Corcoran's rugged Irishmen had not yet been paid for more than ten weeks of service. This pay was desperately needed by their poor Irish families in New York. On July 5, Captain John Breslin's Company F and the engineer company refused to leave their cantonments until they were paid.[50] Colonel Corcoran then paraded the remainder of the regiment before the mutineers, threatening to fire if they refused duty.[51] With that the uprising fizzled and no charges were ever filed against the mutineers.[52] Yet, their reputation for high spirits and drill-field excellence remained untarnished. In a letter written the next day by Major General Patterson, in the Shenandoah Valley, to General Winfield Scott requesting reinforcements, for instance, he specifically asked for the "New York Sixty-Ninth."[53]

Corcoran's gallant Irishmen had volunteered for three months, and that term of service was rapidly coming to a end. The public at large and, especially, the Irish community, wanted to know the future course of the Irish Regiment. Would these Irishmen be patriotic and re-enlist for the

---

[45] Butler. Also General McDowell's report on the action at Vienna June 18, 1861. OR II, 125.

[46] Butler. Also General McDowell to Brigadier General Schenck June 18, 1881, 1:35 a.m.. OR II, 700. It is interesting to note that Captain Butler asserts that five companies were sent up and McDowell states that four were sent up.

[47] General McDowell to Col. Hunter June 20, 1861 OR II, 710. Also see Butler.

[48] Butler.

[49] Ibid.

[50] Jones, 75-6.

[51] Ibid.

[52] Ibid.

[53] Major General Patterson to General Winfield Scott, July 6, 1861. OR II, 159.

duration of the war, or would they come home? As one of the first regiments to volunteer for service, the 69th might well set an example for the other three-month militia units. In a July 8th letter to Judge Daly, Corcoran wrote, "I have to say, that just now, it would be premature for me, or for anyone, to say what the 69th will do at the expiration of three months term of service - their action will be determined by events."[54]

If Colonel Corcoran's motive had purely been patriotic, no doubt he would have had more to say. Corcoran might have remained as long as possible to redeem his name and that of his Irish Regiment. In preparation for their muster out of Federal service, Father Mooney departed for New York City on July 9.[55] The next day, the 69th New York was visited by its division commander, General Daniel Tyler, who inspected the ranks minutely; afterwards, he complimented the Colonel on the fine, healthy, and robust body of men which he had the honor of commanding.[56]

Two days later, on July 12, the Army finally paid the Sixty its scheduled muster out on July 20.[57] So as not to damage the regiment's reputation, Colonel Corcoran ordered double sentinels posted, and the canteen closed to prevent the men from buying "the Dutch Man's Lager."[58] Shortly thereafter, Father O'Reilly, who had superseded Father Mooney as chaplain, departed for New York, carrying most of two months' of the 69th Regiment's pay, around $25,000, as well as letters to the wives and families of Corcoran's Irish militiamen.[59]

That evening, the Irish were ordered to prepare to march. Knapsacks were packed, along with the regiment's heavy baggage, which was ordered to Alexandria.[60] The men trimmed down into light marching order, with at least sixty rounds of .69 caliber buck and ball cartridges, and three days rations.[61] Captain Thomas F. Meagher described the hectic scene:

> In every tent men might be seen -- some seated on kegs, others on their knapsacks, others again on rude blocks, and two or three on drums -- writing their last letters home. Whilst morning and evening hundreds were slowly passing through the little

---

[54] Letter from Colonel Michael Corcoran to Judge Charles Daly, July 8, 1861, Charles Daly Papers, Rare Books and Manuscripts Division, New York Public Library, New York. Box 3.
[55] Butler.
[56] Ibid.
[57] Ibid.
[58] Ibid.
[59] *The Irish American*, August 8, 1861.
[60] Ibid.
[61] Ibid.

46

chapel within the Fort, making their confession and receiving absolution.[62]

Three days later, on July 15, at evening parade, the Sons of Erin were ordered to be prepared to march at 2 o'clock the next afternoon. That evening, the Irishmen made preparations for departure with "laughing hearts," long after the lights were extinguished. The sight of free Irishmen, under the command of Irish officers, was one that had not been seen since the days of the Old Irish Brigade in the French service a century before. No doubt all of Corcoran's Irishmen were aware of the decisive role that the exiles of the old Irish Brigade played at the battle of Fontenoy in 1745, and no doubt they desired to emulate those exploits, if not to surpass them. Throughout the night, the silence was broken by "snatches of songs."[63] At Fort Corcoran that night, the festivities ran so high that it seemed that they were out to liberate Ireland, not to save the Union. From their tongues came the lyrics "that Davis wrote for us" (Thomas Davis being the premier Irish Nationalist poet/songwriter of the nineteenth century).[64] "Close on dawn," the camp quieted down.[65]

With only four days remaining of Federal service, on July 16, 1861, Corcoran's Irishmen were ordered to march at 3 p.m.. At 8:30 p.m., they halted in a park adjacent to the Virginia village of Vienna. There, west of Washington, they were issued the day's rations of salt beef, pork and biscuit.[66] Those men not on duty rolled themselves up in their blankets, with their accoutrements on, and went to sleep.[67] On June 17, at 2:30 a.m., Corcoran's Irishmen rolled up their blankets and wiped down their "firelocks."[68] As the day wore on, it became exceedingly hot. In addition, the advance was slowed by felled trees "...causing a great loss of time in their removal."[69] As they marched, the 69th was ordered from Hunter's Brigade to Colonel William T. Sherman's Brigade. Their new brigade commander was "Old Billy" Sherman, who would make Georgia "howl" during his 1864 march to the sea. As they approached Centreville, the New York Irishmen were thrown into line and directed to the left, while other troops advanced on Centreville. At about twelve p.m., the boys of

[62] Ibid.
[63] Ibid.
[64] Ibid. Thomas Davis was the poet laureate of the Young Irelanders of 1848, as well as of the Fenians, and was responsible for writing such songs as *A Nation Once Again, The Battle Eve of the Brigade.*
[65] Ibid.
[66] Butler.
[67] Ibid.
[68] Ibid.
[69] Ibid.

the 69th reached Germantown. But once again, the enemy had fled after burning the town.[70] With the capture of Germantown, the Irish and American colors were placed upon the abandoned earthworks some fifteen paces apart and the 69th passed in triumph, hats and caps waving on bayonet points, and with an Irish cheer, such as had never before shaken the woods of old Virginia.[71]

After halting for the evening, Corcoran's Irish soldiers "...went on the lookout to procure a little water as all hands were suffering from excessive thirst."[72] Water was "scarce" and was of an "indifferent quality."[73] Nevertheless, the muddy water was drunk with a "healthy relish" by the parched New Yorkers.[74]

At dawn, on July 18, 1861, Corcoran's bluecoats advanced on Centreville, which was secured at about noon. Sherman's brigade then halted for four hours in the fields along the dusty road leading west toward the Blue Ridge. The men made sunshades with their blankets and ate hard tack and salt beef.[75] Sherman's brigade was held in reserve 'til 4 p.m., when it was ordered up to support the remainder of Tyler's Division, which had been in action at Blackburn's Ford since that noon. As General Tyler discovered, the vital ford across Bull Run was strongly defended, and he attempted an orderly withdrawal. However, the 12th New York Volunteers, and the 13th New York State Militia regiment of Rochester panicked, running a mile to the rear before they could be rallied. In bright contrast, Michael Corcoran's Irishmen carried themselves "right gallantly:" not one did not feel that the honor of his race and of its military character was staked that hour upon the conduct of the 69th.[76]

As Corcoran's fighting Irishmen advanced, they were met by the retreating 12th New York, and behind them noticed the greyclad militiamen of the 13th New York State Militia from Rochester. These New York greycoats were immediately mistaken for pursuing Southerners. Consequently, the 69th "instinctively" came to "charge bayonets."[77] They were just about to attack these "Rebels," when acting Lieutenant Colonel James Haggerty realized that they were fellow New Yorkers, he dashed along

---

[70] Ibid.
[71] T.F. Meagher, *The Last Days of the 69th in Virginia. A Treasury of Irish Folklore,* ed. Padraic Colum. (Wings Books, New York: 1992), 326-7.
[72] Butler.
[73] Butler's Diary.
[74] Ibid.
[75] Meagher, 328.
[76] Ibid., 329.
[77] Ibid.

the line "and struck the bayonets upwards with his sword," averting a potential disaster.[78]

The Irishmen were then ordered to lie down, falling under a heavy cannonade for forty-five minutes, and remained in position, silent until the cannonade ended.[79] Between six and seven that evening, General McDowell and Governor Sprague, of Rhode Island, viewed the battle field and ordered the 69th back to the commanding hill overlooking Centreville, Virginia.[80]

James Haggerty

Colonel Corcoran's soldiers waited on the hill above Centreville, while General McDowell attempted to fight the battle of First Manassas. July 20, 1861 arrived, and, with it, their three months' service was over. Consequently, several militia regiments, promptly left at the appointed hour, and on the eve of battle. To its credit, the gallant Irish 69th New York chose to remain, while many other American and New York comrades were leaving. Colonel Michael Corcoran had to replace several field officers to fill gaps, not from Rebel bullets, but from accidents and absence. Captain James Haggerty was made acting Lieutenant Colonel, to replace Robert Nugent, who had been injured in a fall from his horse. Major Bagley was absent, and was replaced by Acting Major Thomas F. Meagher.

On July 21, Colonel Corcoran received orders to march at about 3:30 a.m. The 69th New York, unlike the other regiments of Sherman's Brigade, was not allowed to have baggage and provision wagons immediately to its rear, and had only one ambulance.[81] By the time the troops reached

[78] Ibid.
[79] Ibid.
[80] Meagher, 330.
[81] Captain James Kelly's report, July 24, 1861. OR II, 371-2.

Bull Run, they arrived "greatly harassed and fatigued."[82] Sherman's Brigade deployed to the north of the Stone Bridge, taking position in a skirt of woods overlooking Bull Run, with the 69th anchoring the right flank. At around noon, the Irishmen were ordered across Bull Run in single file.[83]

Once across, the cheering Celts chased after the retreating Rebels across Matthew's Hill. Those withdrawing Southerners fell back on the Manassas-Sudley Road to Henry Hill. Corcoran's Irishmen pushed into a meadow and came under fire from the Louisiana Zouaves, who were hidden in a ravine off to the left. Among these Louisiana boys were many Irish Catholics. The Irish Regiment from New York replied with two volleys, leaving the place "strewn with their dead."[84] The devastating volleys caused the hard-hit Louisiana "Tigers" to fall back towards a cluster of pines. Meanwhile, Lieutenant Colonel Haggerty, without orders, rode out ahead of the main line to cut off their retreat. But the Louisiana Zouaves fought back with spirit and, "...one of the enemy, in full view and at short range, shot Haggerty and he fell dead from his horse."[85] Immediately, the 69th resumed firing and Haggerty's "assassin" fell, to rise no more, being hit as many as fifty times. The 69th New York, leading the way, was ordered to cease firing, and to rejoin Hunter's Division.[86] In a letter to Colonel Hunter, General Ambrose Burnside described the arrival of the 69th:

> It was Sherman's Brigade with the 69th New York Militia in advance, that arrived at about twelve-thirty o'clock, and by a most deadly fire assisted in breaking the enemy's lines, and soon after one o'clock the woods which had been so obstinately held were cleared of the enemy.[87]

Burnside had been engaged since 10:30 a.m., and his weary Rhode Island troops were out of ammunition. Sherman then formed his brigade behind Colonel Porter's brigade in line of battle with the 2nd Wisconsin foremost in line, then the 79th New York, and the 69th New York bringing up the rear.[88] The 13th New York advanced as the brigade skirmishers.[89] Meanwhile, the Northerners prepared to assault Henry House Hill.

---

[82] Ibid

[83] Colonel William T. Sherman's report OR II, Captain James Kelly's report, OR II, 371-2. 368-9.

[84] *The Irish American*, August 8, 1861. A letter from a member of Meagher's Zouave company, name given only as "R."

[85] Colonel William T. Sherman's Report. OR II, 369.

[86] Ibid.

[87] Ambrose Burnside to Colonel Hunter, August 3, 1861. OR II, 398.

[88] Sherman's Report. OR II, 369.

[89] Ibid. The Thirteenth New York was detailed as the brigade skirmishers, as they were the only rifle armed regiment in the Brigade. The other regiments being armed with .69 caliber smoothbores.

There, Beauregard's Rebels rallied behind Thomas J. Jackson's Brigade. Sherman's brigade advanced on fire, until reaching the sunken Henry House Hill under heavy Warrenton Turnpike, where they took shelter.[90]

The 2nd Wisconsin Infantry was ordered to attack on the left, leaving the shelter of the sunken road. The Badgers advanced into the leaden storm, but were repulsed. The Wisconsin boys rallied and attacked again, only to be repulsed again, and, finally, fell back.[91] The 2nd Wisconsin lost 112 soldiers in the assault.[92] Next, the 79th New York, "the Cameron Highlanders," were ordered to attack. But they were "...broken in their first assault, leaving 198 Highlanders on the field, the highest loss in Sherman's Brigade that day.[93] Then it was Corcoran's turn.

Prior to going into battle, the lads of the 69th stripped down to their shirtsleeves, and some of the Irishmen went in bare-chested. As Corcoran's fighting Irishmen reached the lip of the hill, they came upon a barren stretch of ground swept by artillery and musket fire. Corcoran was wounded in the leg, yet continued to lead the attacks with courage and spirit. The charging Celts came under heavy flanking fire, yet the attack was "gallantly led and gallantly sustained."[94] Thomas F. Meagher's horse was shot out from under him, but he was unscratched. He leapt up, waving his sword and crying out, "Boys! Look at that flag: Remember Ireland and Fontenoy!"[95] Colonel Corcoran ordered the flag lowered since there was extremely heavy fire. But the color bearer Green Prince of Wales conspicuous and drawing refused to, when he was cut down.[96] It was raised again, only to come down once again.[97] Three times the hard-fighting Irishmen pressed Jackson's batteries, only to be driven off by a scorching fire. M. Crosbie, of Company E, described the bloody struggle for Henry Hill:

> It was nothing but rally charge and repulse. We could see no enemy; they fought from the woods and from masked batteries. When we'd charge to the borders of the woods not one of them was to be seen - all the while their secreted riflemen and artillery, with every advantage of position, pouring their hail over

[90] Ibid.

[91] Ibid. OR II, 3B9-70.

[92] Casualty returns. OR II 351.

[93] Colonel William T. Sherman's Report. OR II, 3B9-70. Also Casualty Returns. OR II 351.

[94] Capt. D. P. Conyngham, A. D. C., *The Irish Brigade and Its Campaigns: With Some Account of the Corcoran Legion. and Sketches of the Principle Officers* (New York: William McSorely & Co., 1867), 36.

[95] Conyngham, 37.

[96] Jones, 85.

[97] Ibid.

and around us . . . . Still the boys went to their work like bricks. Corcoran made a regular target of himself.[98]

But the men were already "worn out," unable to press the attack a fourth time.[99] The intense fire of the enemy, as well as the panic of the 79th New York Infantry, which had preceded them in the assault, effectively thwarted Corcoran's attack.[100] Despite being punished by a flanking fire, the 69th retired in good order; later, the regiment was personally thanked by General McDowell, who had watched the attack.

Meanwhile, General Sherman ordered his brigade back to where it had formed. Colonel Corcoran's active exertions enabled him to form his men into a rough square to guard against cavalry attack, as the whipped Federals re-crossed Bull Run.[101] Importantly, in General Sherman's report, Colonel Corcoran was the only officer mentioned who seriously attempted to rally and form his men in the face of the pursuing Rebel Cavalry and the first major Union defeat of the war.

When they reached Bull Run, the 69th formed a column to pass through a narrow path through the rough terrain. General Sherman, who had been with the square, told the men to flee, fearing the enemy cavalry in pursuit.[102] Corcoran, who was wounded in the leg, vainly attempted to counter this ill-advised "license to run."[103] Consequently, he was cut off with nine men and the National colors. Corcoran and his band of warriors then retired to a nearby house, prepared to fight to the death.[104] Six more men reached Colonel Corcoran, but, realizing the futility of holding out, he surrendered, with the colors, to Adjutant B. H. Burke of the 13th Virginia Cavalry.[105]

While Corcoran and a handful of men rallied around the National Colors, the rest of the Irish Regiment fell back to Centreville. There they rallied around the Regiment's green flag. They returned to Fort Corcoran, which they reached early the next morning, having marched all night.[106] At Fort Corcoran, the officers attempted to put together what was left of the Regiment after the fiasco at Bull Run. One member of Meagher s Zouave company wrote:

---

[98] *The Irish American*, August 8, 1861.
[99] *The Irish American*, August 8, 1861. Letter from "R" a member of Meagher's Zouaves.
[100] Captain James Kelly's Report, July 24, 1861. OR Vol. II, 371-2.
[101] Sherman's Report. OR II, 370-1.
[102] *The Irish American*, October 26, 1861. Letter from James M. Rorty.
[103] Ibid.
[104] Ibid.
[105] Ibid. Also The Report of Col. R.C. Radford (13th VA Cavalry). OR II 352-3. This is contrary to the assertions of some that the 69th "never lost a color, never disobeyed an order.
[106] *The Irish American*, August 8, 1881.

We were taken to the shambles to be slaughtered; we got no chance to fight, but we stood until we were more than half thinned; all we have saved is our honor. We have lost our principle officers, and have made the bravest stand of the day.[107]

On Wednesday, July 24, 1861, President Abraham Lincoln decided to send all the three-month's volunteers home. The 69th, less 192 men, left Fort Corcoran on July 16, and was sent home, having learned of the many harsh realities of war.

Corcoran's "Fighting Irish" arrived in New York early Saturday morning, were immediately greeted by a sixty-nine gun salute from a detachment of the 4th New York Artillery, and were met by the 7th Regiment, New York State Militia and the Fenian Phoenix Brigade at Bowling Green, as well as by numerous Irish civic associations.[108] At Bowling Green, the 7th regiment graciously loaned the 69th a National Color for the occasion.[109] With both American and Irish Escorts, the parade headed up Broadway.

Captain James Kelly held the position of Colonel, while Lieutenant Colonel Robert Nugent marched with the Chaplains. Not having been present at the battles, Nugent felt that it would be inappropriate to take the honor of leading the Regiment, although it was his right. Major James Bagley had no such reservations, and marched in the major's position, even though he also had not been present at the battle. This placed Captain Relly in an awkward position.[110] Later, Major Bagley was publicly criticized in the Irish papers. But that would prove to be only the first of many such criticisms to head his way during the war. Major Bagely would command the 69th New York State Militia for the duration of the war, and never would serve under fire. When the balance of Corcoran's old Regiment volunteered for the Corcoran Legion in 1882, Bagley refused to go.

Two distinct themes resulted from the Battle of First Bull Run. There emerged, a fierce hatred of General William T. Sherman by the Regiment, and the idolization of Captain Thomas Francis Meagher by a vocal minority within the Regiment.

[107] Ibid.
[108] Ibid.
[109] Bernard Kelly, *The Historic Civil War Irish Colors of the 69th Regiment.* Unpublished work in the 69th Regimental Archives.
[110] *The Irish American*, August 8, 1881.

The 69th New York State Militia at Bull Run, July, 1861.

Evidently, the hatred of Sherman among certain members of the Regiment was fallout from the battle, or it may have begun on July 18th, with the accidental wounding of Captain John Breslin. Apparently, Sherman refused to let the Irish Regiment's sole ambulance carry Captain Breslin to the rear, but obliged the severely-wounded Captain to travel with the Regiment for several days.[111]

Meagher described General Sherman as a "rude and envenomed martinety" and, after the incident, "he was hated by the Regiment.[112] Sherman's unpopularity with the regiment, as his inept handling of his Brigade on Henry Hill, and the shifting of the blame of failure to his men and away from himself, caused much unrest and bitterness in a unit that was anxious to vindicate its fair name. The worst part of all was Sherman's "license to run" at Bull Run, where he lost his nerve, while the gallant Colonel Corcoran vainly tried to rally his troops before he was captured.

Following the battle of First Manassas, Meagher decided to organize an "Irish Brigade" and, immediately, five hundred of the 1,300 men who had served with the 69th New York State Militia Infantry at Bull Run signed up for three years' service in three regiments, the 69th, 88th and the 63rd New York Infantry Volunteers. Among the officers to go were Robert Nugent, Colonel of the 69th New York Infantry; Captain James Cavanagh would become Major of the 69th, and Captain James Quinlan would become Colonel of the 88th New York Infantry, until he resigned February 4, 1863. Captain Patrick Kelly would, later, become the Colonel of the 88th and command the Irish Brigade following Meager's resignation in 1863. The 69th New York State Militia provided the cadre for Meagher's later "Irish Brigade," and with the exception of General Thomas Smyth and Colonel Richard Byrnes, all the commanders of the Irish Brigade served as officers of the 69th New York State Militia at Bull Run. In the four years of war, they gained undying glory, and played a pivotal role on battlefields across the south, especially at the Peninsula, Antietam and Fredericksburg.

While Meagher set about creating his Brigade, Corcoran languished in captivity in Virginia and North Carolina and added new fame to a reputation won at Bull Run by refusing to accept parole. In August, 1862, he was exchanged for Confederate ministers James Mason and John Slidell. Corcoran then immediately began organizing his Irish Legion. Upon their return to New York, seven hundred officers and men of the

---

[111] *The Irish American*, August 8, 1881.
[112] Ibid.

old 69th New York State Militia immediately signed up for three years or the duration, becoming the 1st Regiment of the Corcoran Irish Legion, the 69th New York National Guard Artillery (also called the 182nd New York Infantry). Michael Corcoran was promoted to divisional command but died, in December of 1863, in a riding accident.

Lieutenant Matthew Murphy would become colonel of the 69th New York National Guards Artillery at age twenty-three. He would command the Corcoran Irish Legion from January, 1863, until February, 1865. Murphy would die of his wounds, on April 16, 1865, in a hospital at City Point, Virginia. Captain James P. McIvor would become colonel of the 170th New York Infantry, then would succeed Murphy as commander of the Legion, He would be mustered out a brigadier general. Lieutenant William Butler would rise to Lieutenant Colonel of the 69th New York National Guard Artillery, but died of wounds received before Petersburg. Captain John Coonan would later command the 69th New York National Guard Artillery and Captain J. B. Kirker would be the Brigade Quartermaster for the Irish Legion. With only two short interruptions the Irish Legion, like her sister command the Irish Brigade, was commanded solely by 69th Veterans of First Bull Run, demonstrating the legacy of the 69th. Additionally, the 69th Pennsylvania Infantry Volunteers was named in honor of the old 69th New York, and gained undying glory for breaking Picket's charge at the Angle on the third day of Gettysburg.

During the Bull Run campaign, Corcoran's Irishmen proved beyond all doubt that "...they're true to their oaths, but won't honor the Prince."[113] The editors of *Harper's Weekly*, which had so decried Corcoran's actions and slandered the Regiment s name, was like so many others, forced to eat their words. What was considered treasonous but two years earlier was then approved and lauded. Thirteen months after Bull Run, for example, an author at *Harper's Weekly* wrote, "It will suffice to say for that offense no one will be disposed to censure him now. If Prince Albert Edward were to come here to-morrow there is not a colonel in the service who would willingly pay honor to the heir of the throne of a country which has treated us as England has during the past year."[114]

Clearly, the actions and accomplishments of the 69th set the standard. After Bull Run, approximately two hundred thousand sons of Erin were to serve in the Union army, earning the reputation for always being in the thickest of the fight. Perhaps the greatest vindication of Michael Corcoran

---

[113] Col. Corcoran and the Prince of Wales, Anonymous Broadside, (New York, 186?). In the collections of the New York Historical Society .

[114] *Harper's Weekly.* August 30, 1862.

and his 69th New York State Militia, was one of those subtle and symbolic Ironies of history. Three years, ten months, and two weeks to the day that the 69th New York State Militia advanced into Virginia, the senior surviving field officer of the old 69th, Robert Nugent, now Brigadier General commanding the Irish Brigade, took General Ulysses S. Grant's first surrender offer to General Robert E. Lee. Two days later, General Lee surrendered at Appomattox Court House.

THE IRISH BRIGADE

69th New York Infantry, organized at New York and mustered in November 18, 1861, the 1st regiment of the Irish Brigade.

Rare signed photograph of Thomas F. Meagher. (Sergeant Kirkland's Museum and Historical Society)

Chapter III

Sprig of Green: The Irish Brigade

by Kevin E. O'Brien

"How are you today, Yank?" asked the Confederate of the Union man on the other side of the Rappahannock River near Fredericksburg, Virginia, in December, 1862.

"I reckon I feel rather cold, Johnny; I'd like an nip," replied the Federal soldier from the Irish Brigade.

"Any coffee, Yank?" said the Rebel, holding up a canteen of good home-made whiskey. [1]

"Plenty; and tobacco too."

Thus, a trade was established. Both sides crossed over to exchange essential goods in peace. On occasion, old friends and relatives met this way; they were men from Ireland who had emigrated to a new homeland at war with itself.

In November, 1862, President Abraham Lincoln had sacked General George B. McClellan as commander of the Army of the Potomac for failing to pursue General Robert E. Lee and the Army of Northern Virginia after the Battle of Antietam on September 17, 1862. The new chief general of the Union forces, General Ambrose E. Burnside, had distinguished himself in the Carolinas, but was even better-known for his muttonchop

---

[1] Captain Daniel P. Conyngham, *The Irish Brigade And Its Campaigns* (New York: McSorley & Co., 1867, 328. The author served with the Irish Brigade through 1863 before being transferred to Sherman's Army. His friend, Doctor William O'Meagher, surgeon in the 69th New York, completed the book on the Irish Brigade, covering 1864 - 1865.

whiskers. General Burnside seemed a master strategist at first, feinting towards Culpepper, moving southeast, and evading Lee. The Army of the Potomac stole a march to the Rappahannock River, opposite the city of Fredericksburg. Behind Fredericksburg lay Richmond, whose capture would be a mortal blow to the Confederacy.

The Irish Brigade, First Division, Second Corps, advanced south under General Burnside. Its three original regiments, the 63rd, 69th, and 88th New York Infantry, had just been reinforced by the addition of two more regiments to the brigade -- the 28th Massachusetts and the 116th Pennsylvania Infantry.[2] On the way to Fredericksburg, its men distinguished themselves, capturing two guns from a Confederate battery. As they dashed at the Southern cannons, they gave an Irish cheer, and kicked over Rebel kettles, frying pans, coffee pots, and everything else in the way. The enemy fled without firing a shot. Their new Division commander, Winfield Scott Hancock, cried out, "I have never seen anything so splendid."[3]

There was nothing to stop the Army of the Potomac from taking the city of Fredericksburg in late November, 1862. General Sumner, the Union Right Grand Division commander, could have had his troops wade across the Rappahannock at fords and unlock the door to Richmond. Instead, he was ordered by General Burnside to wait for pontoon bridges, so the moment was lost.

A general feeling prevailed as the year's campaign was ended. The soldiers in the Irish Brigade constructed winter quarters in the pine-covered hills and pleasant meadow lands surrounding Falmouth. Yet, some soldiers had a foreboding about Fredericksburg. Corporal William A. Smith, Company D, 116th Pennsylvania Infantry, wrote his parents: ". . . so we have got to Falmouth now and we expect to go a cross the river to[o] and take Frederick[sburg] . . . we have give them orders to give up the town . . . they will not do it yet . . . so I expect the ball will open so we will make them dance . . ."[4]

The Confederates were very busy across the river. Lee moved every soldier that he had into the heights overlooking Fredericksburg. Every hour saw new earthworks rising in front of the Union forces -- redoubts, rifle-pits, lunettes, and other protective positions. Weeks passed, and the Confederate defenses grew even more formidable.

---

[2] Frederick H. Dyer, *Compendium of the War of the Rebellion: Part III, Regimental Histories* (Des Moines: Dyer Publishing Co., 1908; reprint, Dayton: Morningside House, 1978) 1258, 1612.

[3] Conyngham, 327.

[4] Letter from William A. Smith to Parents, November 27, 1862, on file in Irish Brigade Collection, Fredericksburg and Spotsylvania National Military Park (FSNMP).

Early in December, 1862, General Ambrose E. Burnside called a council of war. As one of those present afterwards remarked, the assembled Union commanders talked to General Burnside at "arm's length." There was a total absence of that harmony and unity of purpose, so necessary to success, between the commanding general and his lieutenants.[5] After vacillating over a possible attack on Lee's flank, Burnside decided to assault, frontally, the Confederate defensive works.[6]

On the eve of General Burnside's attack, the boys of the Irish Brigade were sure that there would not be a fight. One of the men went to Father William Corby, the Catholic chaplain of the 88th New York. "Father," said this soldier, "they are going to lead us over in front of those guns which we have seen them placing, unhindered, for the past three weeks."

Father Corby told him: "Do not trouble yourself; your generals know better than that." [7]

On the morning of December 11, twenty-nine Federal batteries with 147 guns opened a bombardment on Fredericksburg. Tons of iron were hurled into the town, raking and sweeping the streets. Flames leapt high out of the mist-covered buildings, with smoke rising above the fog to cover the doomed city like a pall. Volunteers from the 7th Michigan Infantry and the 19th and 20th Massachusetts Infantry crossed the Rappahannock River in open pontoon boats and drove Confederate General Barksdale's Mississippi Regiment from the city limits.[8]

The 1,200 men of the Irish Brigade, loaded with ammunition and field rations, marched into the newly-captured city of Fredericksburg on December 12, 1862. Packed with Union soldiers readying for assault, there were few accommodations available for the waiting troops. Color Sergeant Peter Welsh, of the 28th Massachusetts, wrote to his wife afterwards: ". . . when it became dark, we moved our position a little and stacked arms for the night with mud ankle-deep to lay down and sleep on

---

[5] Letter from William B. Franklin to St. Clair Mulholland, January 5, 1881, Mulholland Papers, Box 1, Civil War Library and Museum, Philadelphia, Pa; St. Clair A. Mulholland, *The Story of the 116th Regiment, Pennsylvania Infantry* (Philadelphia: F. McManus & Jr. & Company Printers, 1903) 29. Hereafter cited as Mulholland. The author served as an officer in the regiment throughout its association with the Irish Brigade and commanded a brigade of his own by the end of the war.

[6] For an analysis of Burnside's strained relations with his Grand Division commanders (Sumner, Franklin, and Hooker) and his indecision on a battle plan, see Edward Stackpole, *The Fredericksburg Campaign: Drama On The Rappahannock* (2nd ed., Harrisburg: Stackpole Books, 1991), 99-171; for a more sympathetic view of Burnside and his strategy, see William Marvel *Burnside* (Chapel Hill: University of North Carolina Press, 1991), 151-217.

[7] Rev. William Corby, *Memoirs of Chaplain Life* (Chicago: LaMonte, O'Donnell & Co. 1893), 131.

[8] St. Clair A. Mulholland, "Annals of the War," *Philadelphia Weekly Times*, April 23, 1881, 9-12 on file in Irish Brigade Collection (FSNMP).

. . . we hunted up pieces of boards and lay them down on the mud and then lay down and covered ourselves up in our blankets . . ."[9]

A cold, damp, misty morning dawned on December 13, 1862. The Irish Brigade was ordered to fall in and wait for orders. Confederate shells were screaming overhead, striking houses, and scattering bricks and stones all around. The wounded from an early Union attack filed past in great numbers. After standing under arms all morning, the Irish Brigade was addressed by its charismatic commander, Brigadier General Thomas Francis Meagher. In burning, eloquent words, he reminded his boys that they were Irish, and every eye in the Union would watch to see how they would uphold their fighting Irish tradition.

The Irish Brigade was known by its distinctive, emerald-green, regimental battle flags. The flags of the three New York regiments had been so riddled with shot and shell in previous battles that they had been returned to New York City for replacement.[10] To make sure that the enemy knew that it was the Irish Brigade, General Meagher ordered sprigs of evergreen to be placed in the caps of both officers and men, himself first setting the example. The men broke ranks and every soldier in the brigade returned with a bit of boxwood in his cap. Major Mulholland, of the 116th Pennsylvania, recalled years later: "Wreaths were made and hung upon the tattered [U.S.] flags, and the national color of the Emerald Isle blended in fair harmony with the red, white, and blue of the Republic."[11] The green regimental banner of the 28th Massachusetts, only recently presented to it, was uncased, decorated with a harp, a sunburst, and a wreath of shamrocks. It bore the Gaelic motto *"Faugh A Ballagh,"* translated as *"Clear The Way."*

At last, the Irish Brigade was ordered to move towards battle. The men moved out on Hanover Street, passing a blasted and ruined city. Union troops had broken into private residences and businesses, looting as they went. Broken furniture, smashed family portraits, and even church pews littered the streets. Long range Rebel artillery began to find its mark, with shells dropping with destructive effect. One shell took out eighteen men in the 88th New York. Another missile wounded the commander of the 116th Pennsylvania, beheaded a sergeant, and killed three men.[12]

---

[9] Lawrence Kohl and Margaret Richard, ed., *Irish Green - Union Blue: The Civil War Letters of Peter Welsh, Color Sergeant, 28th Regiment, Massachusetts Volunteers* (New York: Fordham University Press, 1986), 42.
[10] Conyngham, 330-337.
[11] Mulholland, 44.
[12] Ibid., 45.

The *New York Herald's* front page map of Fredericksburg, December 16, 1862, showing the locations of the Rebel batteries just south of Fredericksburg. (Sergeant Kirkland's Museum and Historical Society)

Still under intense fire, the Irishmen reached a canal which was supposed to have been bridged. Rebel artillery fire had left only the support posts. Some men plunged into the ice-cold water to cross, while others stepped quickly over the few remaining planks. Protected after crossing the canal by a slight fold of ground, the men relieved themselves of haversacks and blankets, and prepared for action. The rising slope of Marye's Heights lay ahead, covered with stubble from the summer's crops and crested by a low stone wall. It was also carpeted with dead and wounded Federal soldiers from earlier attacks by French's Division and Zook's Brigade of Hancock's Division.

Waiting to go in, the men of the Irish Brigade were ordered to lie down on the ground because of intense Confederate rifle and cannon fire. In a few minutes came the word "Attention!" and every man rose upon his feet again. Next came the order "Fix bayonets!" Private William M'Carter, of the 116th Pennsylvania Infantry, recalled that, as the men attached the bayonets to muskets, "...the clink, clink, clink of the cold steel sounding along the line made one's blood run cold."[13] A bold, distinct Gaelic voice, loud enough to be heard above the noise of battle, yelled, "Irish Brigade, advance!" This command was followed by another shout: "Forward double-quick, guide centre!"[14]

The noonday sun glittered on the frozen ground and the long lines of bayonets as the Irishmen rushed up the hill with wild cheers. General Meagher had led the brigade to the field but could not join the charge because of a lame knee. The five infantry regiments advanced from left to right as follows: 116th Pennsylvania, 63rd New York, 28th Massachusetts, 88th New York, and the 69th New York.[15] The Green Flag of the 28th Massachusetts was in the center of the brigade, flying and flapping in the breeze. The soldiers of the Irish Brigade had not gone far when they were struck by whining artillery shells. Shells burst in front, in the rear, above, and in the ranks. Holes opened in their lines, but the Irishmen closed them and pressed on forward. An Irishman in the 8th Ohio Infantry, whose earlier assault on Marye's Heights had failed, observed the Irish Brigade as it passed: "Every man has a sprig of green in his cap, and a

---

[13] William M'Carter, "Annals of the War," *Philadelphia Weekly Times*, September 8, 1883, 9, on file in Irish Brigade Collection (FSNMP).

[14] Ibid., 9, Conyngham, 342.

[15] Report of Brig. Gen. Thomas F. Meagher, U.S. War Department, *War of the Rebellion: A Compilation of the Official Records of the Union and Confederate Armies* series I, vol. 21, (Washington, D.C.: Government Printing Office, 1880-1902) 241-242. Hereafter cited as OR. All references are to Series I unless otherwise noted.

half-laughing, half-murderous look in his eye."[16] The Union wounded littering the ground cheered and waved on the Irishmen. Officers and men fell rapidly, but others ran to take their places.

The stone wall was defended, in part, by Confederate General Thomas R. R. Cobb's Georgia Brigade, many of whom were Irish immigrants. As the Irish Brigade closed on its position, these Confederates recognized the Green Flag of the 28th Massachusetts and the symbolic sprigs of green in the caps of their opponents. "Oh, God, what a pity! Here comes Meagher's fellows!" was the cry in the Confederate ranks. Nevertheless, they opened fire with their rifles. The sharp whiz of minié balls joined the loud scream of exploding shells. Captain John Donovan, in the 69th New York, called the combined cannon and rifle fire "murderous" as gaps opened in his unit's ranks. In the 116th Pennsylvania, Lieutenant Garret Nowlen, commanding Company C, fell with a ball through the thigh. Major George H. Bardwell fell badly wounded and a ball whistled through Lieutenant Robert T. Maguire's lungs.[17] Lieutenant Christian Foltz fell dead with a ball through his brain. The orderly sergeant of Company H wheeled around, gazed upon Lieutenant Quinlan, and a great stream of blood poured from a hole in his forehead, splashing over the young officer. The sergeant fell dead at Quinlan's feet. Captain John O'Neill, Company K, was shot in the lungs, the ball passing completely through his body. Still onward the line pressed steadily, men dropping in twos, threes, and in groups.[18]

The charge was stalled by a wooden rail fence about sixty yards from the Confederate lines. The Rebels, lined up in four ranks, poured volley after volley into the Irishmen, splintering the fence, spattering mud in all directions, and taking down men. Color Sergeant Peter Welsh, in the 28th Massachusetts Infantry, recalled: ". . . the storm of shot was then most galling and our ranks were soon thinned . . ." Private William McCleland, of the 88th New York Infantry, provided an even more graphic description of the brutal Confederate defensive fire: ". . . none of our company fell until we were within thirty or forty yards of the rifle pits, where we met dreadful showers of bullets from three lines of the enemy, besides their

[16] Capt. Thomas F. Galwey, *The Valiant Hours* (Harrisburg: Stackpole Co., 1961), 62.

[17] Discharged, January 16, 1863.

[18] Mulholland, 57. Letter from Capt. John Donovan, *The Irish-American*, January 3, 1863, on file in Irish Brigade Collection (FSNMP). *The Irish-American* was a New York City newspaper published between 1851-1915. Mulholland, 47-48.

enfilading fire. Our men were mowed down like grass before the scythe of the reaper . . . The men lay piled up in all directions."[19]

Bent over in the hail of lead, the men of the Irish Brigade dashed towards the front as if they were dodging a storm. Many men were almost blown off their feet by the concussion from the concentrated fire. Captain Nagle, of the 88th, was literally thrown over when a piece of shell struck his haversack, tearing it off of him.[20] A strange sound was heard above the screams of the wounded and the exploding artillery shells. The Rebels were cheering and applauding, overcome by the bravery of their foe! General George Pickett, best known for his charge at Gettysburg, wrote, after the battle, to his fiancee: "Your soldier's heart almost stood still as he watched those sons of Erin fearlessly rush to their death. The brilliant assault on Marye's Heights of their Irish Brigade was beyond description. Why, my darling, we forgot they were fighting us, and cheer after cheer at their fearlessness went up all along our lines."[21]

The gaps in the lines had become so large and numerous that continued efforts had to be made to close them. Regiments and companies had their third or fourth commanders, and the colors were raised by the third or fourth soldiers who picked them up from the ground. The Irish Brigade halted about thirty yards from the stone wall and delivered a heavy volley into the Confederate line. The Color Sergeant of the 116th Pennsylvania, William H. Tyrell, down on one knee after a minié ball had shattered his other leg, defiantly waved the Stars and Stripes at the enemy. Five more balls struck him in succession; a dozen more ripped through the colors; still another broke the flag-staff. The colors and color sergeant fell together. Lieutenant Quinlan saved the colors and Tyrell, miraculously, survived.[22]

The command to lie down and fire passed through the surviving men. In the 28th Massachusetts, Color Sergeant Peter Welsh wrote: ". . . our troops had to lay down to escape the raking fire of the batteries and we had a poor chance at the enemy who was sheltered in his rifle pits and entrenchments . . . I seen some hot work at south mountain and Antietam in Maryland but they were not to be compared to this . . . every man that was near me in the right of the company was either killed or wounded except one . . ." The Irishmen loaded their muskets on their backs to pres-

---

[19] Kohl and Richard, 43; Letter from Private William H. McCleland, *The Irish American*, January 10, 1863, on file in Irish Brigade Collection (FSNMP).

[20] Letter from Capt. W.J. Nagle, *The Irish-American*, December 27, 1862, on file in Irish Brigade Collection (FSNMP).

[21] George E. Pickett, *The Heart of A Soldier* (New York: Seth Moyle, Inc., 1913), 66.

[22] Mulholland, 50.

ent a smaller target, rolled over, and shot back at the enemy. Major James Cavanagh, who took over command of the 69th New York after Colonel Nugent was wounded, shouted, "Blaze away and stand to it, boys!" Officers from the 69th New York fell all around Captain Jack Donovan. Two bullets pierced his hat, narrowly missing his head. His own turn came when a rifle ball ripped through his overcoat in the left shoulder, striking a metal shoulder strap and leaving a bruise. Donovan was then struck with a piece of spent shell in the chest, knocking him unconscious.[23]

On the other side of the slope, Private William M'Carter, of the 116th Pennsylvania was first struck by a spent bullet on his left shoulder. A second round cut the leather peak from his cap, leaving it dangling by his ear. A comrade at his side fell, having been shot in the stomach. The man died with the exclamation, "Oh, my mother!" on his lips. While ramming a new cartridge down his musket, M'Carter was hit by a ball in the right arm near the shoulder. He fell, unconscious, to the ground. When M'Carter attempted to rise, a bullet skimmed his left wrist and another round ripped open his cartridge box, scattering its contents. Staying flat, he heard more bullets whiz by his head. M'Carter used his blanket roll to shield himself from the flying bullets. After he finally crawled to safety, M'Carter shook over thirty spent Confederate bullets out of the blanket.[24] With its dead, dying, and wounded strewn about the slope, and its survivors' ammunition exhausted, the Irish Brigade fell back in small groups. Many of the men refused to yield the ground that they had already gained. These soldiers had to collect cartridges out of the dead and wounded men's pouches to continue the fight.[25] By nightfall, the last of the Irish Brigade returned from Mayre's Heights, leaving behind their dead and wounded. Among the very last to leave the field was Captain Jack Donovan of the 69th New York, who regained consciousness around twilight. When the Confederate and friendly fire slackened around dusk, he gave the order to fall back. About a dozen men rose from among the dead and followed him, including three members of his own company and the first sergeant. Donovan's hat was shot off his head before he was beyond effective Confederate rifle range. Reaching safety in the rear, Donovan shed tears of gratitude for his own survival and of sorrow for his fallen friends.[26]

---

[23] Kohl and Richard, 43; Letter from Capt. John Donovan.
[24] M'Carter, 9-22..
[25] Letter from Anonymous Irish Brigade Officer, *Irish-American*, December 27, 1862, on file in Irish Brigade Collection (FSNMP)
[26] Letter from Capt. John Donovan.

After the war, Captain John Dwyer, of the 63rd New York Infantry, re-called the order to "...lie down and fire. Fortunately ... or not a man or officer would have lived." Facing the Confederate regiments of Thomas R. R. Cobb's Georgia Infantry and Joseph B. Kershaw's South Carolina Infantry behind the stone wall at Fredericksburg, December 13, 1862. (Sergeant Kirkland's Museum and Historical Society).

A correspondent from the *London Times*, who had viewed the attack from behind the Southern lines, wrote afterwards:

Never at Fontenoy, Albuera, or at Waterloo, was more undaunted courage displayed by the sons of Erin than during those six frantic dashes which they directed against the almost impregnable position of their foe . . . the bodies which lie in dense masses within forty yards of Colonel Walton's guns are the best evidence what manner of men they were who pressed on to death with the dauntlessness of a race which has gained glory on a thousand battlefields, and never more richly deserved it than at the foot of Marye's Heights on the 13th day of December 1862.

General Robert E. Lee stated, of the Irish Brigade's attack at Fredericksburg, "Never were men so brave."[27] On the cold, frosty morning following the assault, the Irish Brigade learned the price of its bravery.

Three out of its five regimental commanders -- Major Joseph O'Neill, of the 63rd New York; Colonel Robert Nugent, of the 69th New York; and Colonel Dennis Heenan, of the 116th Pennsylvania — had been wounded. Colonel Richard Byrnes, commanding the 28th Massachusetts, and Colonel Patrick Kelly, commanding the 88th New York, barely escaped injury. Kelly's uniform was riddled with bullet holes. Out of 1,200 men in the Irish Brigade engaged, 545 were killed, wounded, or missing, a forty-five percent casualty rate.[28] The 69th New York Regiment alone had lost sixteen of its eighteen officers and 112 of its enlisted men, 128 of the 238 who had started the charge.[29]

General Winfield Scott Hancock, First Division commander, rode his horse past the remains of his troops at morning formation. Three privates of the Irish Brigade were off by themselves on parade. "God damn you!" Hancock shouted, "Why don't you close up with your company?" One of the privates saluted and replied, "General, we are a company." "The devil you are!" exclaimed the impressed Hancock. He returned the salute with extra care, his soldierly eye beaming.[30] Hancock rode away, too full of admiration for the three men to inspect them.

---

[27] Conyngham, 349-350; George W. Pepper, *Under Three Flags* (Cincinnati, 1899). 333.

[28] OR, 21, 1.28. According to the Official Records, the 28th Massachusetts lost 158 men killed, wounded, and missing; the 63rd New York's count was 44 casualties; the 69th New York lost 128 men; the 88th New York had 127 casualties; and the 116th Pennsylvania reported 88 men as killed, wounded, or missing. The Irish Brigade had 46 killed, 416 wounded and 74 missing in action.

[29] Colonel Nugent claimed an even higher casualty rate for the 69th at Fredericksburg after the war. After he detailed three officers and 46 enlisted men to protect a knoll on the flank, Nugent counted 16 officers and 168 enlisted men available for the charge. Of this number, Nugent wrote, 141 enlisted men were killed or wounded and all 16 officers were casualties. Letter from Robert Nugent to St. Clair Mulholland, January 5, 1881, Mulholland Papers, Box I, Civil War Library and Museum, Philadelphia, Pa.

[30] Conyngham, 362-363.

THE CASUALTIES.

Additional Names of Killed and Wounded in the Battle of Fredericksburg.

THE KILLED AND WOUNDED IN THE IRISH BRIGADE.

Colonel Nugent, of the Sixty-ninth New York (Irish Brigade), furnishes the following list of casualties from personal recollection:—

In the Sixty-ninth New York were wounded—

Colonel Nugent, severely.
Major Cavanagh, in the hip.
Captain Leddy, arm. He had just recovered from a previous wound.
Captain Towe, not dangerously.
Lieutenant Birmingham, missing.
Lieutenant M. P. Brennan, missing.
Lieutenant Murphy, wounded, severely.
Lieutenant O'Neil, mortally.
Lieutenant Buckley, mortally.
Captain Donovan, mortally.
Lieutenant Manser, mortally.
Lieutenant Burke, mortally.
Lieutenant Kearney, mortally.
Lieutenant Callahan, mortally.
Lieutenant Scully, slightly.

In the Sixty-third New York:—

Major O'Neil, commanding, lost an arm.
Captain Richard Moore, the same.
Captain Sullivan, not dangerously.
Captain Cartwright, killed.

IN THE EIGHTY-EIGHTH NEW YORK.

Major Horgan, killed.
Captain Burke, wounded, severely.
Captain Clark, wounded, severely.

KILLED AND WOUNDED IN FRANKLIN'S GRAND DIVISION.

Corporal Davidson, Co. E, 186th Pennsylvania, foot.
Paul Wil son, Co. B, 26th New York, arm.
Jos. W. Hirsch, Co. H, 136th Pennsylvania, head.
Lieut. H. Barker, Co. G, 136th Pennsylvania, foot.
Lieut. Stewart, Co. I, 11th Pennsylvania, arm.
David Franklin, Co. C, 97th New York, head.
John S. French, Co. C, 19th Pennsylvania, scrotum.
Geo. Bowman, Co. B, 88th Pennsylvania, loss of right arm.

The casualties list of the *New York Herald*, December 16, 1862. Colonel Nugent was "honored" with his name first, followed by the other officers of the 69th New York, 63rd New York, 88th New York, and then the men of Franklin's Grand Division; the list goes on, column after column, until it nearly fills the page. (Sergeant Kirkland's Museum and Historical Society)

The Irish Brigade was born in the teeming immigrant community of New York City. Driven out of their homeland by the Great Potato Famine of the 1840's, the bulk of Irish immigrants lived at the poverty level in cities like New York, Boston, Philadelphia, and New Orleans. The New York Irish were an unlikely recruiting ground for the crusade to save the Union. Democrats and supporters of Mayor Fernando Wood's Mozart Hall political machine, the Irish contributed to Lincoln's loss of New York City in the 1860 election by about 30,000 votes.[31] Fearful of losing their low-paying jobs to newly-freed slaves, the Irish voted against the abolitionist Republican Party.

In the shock following Fort Sumter, an all-Irish unit from New York City, the 69th New York State Militia, was among the first to answer Lincoln's call for volunteers. Led by Colonel Michael Corcoran, who had been court-martialed for refusing to parade the regiment in honor of the visit of England's Prince of Wales, the 69th rushed to the defense of the Capitol. At the First Battle of Bull Run on July 21, 1861, the Irish distinguished themselves under Sherman, making three hopeless attacks against a Rebel battery.[32]

The Irish community in New York City held a spectacular parade and reception for its returning heroes of the 69th, on Broadway, upon the expiration of their three-month enlistment.

One of the veterans of the 69th New York State Militia, Captain Thomas F. Meagher, returned from battle with a grand vision -- the formation of an all-Irish Brigade. Born in Country Waterford, to a prosperous family, Meagher was a leading figure in the Irish uprising of 1848. Condemned to death for his activities in the rebellion, he was exiled for life, by a special act of Parliament, to Tasmania, off the coast of Australia. Escaping English exile, Meagher fled to the United States. After his arrival in New York City, he became a celebrity in the Irish immigrant community, practicing law, editing a newspaper, and marrying the daughter of a wealthy merchant. He was a prominent Democrat, with many friends in the South, when the war began. Yet, he was among the first to answer the call for volunteers to preserve the Union.[33]

---

[31] See Ernest A. McKay, *The Civil War and New York City*, (Syracuse: Syracuse University Press, 1990), 21.

[32] Conyngham, 19-46.

[33] For Meagher's life, see Robert G. Athearn, *Thomas Francis Meagher: An Irish Revolutionary in America* (Boulder: University of Colorado Press, 1949). See also Michael Cavanagh, *Memoirs of Gen. Thomas Francis Meagher* (Worcester: Messenger Press, 1892).

The Reception of the 69th New York State Militia by the 7th New York State Militia.

With other prominent members of the Irish community, such as Archbishop Hughes and Judge Charles P. Daly, Meagher appealed to his fellow immigrants to fight for the nation that had given them asylum and freedom. In rally after rally, his golden oratory won new recruits for the Union Army. Three regiments were formed and became the Irish Brigade -- the 63rd, 69th, and 88th New York Volunteers. Its 2,500 men were a cross-section of the Irish in America. Most of them were brawny workers: canal diggers, track-layers, highway laborers, carpenters, hod carriers, cabmen, porters, and streetcar drivers, with a seasoning of waiters and barkeepers. The "lace-curtain" Irish were represented by lawyers, teachers, newspapermen, merchants, city workers, and even sea captains.[34]

After training at Fort Schulyer on Long Island, the Irish Brigade was dispatched to join the vast Union host gathering on the banks of the Potomac under General George B. McClellan. Meagher was promoted to brigadier general of the brigade. The Irishmen saw their first action during McClellan's Peninsula campaign in the spring and summer of 1862. On the second day of the Battle of Fair Oaks, June 1, 1862, the Irish Brigade was thrown in to stop a Rebel attack. Colonel Nugent, commander of the 69th New York, reported: "Our fire was sustained with fearful consistency until the enemy was silenced, and checking the advance of the rebels had, I am inclined to believe a marked effect on the fortunes of the day."[35]

The brigade was heavily engaged during the battles of the Seven Days from June 25, to July 1, 1862. At Gaines's Mills, on June 26, the Irishmen reinforced the 9th Massachusetts, a fellow Irish unit being destroyed by Stonewall Jackson's men. The Irish Brigade stalled a Confederate charge, saved the 9th Massachusetts, and kept the Union retreat from turning into a rout. Used as a rear guard again at Savage Station, on June 29, and at White Oak Swamp, on June 30, the Irishmen fought fiercely, protecting the withdrawal of McClellan's forces. At Malvern Hill, on July 1, the Irish Brigade's 88th New York Regiment tangled with Lee's Louisiana Tigers. Meeting the New Yorkers at close range and not having time to load their muskets, the Tigers fought with bowie knives and pistols. The Irishmen, equally surprised by the encounter, had no time to fix bayonets, so they used their muskets as clubs and went to work with a half-Gaelic, half-English scream. The battle raged on into darkness, until a gigantic Irishman seized a mounted officer, who was cheering on the Ti-

---

[34] See Conyngham, 47-70, on the recruitment of the Irish Brigade.
[35] OR, 11, pt. 1, 780.

gers. The capture of their officer took the heart out of the Tigers and they retreated, using their six-shooters to hold off the Irish.[36]

The men of the Irish Brigade discovered who the enemy really was during the Seven Days' campaign. At Malvern Hill, on July 1, a company of the Irish Brigade was pinned down by the fire of Rebels who were sheltered in a stand of trees. The company commander of the Confederates, a man of great daring, directed the fire of his men with such skill and accuracy that the Irishmen could not move. The Irish captain turned to Sergeant Driscoll, one of the best shots in the brigade, and stated: "If that officer is not taken down, many of us will fall before we pass that clump." "Leave that to me," said Driscoll. He raised his rifle, took aim, and the Rebel officer fell. The Confederates broke away at once after their commander was shot down.

"Driscoll, see if that officer is dead -- he was a brave fellow," said the Irish captain.

As Driscoll turned him over, the officer murmured, "Father" and then closed his eyes forever. Driscoll laid down the body of his son, who had moved to the South before the war. Ordered to charge a few minutes later, Driscoll rushed on in frantic grief, calling on his men to follow. He fell, jumped up again, and rolled over for the last time, riddled with bullets.[37] His men buried father and son in one grave, set up a rough cross, and went on with their business.

"I wish I had twenty thousand more men like yours," said McClellan to General Meagher after the Army of the Potomac retreated to safety at Harrison's Landing.[38] McClellan had lost 493 men from the Irish Brigade, who had been killed, wounded, or become missing during the Seven Days' series of battles.[39] The 29th Massachusetts Infantry had been attached to the Irish Brigade just before the Seven Days, to give the brigade the standard number of four regiments. A more unlikely marriage of units is difficult to imagine. Most of the men of the 29th were blue-blooded Yankees who could claim direct descent from Mayflower stock. Whenever Meagher tried his golden Celtic tongue on the men of the 29th, they listened in cold silence. They showed their true colors when a party

---

[36] Rev. Patrick D. O'Flaherty, *The History of the Sixty-Ninth Regiment in the Irish Brigade* (New York: Privately printed, 1986), 112. O'Flaherty is an excellent resource in that he uses much material from the *Irish-American*. Irish Brigade soldiers wrote articles for the *Irish-American* during the war; the newspaper also printed many of their letters. See also Cavanagh, 450-451.

[37] Conyngham, 237-238.

[38] Ibid., 249.

[39] OR, 11, pt. 2, 24. The casualties were as follows: 29th Massachusetts, 85 men; 63rd New York, 70 men; 69th New York, 208 men; and 88th New York, 129 men.

of them raided the general's headquarters, making off with most of the whiskey. Meagher called them "Irishmen in disguise" after that.[40]

Bloody Lane at Antietam, on September 17, 1862, was the Irish Brigade's next major engagement. Reinforcing the attack on Lee's center, the Irish Brigade, its Green Flags snapping in the breeze, led Richardson's Division into battle. The Confederates were well-protected by a sunken road, which served as an effective rifle pit.

When the Irish Brigade arrived on the scene, Posey's Mississippi Brigade and the 7th West Virginia Infantry had advanced into the field in front of the sunken road. These troops threatened to flank the entire Union position in the center of Antietam. This movement was checked by the appearance and deployment of the Irish Brigade in attack formation. A split rail fence, at the edge of a plowed field, blocked the Irish Brigade's forward progress. Volunteers stepped forward to tear down the fence. These men ran into a galling hail of lead from the direction of the sunken road. Bullets literally snatched fence rails from their hands and most of the volunteers fell, shredded and dead on the fence. The obstruction removed, the officers and men of the Irish Brigade dashed forward, cheering and waving swords and hats.[41]

Confederate sharpshooters in treetops started to pick off color-bearers and officers among the onrushing Irish. Armed with old muskets, the Irish could not reply to this long-range rifle fire. Captain Felix Duffy, who had procured an unauthorized modern rifle as a personal weapon, moved about the front, knocking the snipers out of their perches. Duffy went down and died as he fell, the victim of a vengeful sniper.[42]

When the Irishmen reached the brow of a hill and closed on the sunken road, they were greeted by Confederate rifles flashing like a quarter-mile long bolt of lightning. The foremost Green Flag of the 69th New York was completely riddled and eight color-bearers fell charging with it. After the last had fallen, and the Irish Green lay on the ground; General Meagher shouted: "Boys, raise the colors, and follow me!" Captain James McGee, of the 69th, gathered up the flag and raced forward. A bullet cut the flag's standard in half; as McGee retrieved the flag, another bullet tore through his cap. He jumped up, waved the flag at the Rebels, and, miraculously, escaped injury. Lieutenant Colonel Henry Fowler re-

---

[40] Paul Jones, *The Irish Brigade* (New York: Robert B. Luce, 1969), 121.
[41] Report of Brig. Gen. Thomas F. Meagher, OR, 19, pt. 1,294; Conyngham 305; see also John M. Priest, *Antietam: The Soldiers' Battle* (Shippensburg: White Mane Publishing Co., 1989), 159-160.
[42] O'Flaherty, 157-158.

ported that sixteen men fell bearing the colors of the 63rd New York Regiment.[43]

The Irishmen darted into the rifle fire with their heads lowered. They paused at intervals to fire five or six volleys, catching Posey's Mississippi Brigade on the flanks as it bolted towards the sunken road, and turning the left wing of the 7th West Virginia. Their attack nearly annihilated the 16th Mississippi Regiment and drove the Confederates back into the safety of the sunken road.[44]

In the words of General Meagher: "Despite a fire of musketry, which literally cut lanes through our approaching line, the Brigade advanced under my personal command within thirty paces of the enemy. . ." Halting and forming a line in front of the sunken lane, the Irish Brigade cut loose with a murderous blast from its muskets, dropping the tightly-packed Confederates in rows. The Irishmen's buck and ball rounds -- .69 caliber lead balls reinforced by three buckshot -- tore bodies apart like they had been hit by shotguns at that close range. Anderson's North Carolina Brigade -- the 2nd, 14th, 4th, and 30th North Carolina -- returned a vicious fire in one of the most brutal exchanges of musketry that occurred during the Civil War. Captain Thomas F. Galwey, whose 8th Ohio Regiment fought next to the Irish Brigade at Bloody Lane, recalled: "The air is alive with the concussion of all sorts of explosions. We are kneeling in the soft grass and I notice for a long time that every blade of grass is moving. For some time I supposed that this is caused by the merry crickets; and it is not until I have made a remark to that effect to one of our boys near me and notice him laugh, that I know it is the bullets that are falling thickly around us!"[45]

Lieutenant Colonel Henry Fowler saw more than half of the enlisted men and every officer but one in the right wing of his 63rd New York Regiment fall from a single Confederate volley. He moved to the left, where he found Major Bentley, up on the firing line being assisted by Captain Joseph O'Neill, of Company A, whose company, on the right wing, was destroyed. Lieutenant Gleason, Company H, repeatedly raised and supported the falling colors as Fowler caught glimpses of him. Lieutenant John Sullivan pushed his Company K forward; the slender form of Captain Kavanagh, Company I, laid on the ground, cold in death. Lieutenant R. P. Moore, Company E, passed from right to left, boldly urging his men to stand firm. Fowler watched Lieutenant George Lynch, Com-

---

[43] OR, 19, pt. 1, 297; Conyngham, 305-306; OR, 19, pt. 1, 296.
[44] Report of Brig. Gen. Thomas F. Meagher, OR, 19, pt. 1, 294; Priest, 159.
[45] OR, 19, pt. 1, 294; Galwey. 42.

pany G, press his men forward until he fell, mortally wounded. When Lieutenant Colonel Fowler was forced to retire by a severe wound, he estimated that his regiment had only fifty men left standing.[46]

Volley after volley was fired until the Irish Brigade ran out of ammunition. The Irishmen fell back in columns of four through the advancing ranks of Caldwell's Brigade, who took their places on the front line. The exchange of gunfire in front of Bloody Lane had taken only ten to fifteen minutes. Meagher had been carried off the field, unconscious, after his horse was shot beneath him. Lieutenant Colonel James Kelly, commanding the 69th, and Lieutenant Colonel Fowler, of the 63rd, were wounded. Captains Patrick F. Clooney (88th), John C. Joyce (88th), John Kavanagh (63rd), and Felix Duffy (69th) lay dead on the field, surrounded by other dead and dying men of the Irish Brigade. In all, 540 Irishmen fell, killed and wounded, in the assault on Bloody Lane. General McClellan himself praised the bravery of the Irish Brigade for its performance at Antietam, noting that it ". . . sustained its well-earned reputation."[47]

The Irish Brigade recouped from the terrible losses at Antietam after being withdrawn to garrison Harper's Ferry. The 29th Massachusetts refused to carry a Green Flag presented to it by General Meagher shortly after the battle. An uneasy feeling arose between the 29th and the rest of the brigade, resolved by the reassignment of the Massachusetts men to the Ninth Corps.[48] Two new regiments joined the depleted Irish Brigade in the fall of 1862. The 116th Pennsylvania, recruited in Philadelphia, was a mixture of Irish immigrants and native-born Germans from the countryside.[49] The 28th Massachusetts was a predominantly-Irish regiment from Boston, its men already veterans of James Island in South Carolina, Second Bull Run, South Mountain, and Antietam.

Throughout the war, the Irish Brigade was noted for its hospitality and ability to hold an unforgettable party. After Fredericksburg, the brigade sponsored a St. Patrick's Day spectacular in 1863 that included a steeplechase and mountains of food and drink. The race was attended by Fighting Joe Hooker, the new commander of the Army of the Potomac, and many other high-ranking officers. The fare included thirty-five hams; the side of an ox roasted; an entire pig stuffed with boiled turkeys; and an

---

[46] OR, 19, pt. 1, 296.
[47] OR, 19, pt. 1, 192. The casualties were as follows: 29th Massachusetts, 39; 63rd New York, 202; 69th New York, 196; 88th New York, 102; Conyngham, 308.
[48] O'Flaherty, 180.
[49] See Robert I. Alotta, *Stop the Evil* (San Rafael: Presidio Press, 1978), 11-17, on the recruitment and composition of the 116th Pennsylvania. Alotta documents the desertion, court-martial, and execution of a soldier from the regiment.

unlimited number of chickens, ducks, and small game. The drinking material consisted of eight baskets of champagne, ten gallons of rum, and twenty-two gallons of whiskey.[50] Few who attended forgot either the splendor of the affair or their colossal hangovers!

Perhaps the Irish Brigade lived on better terms with the Confederates than did any others in the Army of the Potomac. Rebel pickets, bitterly firing on their counterparts, would often cease fire when the Irish Brigade came on the line.[51] The Confederates knew that they could count on a lively barter for coffee, sugar, whiskey, and tobacco. Frequently, Union and Rebel Irish immigrants exchanged news on the fate of family and friends in the war. Corporal William A. Smith, of the 116th Pennsylvania, wrote to his sister that both sides stuck muskets into the ground as a sign of truce before exchanging goods and written notes. Smith discovered that he had a Confederate namesake during one of these truces. It was customary for Irish Brigade soldiers to warn the Confederates that relief pickets were on duty by yelling, "Hardtacks," a Rebel nickname for the nine-month Federal volunteers who shot, rather than traded.[52]

During the Union disaster at the Battle of Chancellorsville, May 1-5, 1863, the Irish Brigade distinguished itself by saving the guns of the 5th Maine Battery. Shelled in an exposed position, all but two of the battery's men were killed, wounded, or had run away. Major Mulholland, of the 116th Pennsylvania, led a detachment of volunteers who hauled four of the cannons away with ropes.[53] The Irish Brigade lost one hundred and two men, who were killed, wounded, or found to be missing during the Chancellorsville campaign, leaving about four hundred men present for duty.[54]

After Chancellorsville, General Meagher, who had repeatedly petitioned higher command to recruit replacements for the Irish Brigade, resigned his commission in protest. In a tearful farewell, on May 19, 1863, he relinquished command to Colonel Patrick Kelly, of the 88th New York. Meagher was restored to command in Sherman's Army during 1864. After the war, Meagher was appointed Secretary of the Territory of Montana and became Acting Governor from 1865-1867. Meagher drowned in the Missouri River in Montana when he accidentally fell off a riverboat

---

[50] Conyngham, 373.

[51] Ibid., 87.

[52] Letter from William A. Smith to his Sister, April 3, 1863, on file in Irish Brigade Collection (FSNMP).

[53] OR 25, pt. 1, 278; Mulholland, 100-101.

[54] OR 25, pt. 1, 102. The casualties were by regiment: 28th Massachusetts, 16; 63rd New York, 6; 69th New York, 10; 88th New York, 46; 116th Pennsylvania, 24.

steamer, far from the Ireland which he had hoped to free as a young man.[55]

When the Irish Brigade joined the rest of the Army of the Potomac in the long march north to Gettysburg, it was a brigade in name only. Captain Thomas Touhy, Company A, 63rd New York, reported that the three original regiments of the Irish Brigade -- the 63rd, 69th, and 88th New York -- were consolidated into three battalions composed of two companies each.[56] The combined strength of the three regiments was 240 men. The 28th Massachusetts counted 224 men available for action. The 116th Pennsylvania could muster only sixty-six men, less than the full complement of a single company.[57] Colonel Patrick Kelly led 530 men of the Irish Brigade into the Union lines at Gettysburg early on the morning of July 2, 1863.

The Irish Brigade was posted on Cemetery Ridge near Plum Run. Major Mulholland recalled: ". . . the men enjoyed a grateful rest. Arms were stacked and the colors lay folded on the upturned bayonets. Every movement of the enemy was watched with interest, and the hours seemed long on that bright summer day."[58] The men of the Irish Brigade saw Major General Daniel Sickles advance his Third Corps forward into Devil's Den, the Wheatfield, and the Peach Orchard. The Irishmen knew it was only a matter of time before they would enter the fray when smoke rose in the distance, the rattle of musketry was heard, and the crash of canister reverberated through the woods. At about 4:30 p.m., the men were ordered to stand to arms.

Standing on a large rock, Father Corby, the 88th New York's Catholic chaplain, waited at the assembly point. He addressed the men, explaining that he was about to offer a general absolution for their sins. This benediction, familiar to generations of European soldiers, had rarely been performed on the North American continent. The men of the Irish Brigade knelt with their heads bowed, each man holding his cap in one hand while the other hand cradled a musket. There was profound silence in the entire Second Corps, as Catholic and non-Catholic alike received the benefit of the blessing. Father Corby's words rang out over the noise of exploding artillery shells: "*Dominus noster Jesus Christus vos absolvat . . .*"

---

[55] Conyngham, 406-408; see Athearn, 165-167, for the details of Meagher's death.
[56] OR 27, pt. 1, 338.
[57] OR 27, pt. 1, 386; John W. Busey and David G. Martin, *Regimental Strengths and Losses at Gettysburg* (Highstown: Longstreet House, 1986), 36.
[58] Mulholland, 123.

Major General Winfield Scott Hancock, then Second Corps commander, and his staff of officers, removed their hats and bowed their heads.[59]

The Irish Brigade moved to the front under a new Division commander, Brigadier General John Curtis Caldwell, who had replaced General Hancock after his promotion. Caldwell led his four brigades into the Wheatfield to reinforce Sickles' broken Third Corps. Zook's Brigade was the first unit of Caldwell's command to advance and engage the enemy. Kelly's Irish Brigade quickly followed Zook's men into the bullet-swept field, the regiments aligned from left to right as follows: 88th New York, 69th New York, 63rd New York, 28th Massachusetts, and 116th Pennsylvania. Remnants of the beaten Third Corps retired to the rear through intervals in the Irish Brigade's line. The Irishmen swept rapidly through the waist-high wheat in two ranks with their Green Flags unfurled and arms at "right shoulder shift." Confederate Lieutenant Colonel Elbert Bland, of Kershaw's South Carolina Brigade, remarked: "Is that not a magnificent sight?" as he observed the Irish Brigade close on his defensive position.[60]

General Joseph Kershaw's 3rd and 7th South Carolina Infantry Regiments, numbering over eight hundred men, were posted on Stony Hill, a belt of woods interspersed with boulders on the edge of the Wheatfield. The South Carolinians opened fire on the Irish Brigade when its men were about twenty yards from the woods. Shooting down from a slope, the Confederates naturally aimed high and most of their rounds passed over the heads of the Irishmen. The men of the 63rd, 88th, and 69th New York, as well as the 116th Pennsylvania, replied with a devastating volley from their muskets, loaded with "buck and ball." Its effect was overwhelming at that close range.

According to Major Mulholland, of the 116th Pennsylvania: "When the Regiment charged and gained the ground on which the enemy stood, it was found covered with their dead, nearly every one of them being hit in the head or upper part of the body. Behind one large rock, five men lay dead in a heap."[61]

After the Green Flags ascended the slope and the Irishmen entered the woods, a wild melee ensued. "It was a hot place. . . our little brigade fought like heroes" wrote Color Sergeant Welsh, of the 28th Massachusetts, to his wife. Captain Nowlen, 116th Pennsylvania, drew his revolver

---

[59] Corby, 182-184.

[60] Mulholland, 125, 132; *Gettysburg Sources, vol.* 2 (Baltimore: Butternut and Blue, 1987), 175.

[61] Busey and Martin, 138, on Kershaw's South Carolina regimental strengths and 203, on Irish Brigade weapons. Only the 28th Massachusetts Regiment of the Irish Brigade carried modern rifles at Gettysburg, being armed with .58 caliber Enfields. The other regiments still carried .69 caliber muskets. See Mulholland, 126, on the effect of the buck and ball volley.

and opened fire; nearly all the other officers followed his example. Private Jeff Carl, Company C of the 116th, shot a man within six feet of his bayonet. Sergeant Francis Malin, 116th Pennsylvania, was conspicuous in his dash and bravery. He soon fell dead with a bullet through his brain. In the dark woods, individual blazes of light from discharging weapons revealed the opponents to one another. Well-aimed fire from Irish Brigade soldiers dropped four color-bearers in the 3rd South Carolina Regiment. The entire color party of the 7th South Carolina was shot down. Major Mulholland sprang up on a boulder and ordered the Confederates to throw down their weapons.[62]

After a number of the Confederates surrendered and were sent to the rear as prisoners, the Irish Brigade halted and reformed to repel new Rebel attacks. The Confederate troops of Wofford's Brigade suddenly pushed out of the Peach Orchard, sweeping all before them and flanking the Irish Brigade. The remains of Kershaw's South Carolina Brigade and Semme's Brigade threatened the other flank of the Irishmen. Orders were given to retire. Escape lay back through the Wheatfield, with Confederates lining either side of it. Loading and shooting on the run, the Irishmen retreated. Colonel Kelly reported that, during this withdrawal through the Wheatfield, "We here encountered a most terrific fire, and narrowly escaped being captured." Major Mulholland characterized the Confederate gunfire as "severe and destructive" when the men passed through the wheat. So close were the lines of the flanking enemy between which the men ran that the Confederates finally had to stop shooting, as they were hitting each other. Mulholland believed that seven or eight of the 116th Pennsylvania men who were missing after the fight were probably killed in the flight through the Wheatfield. Young "Jersey" Gallagher, of the 116th, fell in the wheat after a ball broke his leg, but managed to crawl to safety despite being hit by six to eight more rounds.[63]

The survivors of the Irish Brigade reformed in a field near Taneytown Road. In a little over two hours, the brigade lost 202 men -- nearly a forty percent casualty rate.[64] Adjutant William McClelland, of the 88th New York, who had encouraged his men in the hottest part of the fight, died of his severe wounds. Lieutenant Colonel Bentley, of the 63rd New

---

[62] Kohl and Richard, 109; Mulholland, 125-126; Mac Wyckoff, "Kershaw's Brigade at Gettysburg," Gettysburg Magazine, No. 5 (July, 1991), 44.

[63] OR 27, pt. 1, 386; Mulholland, 127-128.

[64] OR 27, pt. 1, 386; Busey and Martin, 242. The casualties were by regiment: 28th Massachusetts, 100; 63rd New York, 23; 88th New York, 28; 69th New York, 28; 116th Pennsylvania, 22. For an excellent account of the Irish Brigade's action at Gettysburg, see Eric Campbell, "Caldwell Clears the Wheatfield," Gettysburg Magazine, No. 3 (July, 1990).

York was wounded in the leg by a shell. Captain Richard Moroney, who commanded the 69th New York, was also wounded. Not all of the men in the Irish Brigade were heroes at Gettysburg. On July 4, Lieutenant O'Neil, of the 69th New York, reported back to the regiment with seven or eight enlisted men after being absent without leave during the July 2 engagement. Lieutenant James Smith, temporary regimental commander of the 69th, preferred charges against O'Neil.[65]

The men of the Irish Brigade did no more fighting at Gettysburg. They were in an excellent position to observe the repulse of Pickett's charge, on July 3. After Gettysburg, the shrunken Irish Brigade fought again at Auburn, on October 14, 1863, and during the November, 1863, Mine Run -- Bristoe Station campaign. Lieutenant Louis J. Sacriste, 116th Pennsylvania, was later awarded the Congressional Medal of Honor for rearguard picket action at Auburn.[66]

In early 1864, the surviving veterans of the Irish Brigade were given a thirty-day furlough for re-enlisting. Returning to New York City, Boston, and Philadelphia, the five regiments recruited heavily to fill out their thinned ranks. The three New York regiments faced a particularly difficult task. Irish workingmen had played a large role in the New York City draft riots, and antiwar sentiment in the Irish immigrant community was high.[67] Nevertheless, the 63rd, 69th, and 88th New York regiments had strengths of nearly six hundred men each by April, 1864.[68] The 28th Massachusetts and 116th Pennsylvania recruited large additions to their depleted companies.[69] The new recruits were different from the men who had volunteered in 1861. There were far fewer Irish immigrants and native born Irish-Americans, particularly in the 116th Pennsylvania. The Irish Brigade became less and less Irish as the war dragged on. Most of the new men were boys between eighteen and twenty years of age, far younger, on average, than the mature men who had enlisted in 1861.[70] Bounty money, not patriotism, was often the incentive to enlist. The Irish Brigade was a brigade, in fact, again when it moved south under a new commanding officer, Colonel Thomas Smyth, in the spring of 1864.

[65] OR, 27, pt. 1, 388, 389, 390.

[66] Mulholland, 108-110; O'Flaherty, 279.

[67] McKay, 207-209; see also Iver Bernstein, *The New York City Draft Riots* (New York: Oxford University Press, 1990) on the role of the Irish in the disturbance.

[68] *The Irish-American*, April 16, 1864; O'Flaherty, 290.

[69] The 28th Massachusetts had 505 officers and enlisted men when it crossed the Rapidan River under Grant on May 3, 1864. OR, 36, pt. 1, 388. The 116th Pennsylvania recruited six whole new companies and filled up its four old companies, adding over 600 new recruits to its roster. It became the largest regiment in the Irish Brigade. Mulholland, 177, 186.

[70] Mulholland, 179.

Smyth, an Irish immigrant carriage manufacturer, became Major of the First Delaware Volunteers in the fall of 1861. He rose rapidly and became Colonel of that regiment before assuming command of the Irish Brigade.[71]

On May 5, 1864, the armies of Lee and General Ulysses S. Grant collided in the Wilderness. The Irish Brigade was thrown at a Confederate position near Brock Road late in the afternoon. The new recruits received their baptism under fire in dense, smoky woods. "One by one the boys fell -- some to rise no more, others badly wounded -- but not a groan or complaint," recounted Colonel Mulholland. Sergeant John Cassidy, of the 116th Pennsylvania, bellyached loudly as he exited the field, shot through the lungs, without assistance from his comrades. A broad smile passed along the line when one of the boys said to the sergeant, "Why, Cassidy, there's a man with all of his head blown off and he is not making half as much fuss as you are!"[72]

Corporal Samuel Clear, Company K, 116th Pennsylvania, reported that the Confederate fire in the woods was so heavy that two of his regiment's color guards were killed and another three wounded at one time. Company K, composed of new recruits from Uniontown, Pennsylvania, lost nine men in its first encounter with the enemy.[73] The Irish Brigade also lost its Assistant Adjutant, Captain Richard Turner, of the 88th New York, on the first day in the Wilderness. Turner had been badly wounded at Antietam and was given detached duty in New York. Refusing to stay behind, he was struck by a minié ball in the head while riding beside Colonel Smyth. He died instantly.[74]

General Winfield Scott Hancock, newly returned as corps commander after having recovered from wounds at Gettysburg, wrote in his official report, on the first day of the Wilderness, that the Irish Brigade: ". . . attacked the enemy vigorously on his right and drove his line some distance. The Irish Brigade was heavily engaged, and although four-fifths of its members were recruits, it behaved with great steadiness and gallantry, losing largely in killed and wounded."[75] The soldiers of the Irish Brigade

---

[71] Bounty jumpers became a major problem for the Union Army in 1864. The Irish Brigade undoubtedly had its share. On May 3, 1864, the 69th New York had only 406 men present for duty when it crossed the Rapidan. OR, 36, pt. 1, 394. For Smyth's biography, see Conyngham, 541-542.

[72] Mulholland, 186.

[73] W. Springer Menge and J. August Shimrak, ed., *The Civil War Notebook of Daniel Chisholm: A Chronicle of Daily Life in the Union Army, 1864-1865* (New York: Orion Books, 1989), 13. Diary of Samuel Clear and Letters of Daniel Chisholm, soldiers of the 116th Pennsylvania. Private Daniel Chisholm, of the 116th Pennsylvania, transcribed the diary of Sergeant Clear, who served in the same company, into his Civil War Notebook after the war ended. Chisholm's letters are also part of the Notebook.

[74] *The Irish-American*, May 21, 1864. O'Flaherty, 301; Conyngham, 561.

[75] OR, 36, pt. 1, 320.

spent the morning of May 6, building breastworks of dry logs, brush, and fence rails on the Brock Road. At about 4:15 p.m., Confederates from Longstreet's First Corps, with elements of Hill's Third Corps, emerged from the dense thicket fifty yards in front of Hancock's Second Corps.[76] Wright's Georgia Brigade advanced, firing towards the Irish Brigade's defensive position.

The fight was short and sharp. Corporal Samuel Clear in the 116th Pennsylvania, wrote, in his diary: "On they came with a woman-like scream; then we let them have the buck and Ball from behind the old logs and brush. The burning paper fell into our old logs and they took fire. . ." The wind fanned the flames and soon the whole breastworks leapt into a fiery wall, fifteen feet high, scorching the defenders. The Irishmen stood their ground, firing blind volley after blind volley through the blazing barrier until the Confederates withdrew.[77]

Lee's Army of Northern Virginia withdrew to a new defensive position at Spotsylvania. On May 11, 1864, Grant decided to assault the Confederate works at the "Mule Shoe," a heavily-fortified salient, with two divisions of Hancock's Second Corps. Smyth's Irish Brigade, as part of Francis C. Barlow's First Division, marched in black darkness through dense woods, the rain falling in torrents, to the assembly point for the attack. Stepping off at quick time before dawn in a fog, the Union forces completely surprised the Confederates on the morning of May 12. Smyth's Irishmen charged into the defensive abatis. Corporal Samuel Clear, 116th Pennsylvania, described what happened next: "Then such a yell as only the old Irish Brigade can give, and in we went, like as if the devil had broke loose, over the works in among the Johnnies, and many of them lost their lives by the bayonet. We captured and sent to the rear hundreds of prisoners. . ."[78]

Lieutenant Fraley, Company F of the 116th, ran a color-bearer through with his sword. A Confederate shot one of the men in the 116th when almost within touch of his musket, then threw down his piece and called out, "I surrender." Dan Crawford, Company K of the 116th, shot him dead. Captain James Fleming, 28th Massachusetts, reported that a private from his regiment captured a Confederate general in his tent.[79] "We

---

[76] See Robert Garth Scott, *Into the Wilderness with the Army of the Potomac* (Bloomington: Indiana University Press, 1985), 164-170, for details of the assault on the Second Corps.

[77] Menge and Shimrak, 13; Mulholland, 188-190; Conyngham, 446:447.

[78] Mulholland 206-210; Menge and Shimrak, 15; Conyngham, 448.

[79] Mulholland 210; OR, 36, pt. 1, 389. The Confederate general had to be Maj. General Edward Johnson, Division commander, Second Corps, since the 14th Pennsylvania captured Brigadier General George Steuart. Only two Confederate general officers were taken prisoner in the assault on the Mule Shoe. See

licked saucepans out of them," wrote Color Sergeant Peter Welsh of the 28th Massachusetts, to his wife, from a hospital bed after the battle. His arm shattered by a Confederate bullet, Welsh had been carried to the rear early in the fight. Welsh, an immigrant carpenter who had carried the Green Flag of the 28th Massachusetts through Chancellorsville, Gettysburg, and the Wilderness, died two weeks later.[80]

Flushed with victory, the men of the Second Corps pressed forward to the Confederate reserve line of works. Lee himself led in reinforcements to stop the Union drive. General John B. Gordon counterattacked with Pegram's Virginia Brigade and Evans' Georgia Brigade. These units, joined by Perrin's Alabama Brigade, Ramseur's North Carolina Brigade, and Harris' Mississippi Brigade, drove the Federal forces, many units mingled together in confusion, back to the breastworks which they had carried only one hour before. Lieutenant Colonel Richard C. Dale, commanding the 116th, fell, sword in hand, while calling for his troops to stand firm. He was never seen again. The men of Smyth's Irish Brigade, scattered along the captured log revetment, fought furious Confederate attacks all day long.

A drenching, chilling rain began to fall, but it had no effect on the incessant fire. Men fired into each other's faces across the barrier, were shot through crevices in the logs, and bayonetted each other over the top of the works. In the battle frenzy, men would leap up on the works and fire down on the enemy, while freshly-loaded muskets were handed up to them, maintaining a steady fire until they, too, were shot down. The dead and dying were piled on both sides of the log barrier, and, several times during the day, the dead had to be tossed out of the trenches so that the living could stand and fight. Corporal Samuel Clear, of the 116th Pennsylvania thought that the artillery was worst of all: ". . .from dawn until after dark, the roar of the guns was ceaseless. A tempest of shells shrieked through the forests and ploughed through the fields; I went over the works and seen the Johnnies laying in piles, the dead laying on the wounded holding them tight, and hundreds torn into pieces by shells after they was dead." The Confederates finally abandoned the struggle at about midnight, leaving the bloody ground in possession of the Union troops, as they fell back from that part of the salient to Lee's new line.[81]

William D. Matter, *If It Takes All Summer: The Battle of Spotsylvania* (Chapel Hill: University of North Carolina Press, 1988), 197.
[80] Kohl and Richard, 156.
[81] Matter, 199-268; Mulholland, 211-214; O'Flaherty, 315-317; Menge and Shimrak, 15-16; OR 36, pt. 1, 389, 391, 394, 395, 397, 398.

On May 18, 1864, Hancock's Second Corps attacked this new Confederate line at dawn. The Rebels, who had little to do but strengthen their works since May 13, were wide awake and waiting. Well-placed batteries raked the advancing Federal troops with shells and canister, taking a toll in the Irish Brigade. Pressing forward, the men of the Irish Brigade were confronted with a defensive abatis over one hundred yards deep. One sergeant, from the 116th Pennsylvania, penetrated the abatis eight or ten feet beyond any of his comrades and stood there, waist-deep in the abatis, while he loaded and fired three or four times. Captain Blake, of the 69th New York, grabbed the regimental flag and waved it, shouting, "Come on boys, and I will show you how to fight." He soon fell, mortally wounded. Corporal Samuel Clear, of the 116th Pennsylvania, was struck and knocked senseless. When he regained consciousness, he discovered that his belt buckle had stopped a minie ball and saved his life. In the 28th Massachusetts, Major Andrew J. Lawler, commanding the regiment, and Captains James Magner and William F. Cochrane were killed. The hopeless attack was finally called off at about nine a.m. The Battle of Spotsylvania ended, at last, for the Irish Brigade.[82]

Colonel Richard Byrnes, former regimental commander of the 28th Massachusetts, returned to command the Irish Brigade after extended recruiting duty in Boston at the end of May. Byrnes was an officer from the Regular Army, having served about fifteen years. He was promoted from the ranks for gallant and meritorious service. Colonel Smyth, who was outranked by Byrnes, was given command of Carroll's Brigade in the Second Division. Grant's relentless pursuit of Lee's Army continued. The Irish Brigade participated in the battles of North Anna, Pamunkey, and Totopotomoy between May 22 and June 1.[83]

After an exhausting night march in stifling heat and with no water to be had, the Irish Brigade reached Cold Harbor on the morning of June 2, 1864. At 4:40 a.m., on June 3, Hancock's Second Corps, with the Irish Brigade in the second line, joined the general Union assault on Lee's well-dug and protected defensive position.

---

[82] Matter, 306-3;1; Mulholland, 222; Conyngham, 451-453; Menge and Shimrak; 17, OR, 36, pt. 1, 389.
[83] Conyngham, 455, 542,586; Mulholland, 227-233; OR, 36, pt. 1, 389, 390, 393, 394, 397, 399.

Captain James Magner, Company I, 28th Massachusetts. He was killed in action at the Battle of Spotsylvania, on May 18, 1864. (U.S. Military History Institute)

The Federal troops were greeted by a curtain of steel and lead from Confederate batteries and riflemen. Colonel Richard Byrnes, leading his Irish Brigade from the front, fell, mortally wounded. Captain James Fleming, of the 28th Massachusetts, wrote that his regiment: ". . . suffered much in the loss of officers and men without having the satisfaction of punishing the enemy in return. We formed in line and charged the enemy over the earth-works, and our men fell in heaps." The Irish Brigade reached the first line of Confederate rifle-pits but was soon forced out by heavy rifle and artillery fire. Falling back about seventy-five yards, the men of the Irish Brigade dug in, using bayonets, cups, plates, and bare hands to scoop out shallow trenches. Corporal Samuel Clear, 116th Pennsylvania, noted in his diary: ". . .we dug holes with our bayonets to protect ourselves and more than one poor fellow was shot before his little dugout would protect him. We lay there expecting every minute to be gobbled up and sent south."[84]

When the Irish Brigade attempted to retreat, on the run, from the position, its men felt the full force of Confederate cannon fire and musketry, falling in great numbers. The soldiers of the Irish Brigade rallied in the rear, reformed their ranks, and spent the rest of the day digging defensive works. At that point in the war, the spade was as important to a soldier as his rifle. In addition to the killed and wounded, Cold Harbor produced psychological casualties in the Irish Brigade. Lieutenant Peter S. Frailey, Company E of the 116th Pennsylvania, had been one of the bravest men in the regiment. But, at Cold Harbor, his mind gave way and he was compelled to resign his commission. Captain Michael Schoales and Lieutenant Robert J. Grogan, of the 116th, also broke down after Cold Harbor and resigned.[85]

After Cold Harbor, the Irish Brigade was once again a shadow of itself. Thirty days of constant marching, non-stop fighting, lack of sleep, and the absence of food and water had diminished the ranks of all five regiments. The Irish Brigade had lost 974 men who were killed, wounded, missing or captured at the Wilderness, Spotsylvania, North Anna, Pamunkey, Totopotomoy, and Cold Harbor.[86] Galway-born Colonel Patrick

---

[84] "Brave almost to rashness, he always led his men, who knew no fear under his eye. . ." wrote Conyngham about Colonel Byrnes. Conyngham, 568; OR, 36, pt. 1, 390; Mulholland, 253-257; O'Flaherty, 324-327; Menge and Shimrak, 20.

[85] Mulholland, 257, 261.

[86] OR, 36, pt. 1, 120, 137, 154, 166. The casualties were as follows: The Wilderness, 349; Spotsylvania, 378; North Anna, Pamunkey and Totopotomoy, 53; Cold Harbor, 194. The losses by regiment were: 28th Massachusetts, 286; 63rd New York, 167; 69th New York, 221; 88th New York, 98; 116th Pennsylvania, 201.

Kelly, of the 88th New York, who had led the Irish Brigade at Gettysburg, took over command of the brigade once more after Byrnes died.

The entire Army of the Potomac moved along dusty roads on the hot night of June 12, 1864. Grant hoped to flank Lee's Army of Northern Virginia and capture the City of Petersburg, a vital railroad hub which provided the Confederates with their supplies. Hot and hungry, the soldiers of the Irish Brigade reached the Confederate defensive entrenchments at Petersburg on the morning of June 16. The Irish Brigade was ordered to assault the Confederate works near the Hare House, where Fort Stedman was later built, on the afternoon of the 16th. Charging at dusk over broken ground, the men of the Irish Brigade moved forward in quick-time, keeping their alignment while exposed to heavy shellfire and musketry. When within a hundred yards of the enemy, the five regiments took to the double-quick, went through the slight abatis, and ran over the works. For a few moments, there was a hand-to-hand fight with bayonets.

The fight was soon over and the Irish Brigade took possession of the Confederate works. But the defenders had exacted a heavy toll on the assaulting Irishmen. Colonel Patrick Kelly, commanding the Irish Brigade, was shot through the head and killed. One of the Union forts built during the siege of Petersburg was named after him. Lieutenant Colonel McGee, commanding the 69th New York, was wounded. Captain B. S. O'Neill, of the 69th New York, was left dead on the field, as was Adjutant Miles McDonald of the 63rd. Among the many wounded were Captains O'Shea and O'Driscoll of the 88th New York, and Lieutenants Brennan, Coloney, and Murphy of the 69th. Captain Fleming, of the 28th Massachusetts, wrote that, after the battle: "The men were utterly used up, and dropped asleep in the pits. The utmost exertions of the officers were most ineffectual in keeping them in a wakeful condition."[87]

On June 17, the Second Corps renewed its attack on the Confederate defense line at Petersburg. The few men of the Irish Brigade who penetrated the abatis in this second line of Confederate works were either killed or captured. After that direct attack on Confederate defenses failed, Grant withdrew the whole Second Corps from the trenches and sent it to wreck the railroads south of Petersburg. On June 22, the Irish Brigade was forced to retreat without accomplishing its mission with the rest of the Second Corps, after a Confederate surprise attack on the Union position at William's Farm succeeded. Between June 15, and June 30, the five

---

[87] OR, 40, pt. 1, 334 348, 349, 351, 360; Mulholland, 267-270; O'Flaherty, 338-339; "Gentle, brave and unassuming, no truer man nor braver officer fell during the war," wrote Conyngham in his biography of Colonel Patrick Kelly. Conyngham, 558.

regiments in the brigade lost another 248 men killed, wounded, captured, or missing.[88]

June, 1864, turned into the blackest month in the history of the Irish Brigade. After the June 16, Petersburg assault, command of the Irish Brigade had been assumed by Captain Richard Moroney, of the 69th New York. Six of the ten field officers in the Irish Brigade who had started the spring campaign under Grant had been killed, and the other four severely wounded. Corporal Samuel Clear noted in his diary that less than one hundred men were available for duty in the 116th Pennsylvania on June 24, out of the 867 who had crossed the Rapidan in May. The Army of the Potomac reorganized its units due to the heavy losses in men and officers. On June 20, the 28th Massachusetts was transferred out of the Irish Brigade to the First Brigade, First Division, Second Corps, under the command of General Nelson A. Miles. Following this transfer, the men of the 116th Pennsylvania were shifted to the Fourth Brigade, First Division, Second Army Corps, under the command of General John R. Brooke. The remainder of the Irish Brigade -- the 63rd, 69th, and 88th New York -- became part of the "Consolidated Brigade," which included elements of the Third Brigade of the Second Corps. The proud men of the Irish Brigade were furious. Corporal Samuel Clear, 116th Pennsylvania, wrote in his diary: "It was awful to hear the men swear when they found the Regiments forming the Irish Brigade had to separate, some of the men swore they would never charge again."[89]

The reaction in New York City was also negative. Colonel Nugent, former commander of the 69th, had been appointed to administer the draft in New York. Lieutenant-Colonel James McGee, also of the 69th and in New York recovering from his wounds, joined with Nugent in appealing to the Irish immigrant community to rebuild the Irish Brigade. Recruiting was extraordinarily successful, and a large number of new men was added to the truncated New York units who preserved the memory of the Irish Brigade.[90]

The surviving men of the 63rd, 69th, and 88th New York participated in several engagements with the enemy while assigned to the "Consolidated

---

[88] OR, 40, pt. 1, 351; Mulholland, 270-279; O'Flaherty, 339-344; see also Noah A. Trudeau, *The Last Citadel: Petersburg, Virginia, June 1864-April 1865* (Boston: Little, Brown, and Co., 1991), 62-80. The losses by regiment for June 15-30, 1864, were as follows: 28th Massachusetts, 27; 63rd New York (six companies), 53; 69th New York (six companies), 43; 88th New York (three companies), 55; 116th Pennsylvania, 70. The 28th Massachusetts was removed from the Irish Brigade on June 20, so some of its casualties were incurred afterwards. OR, 40, pt. 1, 219, 220.

[89] OR, 40, pt. 1, 350; Mulholland, 279; Dyer, 1258, 1612; OR, 40, pt. 1, 117; Menge and Shimrak, 26.

[90] Conyngham 465-466; see also Corby, 252.

Brigade." They took part in the first Deep Bottom expedition by the Second Corps from July 26-29, 1864. During the second Deep Bottom expedition by the Second Corps, the three New York regiments were thrown at a Confederate line of rifle pits placed in a ridge on August 14. The Irishmen pushed forward without shooting and took the line of works with the bayonet. Complete silence followed. General Francis C. Barlow, commanding the First Division, jumped up to find the cause and, misjudging the reason, shouted, "That damned Irish Brigade has broken at last!" Just as he uttered the words, Adjutant Smith, of the 69th New York, rode up, covered with sweat and black with the smoke of battle. Swinging his horse close to General Barlow, he said disdainfully, "General, the Irish Brigade has taken the first line of the enemy's works, and I have come back for further orders." Barlow was so confounded that it was some time before he could issue further orders. The General had developed a dislike for the Irish Brigade because of the Irishmen's love of fun and drink in rear area camps.[91]

On August 22, the New York Irish regiments were sent, with the rest of the Second Corps, to tear up the Weldon Railroad. Lee sent an eight-brigade strike force to hit the exposed Second Corps at its entrenchments at Reams Station. On August 25, the Confederates rolled up the Federal troops when several of the defending regiments panicked. The battle was a complete disaster for the Second Corps. The Confederates captured over 2,000 soldiers from the Second Corps, including Major John W. Byron, of the 88th New York, commanding the three New York Irish regiments, and eighty-four veteran officers and enlisted men from the 63rd, 69th, and 88th New York.[92]

The men of the three New York Irish Brigade regiments spent most of their time in the "Consolidated Brigade," assigned to the trenches at Petersburg, combatting lice, snipers, and boredom. On October 30, 1864, a detail from the 69th New York was assigned to routine picket duty opposite Confederate Fort Davis. A detachment from Confederate General William Mahone's Division, Third Corps, slipped into the Union picket line. The raiding party, probably made up, for the most part of Irishmen, spread out, using the brogue and acting as if they were the expected relief pickets. Before anyone could react, the Confederates captured most of the Union pickets; finally, an alert was sounded. Lieutenant Murtha Murphy,

---

[91] OR, 40 pt. 1 348, 349, 350; OR, 42, pt. 1, 290; see Conyngham, 472, 473 for the incident with General Barlow. General Barlow got even by launching an inquiry into the Irish Brigade's alleged violation of his orders. See Report of Major John W. Byron, 88th New York, August 17, 1864, OR, 42, pt. 1, 291.

[92] OR, 42, pt. 1, 129; Conyngham, 477; see also Trudeau, 179-189, on the unfolding of the Union debacle.

Company G of the 69th, told his men who remained to fire, and a brisk action started in the darkness. There was a great deal of firing, but the Rebels withdrew without the loss of a single man. They brought back with them 168 prisoners from the 69th New York, most of them new recruits. The action caused a sensation in both armies. Lee praised General Mahone for his bloodless victory. There was much talk in the Union Army about the enemy being led over by Irish deserters. Nothing was ever proven about these allegations. The Irish from the South had prevailed that time.[93]

Early in November, 1864, Colonel Nugent arrived from New York to reorganize the Irish Brigade. The 63[rd,] 69[th,] and 88th New York were pulled out of the "Consolidated Brigade" and reconstituted as the Irish Brigade. The 28th Massachusetts was also returned to the brigade. A new regiment, the 7th New York Heavy Artillery, was added to the Irish Brigade. The 7th was an oversized regiment, numbering 1,835 men, who had served in the forts guarding Washington, District of Columbia. General U. S. Grant, desperate for new infantry to man his spring campaign, had sent militia to replace the 7th and other large, heavy, artillery units guarding the Capitol. Fighting with great bravery, the 7th had lost a large number of its men between Spotsylvania and Petersburg. Only four companies were available to serve in the new Irish Brigade.[94]

The Irish Brigade went on two Second Corps operations at Hatcher's Run during the siege of Petersburg -- October 27-28, 1864, and February 5-7, 1865. On both occasions, the men of the Irish Brigade encountered Mahone's Confederate Division, which had a large number of Irish immigrants. Even though Mahone's men had captured several flags from the Second Corps, the men of the Irish Brigade could not help but like them. A truce was declared on the picket line and both sides mingled freely, exchanging newspapers, coffee, tobacco, and whiskey. The Northern and Southern Irishmen argued about the war when they had a chance. "A fine bunch of Irishmen you are, coming into the South and burning our farms and acting worse than the English ever did in Ireland," said one of Mahone's Irish immigrant Confederates after he had been captured by a group of soldiers from the 69th New York.

"Ah, hold yer whict," replied one of the New York Irishmen. "A fine bunch of Irishmen you are, trying to break up the Union that gave ye a home and fighting for the rich slave owners." The New Yorker shared his canteen of whiskey with the prisoner and soon the two men were toasting

---

[93] OR, 42, pt. 1, 257-260; Conyngham, 503-504; O'Flaherty, 358.
[94] Dyer, 1385; Conyngham, 505; O'Flaherty, 358.

the health of General Meagher of the Irish Brigade and the memory of Confederate General Patrick Cleburne, an Irish immigrant.[95]

In February, 1865, the 7th New York Heavy Artillery was detached from the Irish Brigade. It was replaced by the 4th New York Heavy Artillery. These former garrison soldiers from the Capitol served with the Irish Brigade until the end of the war.[96] Thus reinforced, the Irish Brigade participated in the last campaign of the war. The Irish Brigade joined the general assault on the Petersburg lines which Grant ordered on April 1, 1865. On April 2, Nugent's Irish Brigade found the rear guard of Lee's retreating army at Sutherland Station in front of the South Side Railroad. Colonel Nugent reported that the Irish Brigade charged the works with the Third Brigade and, owing to a terrific enfilading fire of artillery and musketry, was repulsed. The men of the brigade immediately reformed, charged again, and captured the Confederate defensive works with some 150 prisoners, two cannon, and one battle flag. The Confederate colors were captured by a private in the 4th New York Heavy Artillery with a very non-Irish name -- Frank Denio. In this engagement, which was the last major battle of the Irish Brigade, 124 men were killed, wounded, or missing.[97]

Following the Union cavalry and the Fifth Corps, the Irish Brigade joined the pursuit of Lee's fleeing army. On the afternoon of April 4, Irishman General Philip Sheridan rode up and asked Colonel Nugent what troops he was leading. Nugent replied, "The Irish Brigade, First Division, Second Corps." Sheridan replied, "Ah, indeed!" with a smile. A spontaneous cheer rose from the throats of over 1,000 men in the Irish Brigade while General Sheridan rode away, acknowledging the compliment.[98] After Lee's surrender, the remnant of the Irish Brigade marched in the Grand Review of the Union Armies at Washington, D.C., with every man sporting a sprig of evergreen in his cap. The Irish Brigade lost over 4,000 men who had been killed or wounded during the Civil War. There were never 4,000 soldiers in the brigade at any one time. The five regiments which were the core of the Irish Brigade -- the 63[rd,] 69[th,] and 88th New York, the 28th Massachusetts, and the 116th Pennsylvania -- had 961 men killed or mortally wounded in action. The 69th New York ended up

[95] Conyngham, 510; The Irish-American, December 11, 1864; O'Flaherty, 362.
[96] OR, 46, pt. I, 566, 582; Dyer, 1383.
[97] OR, 46, pt. 1, 724-733; Conyngham, 520; see also Trudeau., 390-397, on the Sutherland Station action.
[98] Conyngham, 522-523.

sixth among all Union regiments in the number of men killed or mortally wounded. The 28th Massachusetts was seventh on the list.[99]

Of the five field-grade officers who commanded the Irish Brigade, three were killed in action and the other two were wounded. Colonel Richard Byrnes was killed at Cold Harbor. Colonel Patrick Kelly died at Petersburg. Brigadier General Thomas A. Smyth, who commanded the Irish Brigade before his transfer back to the Second Division, was the last Federal general to be killed in the Civil War. He fell at Farmville, a few days before the surrender at Appomattox. Both Generals Thomas Meagher and Robert Nugent were wounded.[100]

In 1869, the U. S. Sanitary Commission reported that 144,221 Irish-born Americans had served in the Union Army during the Civil War. Some were Fenians, who hoped to apply their military experience from the Civil War in armed rebellion against English rule in Ireland. But most were committed to America itself and the future of their adopted country. On June 1, 1863, Color Sergeant Peter Welsh, of the 28th Massachusetts wrote a letter to his father-in-law in Ireland explaining why he had left his dear wife Margaret to fight for the Union. His simple words summarize the reasons for the shedding of so much blood by the Irish Brigade: "Here we have a free government, just laws and a Constitution which guarantees equal rights and privileges to all. Here thousands of the sons and daughters of Ireland have come to seek a refuge from tyranny and persecution at home. And thousands still continue to come . . . Here Irishmen and their descendants have a claim, a stake in the nation . . . America is Irlands refuge and Irlands last hope. . ."[101]

Corporal Samuel Clear, 116th Pennsylvania, wrote the best epitaph for the fighting Irish Brigade on the day of his transfer to the Fourth Brigade of the First division: "The old Irish Brigade is a thing of the past. There never was a better one pulled their triggers on the Johnnies."[102]

---

[99] Menge and Shimrak, XXII; William F. Fox, *Regimental Losses in the American Civil War, 1861-1865* (Albany: Albany Publishing Company 1889), 118. The losses by regiment in killed or wounded were as follows: 28th Massachusetts, 250; 63rd New York, 156; 69th New York, 259; 88th New York, 151; 116th Pennsylvania, 145. Dyer's *Compendium*, which included deaths from all causes, reported that 1,494 men in the Irish Brigade died during the Civil War. The losses were, by regiment: 28th Massachusetts, 387; 63rd New York, 249; 69th New York, 401; 88th New York, 223; 116th Pennsylvania, 234.

[100] Conyngham, 532, 541, 547, 558, and 586.

[101] Jones, Foreword; Kohl and Richard, 100-102; for an assessment of the Irish contribution to the Union war effort, see William L. Burton, *Melting Pot Soldiers: The Union's Ethic Regiments* (Ames: Iowa University Press, 1988), 112-154.

[102] Menge and Shimrak, 26.

Chapter IV

THE IRISH BRIGADE
IN THE
WHEATFIELD

by Kevin E. O'Brien

It was hot and quiet at midday on July 2, 1863, in Gettysburg, Pennsylvania. Except for the occasional popping of skirmishers' rifles between the lines, neither the North's Army of the Potomac or the South's Army of Northern Virginia seemed eager to renew the deadly conflict commenced on July 1. Some soldiers of the Union Army's Irish Brigade, posted with the rest of the Federal Second Corps to defend Cemetery Ridge, played cards, while others napped, talked, or fried their hardtack and bacon at small fires in the rear of the lines. Shortly after 1 p.m., the afternoon's lassitude was shaken by a flurry of motion on the southern end of the Union line to the left of the Irish Brigade. The young Irishmen dropped their cards, regardless of what was trump, and gathered for a good look at the opening of the action.[1]

Major General Daniel Sickles' Union Third Corps advanced forward from Cemetery Ridge and the Round Tops. Ten thousand men, in perfect order, flags flying, rolled majestically towards the Peach Orchard and Emmitsburg Road. Cannons and caissons rumbled over the swells in the ground. A heavy line of skirmishers preceded the main body and cleared away enemy scouts. Major General Winfield Scott Hancock, commanding the Union Second Corps, rode up to the right of the Irish Brigade and dismounted to witness the spectacle. Surrounded by field officers, including Colonel Patrick Kelly; Colonel Richard Byrnes; and Major Mul-

---

[1] "Address of Brevet Maj.-Gen. St. Clair A. Mulholland" in John P. Nicholson, ed., *Pennsylvania at Gettysburg: Ceremonies at the Dedication of the Monuments Erected by the Commonwealth of Pennsylvania to Mark the Positions of the Pennsylvania Commands Ennaned in the Battle,* 2 vols. (Harrisburg: W.S. Ray, State Printer, 1904), vol. 2, 662, 623.

holland, of the Irish Brigade; Hancock watched for awhile, resting on one knee and leaning on his sword. Turning to the officers assembled around him, he smiled and remarked: "Wait a moment, you will soon see them tumbling back."[2]

At that point in its history, the Irish Brigade was a brigade in name only. Nearly one unremitting year of hard fighting at places like Malvern Hill, Antietam, Fredericksburg, and Chancellorsville had decimated the ranks. The three original regiments of the Irish Brigade -- the 63rd, 69th, and 88th New York Volunteer Infantry -- had numbered close to 2,500 men when they left New York City in 1861 to fight for the Union.[3] Captain Thomas T. Touley, Company A, 63rd New York, reported that these three regiments were consolidated into three battalions of two companies each on the eve of the Gettysburg campaign.[4] The combined strength of the three regiments was 240 men -- less than ten percent of those who had originally volunteered.[5] The 28th Massachusetts Volunteer Infantry, a predominantly Irish regiment from Boston, transferred to the Irish Brigade in November, 1862. This regiment counted only 224 men ready for action when it marched towards Gettysburg. The 116th Pennsylvania Volunteer Infantry, a mixture of Irish immigrants from Philadelphia, and native-born Germans from the Keystone State's countryside, had also been added to the Irish Brigade in late 1862. Disease and casualties had reduced the 116th Pennsylvania to sixty-six men available for combat, less than the full complement of a single company, when it joined the pursuit of Lee's invading army. In all, the Irish Brigade, the Second Brigade of the First Division, Second Corps, mustered 530 men present for action on July 2, 1863.[6]

The Irish Brigade had lost its commanding officer and founder just two months before Gettysburg. Brigadier General Thomas F. Meagher had repeatedly petitioned headquarters for permission to recruit replacements for the Irish Brigade. He resigned his commission in protest

---

[2] For background on the ill-fated advance of Sickles' Third Corps into the Peach Orchard, see Harry W. Pfanz, *Gettysburg: The Second Day* (Chapel Hill: University of North Carolina Press, 1987), 124-148 and Richard A. Sauers, *Casoian Sea of Ink* (Baltimore: Butternut and Blue,1989); Hancock quote from Nicholson, *Pennsylvania at Gettysburg*, vol. 2, 623.

[3] Captain Daniel P. Conyngham, *The Irish Brigade and Its Campaigns* (New York: McSorley & Co. Publishers, 1867; reprint, Gaithersburg: Old Soldiers Books, undated), 597. The author served with the Irish Brigade from its formation through 1863. His book remains the best source on the unit.

[4] United States War Department, *The War of the Rebellion: A Compilation of the Official Records of the Union and Confederate Armies*, 70 vols. in 128 parts (Washington, D.C.: Government Printing Office.1880-1901). series 1. vol. 27. part 1. 386. Hereinafter cited as O.R.

[5] John W. Busey and David G. Martin, *Regimental Strengths and Losses at Gettysburg* (Highstown: Longstreet House, 1986), 94.

[6] Ibid., 36.

on May 8, 1863, after his brigade lost one hundred more men at the Battle of Chancellorsville, May 1-5. Meagher stated in his resignation that "...the Irish Brigade no longer exists."[7] Born in County Waterford to prosperous parents in 1823, Meagher was a leading figure in the Irish uprising of 1848. Condemned to death for his activities in the rebellion, he was exiled for life, instead, by special act of Parliament, to Tasmania, off the coast of Australia. Escaping English exile, Meagher fled to the United States. After his arrival in New York City, he became a celebrity in the Irish immigrant community, practicing law, editing a newspaper, and marrying the daughter of a wealthy merchant. He was a prominent Democrat with many friends in the South when the war began. Yet Meagher was among the first to answer the call for volunteers to preserve the Union.

Thomas Meagher fought as a captain in the Irish Zouave company of the 69th New York State Militia at First Bull Run on June 21, 1861. Returning to New York City, he was commissioned a colonel and set about raising an all-Irish brigade. In rally after rally, Meagher's golden oratory won new recruits from the immigrant community. President Lincoln promoted Meagher to brigadier general and command of the Irish Brigade in February, 1862. General Meagher's colorful field headquarters, his dashing Irish staff officers, many of whom had served with European armies, and his personal bravery on the battlefield all had contributed to make the Irish Brigade one of the most famous fighting units in the Army of the Potomac.[8] His loss was mourned by both officers and enlisted men in the brigade. Captain William J. Nagle, of the 88th New York wrote his father: "The resignation of our beloved chief, General Meagher, has been accepted, and with him go our hearts, our hopes and our inspiration. Every man in the camp -- officers and privates -- caught the spirit and vivacity from him."[9]

Colonel Patrick Kelly, of the 88th New York, took command of the dispirited Irish Brigade after Meagher's resignation. Kelly was a farmer in Castlehackett, County Galway, before he emigrated to America in 1849. He rose from private to captain in the 69th New York State Militia before

---

[7] *The Irish-American*, May 23, 1863. This newspaper was published in New York City between 1851 and 1915. It printed numerous letters from Irish Brigade soldiers during the Civil War.

[8] For Meagher's life, see Michael Cavanagh, *Memoirs of General Thomas Francis Meagher* (Worcester: Messenger Press, 1892) and Capt. W. F. Lyons, *Brigadier-General Thomas Francis Meagher: His Political and Military Career* (New York: D. & J. Sadler Co., 1870); for a modern biography of Meagher, see Robert G. Athearn, *Thomas Francis Meagher: An Irish Revolutionary in America* (Boulder: University of Colorado Press, 1 949).

[9] Letter from Wm. J. Nagle to father, May 18, 1863. *The Pilot*, May 30, 1863. This newspaper was an Irish-American weekly published in Boston, Massachusetts.

the war. After fighting as a company commander at First Bull Run, Kelly was mustered out with his militia regiment after three months of service on August 3, 1861. Commissioned at the same rank in one of the Regular Army's new infantry regiments, he was elevated to brevet major for his bravery at the Battle of Shiloh in Tennessee.

Upon the organization of the Irish Brigade, Kelly was promoted to lieutenant colonel and appointed second-in-command of the 88th New York. Joining his regiment, he led the 88th New York at Seven Pines in Virginia, and at Antietam. Promoted to colonel, Kelly commanded the 88th at Fredericksburg, where his uniform was riddled with bullet holes, and at Chancellorsville. General Meagher had the highest praise for Colonel Kelly, "...a true, conscientious, unwearied, uncomplaining, indomitable, absolutely fearless soldier -- one whose positive truthfulness, devotion to duty, innocent and immaculate relations with his superiors and subordinates might be studied with singular edification . . . "[10]

Colonel Kelly's regimental commanders were tried combat veterans. Colonel Richard Byrnes led the 28th Massachusetts Regiment. Born in County Cavan, Byrnes emigrated to the United States at age twelve. He joined the U.S. Cavalry in 1856 and served on the Western frontier. During this enlistment, he was wounded in the thigh by a lance during an engagement with the Indians in the Rocky Mountains. Byrnes also served in the 17th U.S. Infantry and 5th U.S. Cavalry. Originally commissioned a lieutenant in the cavalry at the outbreak of the war, he was promoted to colonel and command of the 28th Massachusetts by Governor Andrew. Byrnes led the 28th at both Fredericksburg and Chancellorsville.[11]

Lieutenant Colonel Richard Charles Bentley commanded the 63rd New York, also known as the "Third Regiment, Irish Volunteers." Bentley was born in the United States at Albany, New York, and earned his living as a commission and shipping merchant in Albany before the war. He served as adjutant with the 30th New York prior to joining the Irish Brigade. Lieutenant Colonel Bentley was wounded on May 3, 1863, during the Chancellorsville campaign. He chose, nevertheless, to lead the 63rd towards the encounter with Lee in Pennsylvania. The 63rd New York had seventy-five veterans available for battle on July 2, 1863.

Like Lieutenant Colonel Bentley, Captain Richard Moroney, who commanded the 69th New York, was a native-born American. Moroney,

---

[10] The Irish-American, July 2, 1864, and July 16, 1864; see also Stewart Sifkasis, Who Was Who in the Union (New York: Facts on File, 1988), 219.

[11] The Irish-American, June 25, 1864; see also Edmond Raus, Jr., A Generation on the March -- The Union Army at Gettysburg (Lynchburg: H. E. Howard, Inc., 1987), 37.

born in Lockport, New York, was a veteran of the Mexican War. He had worked as a machinist in New York City and had served in the militia before the outbreak of hostilities between North and South. "He was a brave, active, and efficient officer," wrote Captain David Power Conyngham, historian of the Irish Brigade, "witty, genial, and a universal favorite." Moroney led seventy-five men from the 69th New York, also known as the "First Regiment, Irish Brigade," into action at Gettysburg.

Born in County Cork, Captain Denis Francis Burke, commander of the 88th New York, emigrated to New York City. He worked in the dry goods business before the Civil War. Commissioned as a second lieutenant at the outbreak of the war, Burke was promoted after being wounded at Fredericksburg on December 13, 1862, and at Chancellorsville on May 3, 1863. The 88th New York, nicknamed the "Connaught Rangers," as well as "Faugh A Ballaghs," and "Fourth Irish," numbered seventy men on the day of reckoning at Cemetery Ridge.

Major St. Clair Mulholland, born in County Antrim, commanded the 116th Pennsylvania. He became a painter in Philadelphia after having immigrated to America. Mulholland was, originally, commissioned as lieutenant colonel and was second-in-command of the regiment in 1862. He was wounded at Fredericksburg on December 13, 1862. After the 116th was consolidated as a battalion due to losses, Mulholland was demoted to major. Mulholland received letters of commendation from Major General Hancock and General Meagher for his conduct at Chancellorsville.[12]

Thanks to the resignation of Meagher and the reduced size of the brigade, the mood of the rank and file in the Irish Brigade was black as the men started their march from the Fredericksburg, Virginia, area towards Pennsylvania late in June. Color Sergeant Peter Welsh, of the 28th Massachusetts, complained bitterly to his wife that, "...our number is so low that our regiment will be consolidated into six companys."[13] The march to Gettysburg in pursuit of the invading Confederate Army turned into one of the longest and most severe ordeals that the soldiers of the Irish Brigade had faced. On some days the soldiers marched fifteen miles, on others 18, and, on June 29, a distance of thirty-four miles.[14]

The Irish Brigade passed grim reminders of the war along the way. Marching through Bull Run, where two battles had been fought, the sol-

[12] Biographical information on Bentley, Moroney, Burke, and Mulholland from Conyngham, *The Irish Brigade*, 550, 559, 566, 594 and Raus, *A Generation on the March*, 66, 68, 74, 132.
[13] Letter from Sergeant Peter Welsh to wife, May 13, 1863, in Lawrence Kohl and Margaret Richard, *Irish Green and Union Blue: The Civil War Letters of Peter Welsh, Color Sergeant. 28th Regiment. Massachusetts Volunteers* (New York: Fordham University Press, 1986), 96.
[14] Nicholson, *Pennsylvania at Gettysburg*, vol. 2, 619.

diers saw exposed skeletons and rusted gear scattered over the battle-ground. Private William A. Smith, 116th Pennsylvania, wrote his parents and sister: "I came over the battle fields of Bull Run and Antietam and seen the brains of the dead on the field that was not half-buried."[15] Private Allen Landis, Company C of the 116th Pennsylvania, whose brother, Aaron, had been killed in the Irish Brigade's assault at Fredericksburg, reported the numbing fatigue of the forced marches. In a letter to his parents penned late in June, he wrote: "I have slept very little for the last couple of days, and think if we march for today I can sleep on a clothes line tonight."[16]

After spending over a year in Virginia where the only civilians encountered were sullen supporters of the rebellion, the men of the Irish Brigade enjoyed the welcome of loyal Union citizens in Maryland. When the brigade rested near Frederick, Maryland, farmers flocked into camp with produce, and townspeople provided the soldiers with candy and doughnuts.[17] Private William A. Smith, 116th Pennsylvania, noted, "We come through Frederick City. It was a nice place as the people use us first-rate. Their every house had a flag hung out of the window as we come through it..."[18] At Frederick, the Irishmen learned that General George G. Meade had relieved General Hooker as commander of the Army of the Potomac.

The Irish Brigade crossed the Pennsylvania state line on June 30. Rumors flew as to the whereabouts of Lee's Army of Northern Virginia. On the morning of July 1, while the entire Second Corps filed into fields to rest and wait for orders, a mounted officer dashed up bringing the intelligence that fighting had begun at Gettysburg -- thirteen miles distant. The news was meager, only that there was fighting. Early in the afternoon, another messenger appeared out of a cloud of dust. He told the soldiers of the Irish Brigade that General Reynolds, commanding the First Corps, was dead, the First and Eleventh Corps were fighting hard, and the battle was going against the Union.[19] General Winfield Scott Hancock and his staff were soon mounted and on the road to Gettysburg. The en-

[15] Letter from William A. Smith to parents and sister, July 12, 1863, William A. Smith Letters, Lewis Leigh Collection, U.S. Army Military History Institute, Carlisle Barracks, Pennsylvania, hereinafter cited as USAMHI.

[16] Letter from Allen Landis to parents, June 27, 1863, Allen Landis Letters, Manuscript Division, Library of Congress.

[17] St. Clair A. Mulholland, *The Story of the 116th Regiment, Pennsylvania Infantry* (Philadelphia: F. McManus, Jr. & Company Printers, 1903), 117, 118.

[18] Letter from William A. Smith to parents and sister, July 12, 1863, William A. Smith Letters, Lewis Leigh Collection, USAMHI.

[19] Nicholson, *Pennsylvania at Gettysburg*, vol. 2, 620.

tire Second Corps promptly followed Hancock on foot. Colonel Patrick Kelly reported that the Irish Brigade had arrived within two or three miles of Gettysburg at 10 p.m., bivouacked in a field, and threw out pickets to look for the enemy.[20]

The first day of the battle for Gettysburg had gone badly for the Union Army. Confederate infantry regiments in search of a rumored cache of shoes at Gettysburg bumped into Federal cavalry pickets on the outskirts of town early on the morning of July 1. The Union cavalrymen managed to contain the Rebel attackers until reinforcements from the Federal First Corps arrived. Meade and Lee fed reinforcements into the desperate fighting at places like Oak Ridge, Seminary Ridge, and the Bloody Railroad Cut all afternoon. Lee concentrated his forces better and faster than the Federals. Late in the day, the Union Eleventh Corps broke, after being flanked by the Confederates, and fled through the town of Gettysburg, losing thousands of men who were taken as prisoners. Reaching the safety of Cemetery Ridge, the survivors of the Eleventh Corps combined with the troops of the First Corps who had retreated, fighting, from Seminary Ridge. General Winfield Scott Hancock, of the Second Corps, rallied these beaten men, formed them into a defensive line, and placed batteries of artillery to cover likely Confederate avenues of approach. If Lee had pressed the attack early on the evening of July 1, the battle might have ended as a Southern victory.[21]

At 4:30 in the morning, on July 2, Kelly's Irish Brigade filed off towards Gettysburg and, shortly, reached the Union defensive line at Cemetery Ridge near Plum Run.[22] "The division was massed in brigade columns," recalled Major Mulholland, "and the men enjoyed a grateful rest. Arms were stacked and the colors lay folded on the upturned bayonets. Every movement of the enemy was watched with interest, and the hours seemed long on that bright summer day. The pickets were more or less engaged all the morning -- sometimes stray shots, then again volleys, now a rattling fire all along the front, and smoke would be seen here and there in the distant foliage."[23] The soldiers of the 69th New York spent the morning tearing down fences and using the rails to build defensive entrenchments.[24]

---

[20] O.R., vol. 27, part 1, 386.
[21] On the July 1 fighting, see Warren W. Hassler, Jr., *Crisis at the Crossroads: The First Day at Gettysburg* (Montgomery: University of Alabama Press, 1970; reprint, Gettysburg: Stan Clark Military Books, 1991).
[22] O.R., vol. 27, part 1, 386.
[23] Mulholland, *The Story of the 116th Regiment*, 123.
[24] J. Noonan, *The 69th New York*, Kenneth H. Powers Collection, USAMHI.

Not a shot was fired as Sickles' Third Corps formed an exposed salient in the Union line on Emmitsburg Pike, the Peach Orchard, Devil's Den, and the Wheatfield. Shortly after General Hancock uttered his prophetic words, someone in the Irish Brigade called out, "There!" and pointed to where a puff of smoke was seen rising against the dark green of the woods beyond the Emmitsburg Pike. The Irishmen knew it was only a matter of time before they would enter the fray when the whole face of the forest was enveloped in smoke, the rattle of musketry roared in the distance, and the crash of canister reverberated through the woods. Lieutenant General James Longstreet's Confederate Corps of nearly 15,000 men struck Sickles' position with a fury. Less than an hour passed before the soldiers of the Irish Brigade observed Union troops recoiling and retreating.[25]

A staff officer rode up to General Hancock with orders to send a division to reinforce the Union left. Hancock quietly remarked, "Caldwell, you get your division ready." Kelly's Irish Brigade was one of the four small brigades in Caldwell's Division. "Fall in," was the command and each man rushed to his equipment.[26] Muskets and cartridge boxes were soon in place, and the Irish Brigade was ready to move at about 4:30 that evening. Captain Thomas Touley, Company A, of the 63rd New York, reported that each man was provided with sixty rounds of ammunition.[27]

A few minutes remained before the advance. Father William Corby, chaplain of the 88th New York, asked Colonel Kelly if he could give the men a general absolution for their sins. Born in Detroit to an Irish immigrant father, Father Corby taught at the fledgling Notre Dame University before the war.[28] At Gettysburg, the Reverend William Corby was the only priest seen in the Army of the Potomac. After receiving Colonel Kelly's permission, Father Corby reached into a pocket and pulled out a purple stole which he placed around his neck. Then he climbed up onto a large boulder so that the whole brigade might see him.

Father Corby addressed the men as follows:

My dear Christian friends! In consideration of the want of time for each one to confess his sins in due order as required for the reception of the sacrament of penance, I will give you general absolution. But my dear friends while we stand here in the pres-

---

[25] Nicholson, *Pennsylvania at Gettysburg*, vol. 2, 622, 623.

[26] Ibid., 623.

[27] O.R., vol. 27, part 1, 388.

[28] William Corby, *Memoirs of Chaplain Life: Three Years with the Irish Brigade in the Army of the Potomac* (Chicago: La Monte, O'Donell & Co., 1893; reprint, Lawrence F. Kohl, ed., New York: Fordham University Press, 1992), DD. Xi, Xii, Xiii.

ence of eternity -- so to speak -- with a well armed force in front and with missiles of death in the form of shells bursting over our heads, we must humble ourselves before the *Great Creator* of all men and acknowledge our unworthiness and conceive a heart-felt sorrow for the sins by which we ungratefully offended the Divine Author of all good things . . .[29]

Corby reminded the men of the noble cause for which they fought, and declared that the Church would refuse Christian burial to those who deserted their flag. As he raised his right hand up in blessing, the men of the brigade knelt with their heads bowed to recite the Act of Contrition, each man holding his cap in one hand while the other hand cradled his musket.[30]

Father Corby's voice rang out over the noise of exploding artillery shells as he pronounced the Latin words of absolution. "The scene was more than impressive," wrote Major Mulholland, "it was awe-inspiring."[31] There was profound silence among the thousands of men and officers in the entire Second Corps, Catholic and non-Catholic alike wishing to receive the benefit of the absolution. Major General Winfield Scott Hancock and his staff removed their hats and reverently bowed their heads. Father Corby recalled: "A more impressive scene perhaps never took place on any battlefield. It was indeed so earnest and truly sublime that non-Catholics prostrated themselves in humble adoration of the true God while they felt that perhaps in less than half an hour their eyes would open to see into the Ocean of Eternity."[32]

The special moment over, the Irish Brigade prepared for battle. The color bearers in four of the regiments uncased their emerald green battle flags, each banner bearing symbols of Ireland -- a harp, a sunburst, and a wreath of shamrocks. The 116th Pennsylvania, because of its mixed composition, carried the state flag rather than a green regimental color. Captain Denis Burke, commanding the 88th New York, recalled that the ad-

---

[29] Letter from Reverend William Corby, C.S.C., to John Bachelder, January 4, 1879. Historian's Office, Gettysburg National Military Park. Colonel Bachelder's correspondence with major participants in the fight for Gettysburg, compiled by the New Hampshire Historical Society, has long been one of the most valuable primary resources on the battle. The letter from Father Corby, however, never became a part of the Bachelder Papers. It surfaced at a 1992 auction of Bachelder's effects sponsored by his descendants and was donated to the National Park Service. See Craig Caba, "Gettysburg Park Among Bachelder Auction Buyers," The Civil War News, vol. 18 (September 1992): 26.

[30] "Notes of a Conversation with Col. Mulholland," John Bachelder Papers, New Hampshire Historical Society, Concord, Microfilm copy, Gettysburg National Military Park. Hereinafter cited as B. P. and G.N.M.P.

[31] Corby, *Memoirs of Chaplain Life*, 183-184.

[32] Letter from Reverend William Corby, C.S.C., to John Bachelder, January 4, 1879. Historian's Office, G.N.M.P.

vance began with each regiment moving out behind the Stars and Stripes and the Old Green Flag of Erin.[33] The Irish Brigade advanced down Cemetery Ridge in a column of regiments, skirted Plum Run, and reached the plowed fields of the Trostle House.[34] Confederate batteries near the Peach Orchard opened fire upon the column. "The solid shot falling on the soft soil of a newly plowed field threw the earth in showers over the men," wrote Major Mulholland.[35]

Lieutenant Colonel Bentley, commanding the 63rd New York, most likely fell wounded there since he had been struck in the left leg by a piece of shell.[36] Captain Thomas Touhy, born in County Clare, took over command of the regiment. The whole Irish Brigade moved to the left and reached the valley in front of Little Round Top. General Caldwell deployed his division as quickly as possible to reinforce the broken Third Corps. Cross' brigade headed to the left of the Irishmen and moved forward. Brooke's brigade went in to the left of Cross. The Irish Brigade counter-marched to the right, passing to the rear of Cross, and, after clearing his line, deployed on the right of the division.[37] Directly ahead was a wheat field, the rows of grain about waist-high. Kelly's Irish soldiers watched Zook's brigade of their own division disappear into the wheat not forty yards ahead of their position.[38]

Directly across the Wheatfield, Kershaw's Confederate 3rd and 7th South Carolina regiments checked their cartridge boxes and anxiously waited for a Union counterattack. General Kershaw's South Carolina brigade spearheaded Longstreet's attack against Sickle's exposed position and swept away the defenders. Kershaw recognized that the key terrain on his front was "...a stony hill, covered with heavy timber and thick undergrowth, interspersed with boulders and large fragments of rock, extending some distance toward the Federal main line, and in the direction of Round Top."[39] Over eight hundred veterans in the 3rd and 7th South Carolina regiments rapidly advanced into the woods and occupied the stony hill on the edge of the Wheatfield.[40] "I am sure that from the time

[33] New York Monuments Commission for the Battlefields of Gettysburg and Chattanooga, *Final Report on the Battlefield of Gettysburg*, 2 vols. (Albany: J.B. Lyon Co. Printers, 1900), vol. 2, 479.

[34] Nicholson, *Pennsylvania at Gettysburg*, vol. 2, 624.

[35] Mulholland, *The Story of the 116th Regiment*, 124.

[36] O.R., vol. 27, part 1, 388.

[37] Mulholland, *The Story of the 116th Regiment*, 124.

[38] Nicholson, *Pennsylvania at Gettysburg*, vol. 2, 624.

[39] J. B. Kershaw, "Kershaw's Brigade at Gettysburg," in Robert Underwood Johnson and Clarence Clough Buel, eds., *Battles and Leaders of the Civil War*, 4 vols. (New York: The Century Co., 1884-1889; reprint, Harrisburg: The Archive Society, 1991), vol. 3, 333.

[40] Busey and Martin, *Regimental Strengths*, 138.

we reached the top of the ridge," wrote General Kershaw, "there was not one moment to take breath. I distinctly noticed that the troops we first engaged seemed to melt away and almost in the same moment heavy bodies of troops bore down upon us."[41]

Colonel Kelly wasted no time in following Zook's brigade into the rows of wheat, his regiments aligned from left to right as follows: 88th New York, 69th New York, 63rd New York, 28th Massachusetts, and 116th Pennsylvania.[42] Soldiers from the beaten Third Corps fled to the rear through intervals in the Irish Brigade's advancing line. The Irishmen swept rapidly through the waist-high wheat in two ranks, with their green regimental flags flying and their weapons at "right shoulder shift."[43] Lieutenant Colonel Elbert Bland of the 7th South Carolina, remarked, "Is that not a magnificent sight?" to his commanding officer as he watched the Irish Brigade closing on his position.[44] Kershaw's Confederates had seen the green flags of the Irish Brigade before -- when they poured a murderous fire into the charging Irishmen at Marye's Heights in Fredericksburg, Virginia, slaughtering hundreds.[45]

Kelly's Irishmen moved quickly from the Wheatfield into the timber covering the stony hill. Strangely, the Southerners had not yet fired a shot at the Irish Brigade, perhaps being preoccupied with repelling Zook's brigade. A soldier in the 116th Pennsylvania cried out, "There they are!"[46] The South Carolinians opened fire on the Irish Brigade from the crest of the stony hill, shooting from behind the protection of the trees and big rocks covering the ground. Aiming downhill, the Confederates fired too high and most of their rounds whistled harmlessly over the heads of the Irishmen. The soldiers of the Irish Brigade immediately replied with a volley. The men of the 63rd, 69th, and 88th New York, as well as the 116th Pennsylvania, were armed with old *.69* caliber muskets, almost useless at long range, but deadly for close hand work, each piece loaded with a *.69* caliber ball and three buckshot.[47] Major Mulholland reported the results of this exchange of gunfire: "When the One Hundred and Sixteenth

[41] B. P., Letter from J. B. Kershaw to Bachelder, April 3, 1876.

[42] O.R. 27, part 3, 1087 and unit position markers at G.N.M.P.

[43] Mulholland, *The Story of the 116th Regiment*, 125.

[44] "The Gettysburg Reunion. What is Necessary and Proper for the South to Do. An Open Letter from Col. D. Wyaff Aiken to Gen. J. B. Kershaw," *Gettysburg Sources*, 2 vols. (Baltimore: Butternut and Blue, 1987), vol. 2, 175.

[45] Mulholland, The Story of the 116th Regiment, 125; see also D. Augustus Dickert, *History of Kershaw's Brigade*, (Newberry: Elbert H. Aull Co., 1899; reprint Dayton: Morningside, 1976).

[46] B. P., "Notes of a Conversation with Colonel Mulholland,"; Nicholson, *Pennsylvania at Gettysburg*. vol. 2. D. 625.

[47] See Busey and Martin, *Regimental Strengths*, 203, on the weapons carried by the Irish Brigade at Gettysburg. Only the 28th Massachusetts was armed with modern rifles, .58 caliber Enfields.

charged and gained the ground on which the enemy stood, it was found covered with their dead. Behind one large rock five men lay dead in a heap. They had evidently fallen at the first volley and all at the same time."[48]

Lieutenant James J. Smith, 69th New York, wrote that, "...after our line delivered one or two volleys, the enemy were noticed to waver, and upon the advance of our line (firing) the enemy fell back, contesting the ground doggedly."[49] After Colonel Kelly ordered the green flags to ascend the slope, a wild melee ensued in the woods.[50] "It was a hot place," penned Color Sergeant Peter Welsh, 28th Massachusetts, in a letter to his wife. "Our little brigade fought like heroes."[51] Captain Nowlen, 116th Pennsylvania, drew his revolver and opened fire; nearly all the other officers followed his example. Private Jeff Carl, Company C of the 116th, shot a Rebel within six feet of his bayonet. Sergeant Francis Malin, 116th Pennsylvania, was conspicuous in his dash and bravery, as his tall form towered above all around him. He soon fell dead with a bullet through the head.[52] In the dark, smoke-filled woodline, individual blazes of light from muzzle flashes revealed the opponents to each other. Adjutant William McClelland, 88th New York, dropped to the ground, mortally wounded, after encouraging and inciting his men in the hottest part of the fight.[53] Colonel Richard Byrnes, commanding the 28th Massachusetts, reported that the Irish Brigade, "...advanced over the top and almost to the other side of the hill, being all the time exposed to a very severe fire of musketry, and losing many men in killed and wounded."[54]

Joseph B. Kershaw's South Carolinians suffered severely in the close quarters combat. Lieutenant Colonel Elbert Bland, commanding the right wing of the 7th South Carolina, fell with a serious thigh wound.[55] Well-aimed fire from Irish Brigade soldiers dropped several color bearers. When Corporal Thomas Harling, the last remaining member of the 7th South Carolina color guard, picked up the flag, he was immediately shot in the head. Four color bearers in the 3rd South Carolina went down.[56] "I

---

[48] Mulholland, *The Story of the 116th Regiment*, 125.

[49] O.R., vol. 27, part 1, 389.

[50] Letter from an Officer of the 116th Pennsylvania, Irish Brigade, *The Irish-American,*August 29, 1863; Letter from Daniel P. Conyngham, Irish-American, October 10, 1863.

[51] Letter from Sergeant Peter Welsh to wife, July 17,1863, in Kohl and Richard, *Irish Green and Union Blue*, 109.

[52] Mulholland, *The Story of the 116th Regiment*, 125-126.

[53] O.R., vol. 27, part 1, 390; Adjutant McClelland rose from private to officer and regimental adjutant because of his merits and courage in battles before Gettysburg. *The Irish-American,* July 25, 1863.

[54] O.R., vol. 27, part 1, 387.

[55] O.R., vol. 27, part 2, 369.

[56] Mac Wycoff, "Kershaw's Brigade at Gettysburg," *The Gettysburg Magazine*, 5 (July 1991).

have never been in a hotter place," said General Kershaw about the fight for the stony hill after the war.[57] Kershaw was determined to hold the hill, but Cross' and Brooke's brigades drove off the Confederate troops supporting him on the right. With Kelly's Irish Brigade curling back his right flank, Kershaw decided "to call off the dogs of war" and retreat.[58] He first ordered the 7th South Carolina to withdraw to the Rose Farm about two hundred yards behind the stony hill. Fearing that the 3rd South Carolina would be surrounded if it fought on alone, Kershaw directed these soldiers to fall back to the safety of the stone buildings and fences of the Rose Farm.[59]

Many of Kershaw's men were too closely engaged with the Irish Brigade to flee to safety. Major Mulholland, 116th Pennsylvania, claimed that he jumped on a boulder and shouted, "Confederate troops, lay down your arms and go to the rear!" According to Mulholland, his order was promptly obeyed and a large number of Confederates surrendered.[60] Colonel Kelly and Captain Thomas Touley, 63rd New York, and Lieutenant Cadwalder Smith, 69th New York Infantry, noted, in their after-action reports, that the Irish Brigade captured a large number of Confederate prisoners, including officers, and sent them back to the Union lines.[61]

Colonel Kelly deployed his troops into a defensive line facing the Rose Farm. The men of the Irish Brigade checked their ammunition, helped the wounded, and kept a careful eye to the front. Fifteen minutes passed without a sign of enemy activity. Major Mulholland reported, to Colonel Kelly, that he had sighted an enemy column passing through the Peach Orchard towards the rear of the Irish Brigade's position. Kelly was not convinced that the troops were really Southerners, considering the smoke and the distance. Major Mulholland was relieved of command to scout on the right of the Irish Brigade's position. He discovered the 140th Pennsylvania to the right and rear of the 116th Pennsylvania and asked its officers to advance with him to discover which troops were moving in the Peach Orchard. Mulholland and the 140th had marched only fifty yards when they distinctly saw that the mobile column consisted of Confederates. Major Mulholland hurried back to Kelly with this intelligence.[62]

---

[57] B.P., Letter from J.B. Kershaw to Bachelder, April 3, 1876.

[58] Ibid.

[59] B.P., Letter form J.B. Kershaw to Bachelder, March 20, 1876; O.R., vol. 27, part 2, 369.

[60] Nicholson, *Pennsylvania at Gettysburg*, vol. 2, 625.

[61] O.R., vol. 27, part 1, 386, 388, 389.

[62] Letter from St. Clair A. Mulholland to John P. Nicholson, November 26, 1894, Civil War Library and Museum, Philadelphia, Pennsylvania; Nicholson, *Pennsylvania at Gettysburg*, vol. 2, 625-627.

General Kershaw quickly identified the advancing Confederate troops: "I saw Wofford advancing splendidly; he was there in the field to the right of the Peach Orchard."[63] Wofford's brigade of 1,400 Georgians headed down a road north of the Wheatfield, sweeping Union troops out of its way. Kershaw sent the 15th South Carolina, reinforced by part of Semmes' Georgia brigade, to press around the southern side of the Wheatfield.[64] Caldwell's entire division, including the Irish Brigade, was about to be surrounded.

"Finding myself in this very disagreeable position," wrote Colonel Kelly, "I ordered the brigade to fall back, firing. We here encountered a most terrific fire, and narrowly escaped being captured."[65] Major Mulholland rolled up the colors and, with about thirty men, ran down through the woods and back into the Wheatfield.[66] With Confederates closing in from the north and the south, the Irishmen drew fire from both sides. The men loaded and shot as they fled through this narrowing alley of death. So close were the lines of the flanking enemy between which the soldiers of the Irish Brigade ran that the Confederates finally had to stop shooting, as they were hitting each other.[67] Lieutenant Dominick I. Connally, 63rd New York, was captured by the Rebels during the withdrawal through the Wheatfield.[68] Captain John Teed, 116th Pennsylvania, ran the wrong way and was taken prisoner. Many wounded, such as Sergeant George Halpin, 116th Pennsylvania, could not get away and became prisoners. Some of the wounded so feared captivity in Southern prisons that they escaped with almost superhuman efforts. Young "Jersey" Gallagher, of the 116th Pennsylvania, fell in the wheat after a Rebel ball broke his leg, but managed to crawl to safety despite being hit by six to eight more rounds.[69] Major Mulholland knew that he was saved when he heard voices calling, "Come here, run this way." A few seconds later, he leapt over a low stone wall with ten of his men and found himself among Sweitzer's Federal brigade. He reported to Colonel Brooke, 53rd Pennsylvania, who directed Mulholland to plant his colors in a field near the Taneytown Road as a rallying point for the Irish Brigade.[70] After he crossed the Wheatfield, Lieutenant James J. Smith, 69th New York, col-

[63] B. P., Letter from J. B. Kershaw to Bachelder, March 20, 1876.

[64] O.R., vol. 27, part 2, 369.

[65] O.R.; vol. 27, part 1, 386.

[66] Nicholson, *Pennsylvania at Gettysburg*, vol. 2, 627.

[67] Mulholland, *The Story of the 116th Regiment*, 127.

[68] O.R., vol. 27, part 1, 388.

[69] Mulholland, *The Story of the 116th Regiment*, 127, 128.

[70] Nicholson, *Pennsylvania at Gettysburg*, vol. 2, 627.

lected about a dozen men from his regiment and presented himself to
Colonel Brooke. Smith learned, at the rallying point, that Captain Richard
Moroney, his regimental commander, had been wounded during the retreat. Lieutenant Smith, an immigrant from County Monaghan, took over
command of the 69th New York.[71] Colonel Richard Byrnes reformed the
28th Massachusetts and rejoined the rest of the Irish Brigade survivors as
darkness fell.[72]

When heads were counted, the officers of the Irish Brigade discovered that losses had been grievous. In a little over two hours of combat,
the Irish Brigade lost 202 killed, wounded, and missing out of 530 engaged -- nearly a forty percent casualty rate.[73] The 28th Massachusetts suffered the worst loss; nearly half of the regiment fell. Adjutant Augustus
Annand, 28th Massachusetts, reported that most of the thirty-five missing
in action from the regiment were ascertained to have been killed because
of the nature of the ground and the severe fire to which the men were exposed.[74] "We lost heavily," wrote Color Sergeant Peter Welsh, 28th Massachusetts. "The killed, wounded and missing of our little regiment is over
a hundred. Out of the five regiments that form this brigade there is but
men enough here to make three full companies."[75]

There was no time to grieve for the dead. General Hancock posted
the Irish Brigade and the rest of Caldwell's division back on Cemetery
Ridge close to their original position.[76] "Few of us slept during this
night," recalled Major Mulholland. "The men gathered rocks and fence-
rails and used them to erect a light breastwork."[77] The soldiers of the Irish
Brigade completed their defensive works on the morning of July 3 as they
listened to the sounds of battle from the fight for Culp's Hill about a mile
to their rear. Spent bullets from that engagement went singing over their
heads. At about 11 that morning, the firing suddenly stopped and a tre-
mendous cheer went up. In a few moments, every man in the Union

---

[71] O.R.. vol. 27, part 1, 389.

[72] O.R., vol. 27, part 1, 387.

[73] The losses were, by regiment: 28th Massachusetts, 8 killed, 57 wounded, 35 missing or captured; 63rd
New York, 5 killed, 10 wounded, 8 missing or captured; 69th New York, 5 killed, 14 wounded, 6 missing
or captured; 88th New York, 7 killed, 17 wounded, 4 missing or captured; 116th Pennsylvania, 2 killed, 11
wounded, 9 missing or captured. In comparison, Kershaw's 3rd and 7th South Carolina regiments lost 197
men. See Busey and Martin, *Regimental Strengths*, 242, 281.

[74] *The Pilot*, August 8, 1863.

[75] Letter from Sergeant Peter Welsh to wife, July 17, 1863, in Kohl and Richard, *Irish Green and Union Blue*,
109.

[76] O.R., vol. 27, part 1, 390.

[77] Nicholson, *Pennsylvania at Gettysburg,* vol. 2, 628.

Army knew through the soldier grapevine, that the fight for Culp's Hill had been won.[78]

A perfect calm followed for about two hours. The quiet was shattered when the Southern artillery, massed to prepare the way for Pickett's Charge opened its bombardment at 1 p.m. Colonel Kelly characterized the shower of shellfire as "...probably the heaviest artillery fire ever heard."[79] Thanks to the protection of the newly-constructed earthworks, only one man in the 63rd New York was wounded by an exploding shell.[80] After two hours of shelling, the Confederate guns fell silent, and the Virginian and North Carolinian infantry, under General George Pickett, began to advance. Major Mulholland described what happened next:

> At this moment, our artillery, which up to this time had remained almost silent, opened with terrible effect upon the advancing lines, tearing great gaps in their ranks and strewing the field with their dead and wounded. Notwithstanding the destructive fire under which they were placed, the enemy continued to advance with a degree of ardor, coolness, and bravery worthy of a better cause, until, reaching a ravine which ran parallel with our line, about midway between us and their artillery, they halted, being under cover and no longer exposed to our fire. They halted but to surrender.[81]

The soldiers of the Irish Brigade had a spectacular view of the repulse of Pickett's Charge.

When the sun rose on the morning of July 4, the Irishmen learned that Lee's Army of Northern Virginia had retreated and that they were victors. The Irish Brigade spent July 4 and 5 celebrating the victory and national holiday, as well as going about the grim task of burying the dead. The enlisted men in the Irish Brigade sensed the enormous importance of the triumph at Gettysburg. "Lee thought that the gates of Washington were opened out for him," wrote Private Allen Landis, 116th Pennsylvania, to his parents, "...in which he was alas very much disappointed."[82] Private William A. Smith, 116th Pennsylvania, told his parents and sister: "Well we give them a hard rube at Gettysburg I think it will

---

[78] Ibid., 628, 629.

[79] O.R., vol. 27, part 1, 386.

[80] O.R., vol. 27, part 1, 388.

[81] O.R., vol. 27, part 1, 392, 393.

[82] Letter from Private Allen Landis to parents, July 12, 1863, Allen Landis Letters, Manuscript Division, Library of Congress.

finish them off."[83] Color Sergeant Peter Welsh, 28th Massachusetts, composed a letter to his wife that contained the most important news for his family about the battle for Gettysburg: "I have come out safe and unhurt where thousands have been wounded and killed."[84]

Not all of the men in the Irish Brigade were heroes at Gettysburg. On July 4, Lieutenant O'Neil, 69th New York, came back to the regiment with seven or eight enlisted men after being absent without leave during the July 2 engagement. Lieutenant James J. Smith, acting regimental commander, preferred charges against O'Neil.[85]

Demoralized by the resignation of General Meagher and their thinned ranks, the soldiers of the Irish Brigade, nevertheless, made a significant contribution to the Union triumph at Gettysburg. Father Corby deserved enormous credit for inspiring the men with his general absolution. The Irish Brigade cleared the Wheatfield and blunted Kershaw's attack. The Irishmen bought precious time with their blood for General Hancock to reinforce the Federal left. Thanks in part to the sacrifice of the Irish Brigade and the other regiments in Caldwell's division, Longstreet's offensive failed and Cemetery Ridge and the Round Tops remained in Union hands.

After Gettysburg, the shrunken Irish Brigade fought again at Auburn on October 13, 1863, and during the November, 1863, Mine Run-Bristoe Station campaign. In early 1864, many of the surviving veterans were given a thirty-day furlough for re-enlisting. The five regiments recruited heavily to fill out their depleted companies. In May, 1864, over 2,000 men in the new Irish Brigade crossed the Rapidan River in Virginia under General Ulysses S. Grant. Even though the Irish Brigade was composed mainly of recruits, it was always in the forefront of action at the Wilderness, Spotsylvania, North Anna, Pamunkey, Totopotomy Creek, Cold Harbor, and Petersburg. In June, 1864, the Irish Brigade was abolished because of its losses. The three New York regiments became part of the "Consolidated Brigade," and the 28th Massachusetts and 116th Pennsylvania transferred to other commands. Protests from the Irish immigrant community in New York City resulted in re-activation of the Irish Brigade in November, 1864, under Colonel Robert Nugent. Rejoined by the 28th Massachusetts and reinforced by the 7th New York Heavy Artillery, the three New York regiments endured the siege of Petersburg and fought in

[83] Letter from Private William A. Smith to parents and sister, July 12, 1863, Lewis Leigh Collection. USAMHI.
[84] Letter from Sergeant Peter Welsh to wife, July 17, 1863, in Kohl and Richard, Irish Green and Union Blue, 110.
[85] O.R., vol. 27, part 1, 389.

the last campaign of the Civil War.[86] After Lee's surrender at Appomattox, the survivors of the Irish Brigade marched in the Grant Review of the Union Armies at Washington, D.C., every man's coat bound with sprigs of evergreen.[87]

General Thomas F. Meagher campaigned for Lincoln's re-election in 1864, much to the chagrin of the Democrat Irish immigrant community in New York City.[88] He returned to active duty in 1864 and held minor commands in the Western theater under General Sherman. After the war, Meagher was appointed Secretary of the Territory of Montana and became Acting Governor from 1865-1867. Poised at the beginning of a promising political career, which might have included a seat in the U.S. Senate, Meagher fell off a riverboat and drowned in the Missouri River. Rumors abounded that his heavy drinking had caught up with him at last.[89]

Colonel Patrick Kelly commanded the Irish Brigade at Bristoe Station and the Mine Run campaign. Reverting to command of the 88th New York in 1864, he led his regiment through Grant's spring campaign. Kelly took command of the Irish Brigade again after Cold Harbor. Two weeks later, he was shot through the head and killed on June 16, 1864, while leading the Irish Brigade in a charge on Confederate trenches at Petersburg. A soldier in the 88th New York wrote: "Over his lifeless body strong old veteran soldiers wept like children and wrung their hands in frenzy."[90] Captain D. P. Conyngham caught the essence of Kelly -- "Gentle, brave, and unassuming, no truer man nor braver officer fell during the war."[91]

Colonel Richard Byrnes, 28th Massachusetts, went back to Boston for extensive recruiting duty after Gettysburg. He returned to the Army of the Potomac at the end of May, 1864, and assumed command of the Irish Brigade. Leading his men from the front in the Union assault at Cold Harbor on June 2, 1864, Byrnes collapsed, mortally wounded.[92] "Brave almost to rashness, he always led his men, who knew no fear under his eye."[93]

Lieutenant Colonel Bentley, 63rd New York, recovered from his leg wound at Gettysburg and returned to active duty. He left the Irish Bri-

---

[86] See Conyngham, *The Irish Brigade*, 438-509; see also Reverend Patrick D. O'Flaherty, *The History of the Sixty-Ninth Regiment in the Irish Brigade*,(New York: privately printed, 1986), 271-389.

[87] *The Irish-American*, June 3, 1865.

[88] *The Irish-American*, November 12, 1864.

[89] *The Irish-American*, July 13, 1867.

[90] *The Irish-American*, July 2, 1864.

[91] Conyngham, *The Irish Brigade*, 558.

[92] *The Irish-American*, June 18, 1864, and June 25, 1864.

[93] Conyngham, *The Irish Brigade*, 586.

gade on sick leave after Cold Harbor and was mustered out of the army on September 18, 1864. Bentley died in Albany on December 1, 1871.[94] Captain Thomas Touhy, who took command of the 63rd New York when Bentley was wounded, was promoted to major after Gettysburg. He was mortally wounded at the Wilderness on May 5, 1864.[95]

Captain Richard Moroney, 69th New York, was promoted to major after he recovered from his wounds. He mustered out with his regiment at the end of the war and died on December 29, 1865.[96] Lieutenant James J. Smith, who took over the 69th New York after Moroney was hit, was wounded on August 14, 1864, in a bayonet charge during the second Deep Bottom expedition and again on August 25, 1864, at Reams Station. Promoted through the officer ranks, he became a lieutenant-colonel and the last commanding officer of his regiment.[97] Smith died in Cleveland on October 7, 1913. Captain Denis F. Burke was promoted to colonel before the war ended. After mustering out of the 88th New York, he became a publisher in New York City. Burke was breveted brigadier general for his war service. He died in New York on October 19, 1893.[98]

Major St. Clair A. Mulholland commanded his own brigade by the end of the war. He was wounded at the Wilderness on May 5, 1864, at Po River on May 10, 1864, and at Totopotomy Creek on May 31, 1864. Mulholland was breveted major general for his war service. He was also awarded the Congressional Medal of Honor for his bravery at Chancellorsville on May 4, 1863. Mulholland became Philadelphia's Chief of Police. He died in Philadelphia on February 17, 1910.[99]

Father William Corby campaigned with the Irish Brigade until September, 1864. He returned to Notre Dame University and served with distinction as its president. Father Corby helped to establish Sacred Heart College in Wisconsin and was elected Provincial General of the Congregation of the Holy Cross for the entire United States. He eventually became Assistant General for the Congregation of the Holy Cross throughout the world. Recommended for the Congressional Medal of Honor, he never received it. Father Corby stayed close to his comrades in the Irish Brigade and attended all of their reunions. He died at Notre Dame on December 28, 1897. In a departure from custom, Father Corby's casket was

---

[94] Raus, *A Generation on the March*, 66.
[95] *The Irish-American*, June 11, 1864.
[96] Raus, *A Generation on the March*, 68.
[97] *The Irish-American*, July 15, 1865.
[98] Raus, *A Generation on the March*, 74.
[99] Ibid., 132.

not borne by Holy Cross priests but instead by aging Civil War veterans, who saluted him with a rifle volley.[100]

On May 12, 1864, Color Sergeant Peter Welsh's arm was shattered by a Rebel bullet at Spotsylvania as he bore the green flag of the 28th Massachusetts. He died two weeks later.[101] Private Allen Landis died in a hospital in Philadelphia on October 2, 1864.[102] Private William A. Smith was not on the muster-out roll of the 116th Pennsylvania. His fate is lost to history.[103]

On July 2, 1888, the 25th anniversary of Gettysburg, survivors of the Irish Brigade gathered to dedicate a memorial to the three New York regiments on the battlefield – it was a Celtic cross with an Irish wolfhound at its base, forever waiting for its fallen master. A poet, Williams Collins, captured the spirit of the brave young Irishmen far better than monuments of bronze and stone:

Here, on the field of Gettysburg, where treason's banner flew,

Where rushed in wrath the Southern Gray to smite the Northern blue,

Where'er that Blue, by valor nerved, in serried ranks was seen,

There flashed between it and the foe the daring Irish Green!

And never yet on any land rush forth to Freedom's aid,

A braver or more dauntless band than Ireland's brave Brigade.

Pause on their graves! Tis holy dust ye tread upon to-day

The dust of Freedom's martyred dead whose souls have passed away.[104] The best epitaph for the fighting Irish Brigade was written by one of its own, Corporal Samuel Clear, 116th Pennsylvania, in 1864. "The old Irish Brigade is a thing of the past. There never was a better one pulled their triggers on the Johnnies."[105]

---

[100] Corby, *Memoirs of Chaplain Life*

[101] Kohl and Richard, *Irish-Green and Union Blue*, 157, xvii-xxv.

[102] Mulholland, *The Story of the 116th Regiment*, 394.

[103] Ibid., 399.

[104] New York Monuments Commission for the Battlefields of Gettysburg and Chattanooga, *Final Report*, 483.

[105] W. Springer Menge and J. August Shimrak, ea., *The Civil War Notebook of Daniel Chisholm: A Chronicle of Daily Life in the Union Army, 1864-1865* (New York: Orion Books, 1989), 26.

Monument of the New York regiments of the Irish Brigade at Gettysburg

Monument of the 28th Massachusetts Volunteers at Gettysburg

Monument of the 116th Pennsylvania Volunteers at Gettysburg

"Scene of a Religious Character on the
Historic Battlefield of Gettysburg"

January 4, 1879

Colonel John Bachelder,

Several days prior to this battle, the "Army of the Potomac,"
under the command of General Meade, was continually on the
March. The day before the battle, the 2nd Army Corps left Frederick City, Maryland about 5 in the morning and halted at 12
(midnight) to rest during the balance of the night on the cold wet
ground and next morning opened fire on the enemy with artillery. The enemy responded in full numbers. Shells were bursting
thick and fast all morning over the 2nd Army Corps until finally
all the troops were drawn up in line of battle.

The men were ordered to "prime" and now everything was
ready for the word "advance." At this moment the Chaplain of
the Irish Brigade, Rev. William Corby, C.S.C. (the only priest
then in the Army of the Potomac) stepped in front of the battle
line and addressed the men and officers in substance as follows:

My Dear Christian Friends! In consideration of the want of
time for each one to confess his sins in due order as required for
the reception of the Sacrament of Penance, I will give you general absolution. But my dear friends, while we stand here and in
the presence of eternity -- so to speak -- with a well armed force
in front and with missiles of death -- in the form of shells bursting over our heads, we must humble ourselves before the *great
Creator* of all men and acknowledge our great unworthiness and
conceive a heartfelt sorrow for the sins by which we have ungratefully offended the Divine Author of all good things. Him
whom we ought to love -- we have despised by sinning against
his laws -- Him whom we should have honored by lives of virtue, we have dishonored by sin.

We stand in debt to our great Lord and Master. He loves us
but we, by sin, have forfeited that love. Now to receive a full

pardon for our sins and regain the favor of God -- do not think it is sufficient to get the priest's absolution. It is true as a minister of God he has received the power to pronounce your sins absolved: Whose sins you shall forgive they are forgiven, John XX. By virtue of this power given the Apostles and their lawful successors, the priest acts. But the absolution pronounced by the priest or by St. Peter himself -- would be worthless unless the penitent conceives a true sorrow for his sins which sorrow should include a firm determination never more to *willfully* offend and to do all in his power to atone for the past sins. Therefore, my dear friends, in the Solemn presence of Eternity, excite in your minds a deep sorrow for all the sins, negligences and transgressions of your past lives. "Rend your hearts and not your garments." And I, the consecrated minister of God, will give you general absolution.

At this moment, all fell on their knees and recited an act of *contrition*. Officers mounted waiting to advance removed their hats, and then the Chaplain in solemn fervent tones pronounced the words of absolution (a few minutes after all were plunged into the dense smoke of battle).

A more impressive scene perhaps never took place on any battlefield. It was indeed so *earnest* and truly *sublime* that non-Catholics prostrated themselves in humble adoration of the true God while they felt that perhaps in less than half an hour their eyes would open to see into the Ocean of Eternity.

Reverend William Corby
C.S.C.

Above letter was sold at public auction by Bachelder family on July 19, 1992, and later donated to Gettysburg National Military Park. (Spelling and punctuation are corrected to aid the reader.)

Colonel Richard Byrnes, commanding officer of the 28th Massachusetts Volunteer Infantry Regiment. (U.S. Army Military History Institute)

Chapter V

COLONEL RICHARD BYRNES: IRISH BRIGADE LEADER

by Barry Lee Spink

With the expansion of the Army by President Lincoln's May 3, 1861, Proclamation, nine new infantry units were created. Richard Byrnes received an appointment as a second lieutenant in the new 17th Regiment of Infantry, as of May 14, 1861.[1] As the sergeant major at Headquarters, 1st Cavalry, Byrnes lived with his wife in St. Louis, and did not receive news of his promotion until July 10. He immediately took his family back to New Jersey, and headed for Washington to take the oath of an officer.[2]

Arriving in Washington shortly before the First Battle of Bull Run, Byrnes found companies A and E of his old unit, the 1st Cavalry, attached to Colonel David Hunter's Division. He knew Hunter; Major Innis N. Palmer, commanding the U.S. Cavalry Battalion; and Captain A. V. Colburn, leader of the two 1st Cavalry companies. He had no problem in joining in with these troops, and went to his first battle in the Civil War.[3]

Arriving at Bull Run, Hunter's Division held the extreme right of the Union line. Moving towards the Warrenton Turnpike, with cavalry kept in the rear, resistance was soon encountered. Instead of bypassing or enveloping the enemy's strong point, they attacked frontally and piecemeal. Meanwhile, the cavalry felt out the exposed Confederate left flank, and repulsed a Rebel mounted force. In the process, they captured an ac-

---

[1] War Department General Order 33, June 18, 1861.
[2] Letter, Richard Byrnes to Adjutant General Lorenzo Thomas, July 10, 1861, Adjutant General's Office, Letters Received, Microfilm Roll #M619, Roll 7, NARA.
[3] "Flag Presentation."

quaintance of Byrnes from his days in the Dragoons, Colonel George H. Steuart.[4]

During the entire action, the cavalry moved to various points on the field where there was the prospect of having an advantage over the Rebels. Palmer and his troopers found such a prospect when attached to Colonel Samuel P. Heintzelman's Division. The major spied the enemy and pleaded for permission to attack. Palmer was denied the opportunity, due to Heintzelman's belief that the ground was unsuitable for cavalry. Ordered back out of range of the enemy fire, Palmer, Byrnes, and the rest of the cavalry could only watch the disintegration of the Union Army as fresh Confederate troops attacked the Federal right.[5]

The lack of discipline, combined with a general attack against the whole Federal line, broke the Northern volunteers. An orderly retreat towards Centreville ended in a rout back to Washington. The U.S. Cavalry, including Byrnes, tried to oppose retreating volunteers, but utterly failed. Covering the retreat was the only action left to do, and Heintzelman credited the regular cavalry for providing protection during the withdrawal.[6]

Byrnes and other regular army veterans were disgusted by what they had witnessed. None had ever seen such a rout. Any hope that the volunteers would achieve the standards of army regulars fell into the dust, like the many guns flung away by terror-stricken soldiers running headlong toward the capitol. Disdain for volunteer troops was a common trait in the regulars, and Byrnes was no exception. Such feelings would later taint his relationship with the 28th Massachusetts.

On July 27, 1861, Byrnes was sworn in as a second lieutenant in the 17th United States Infantry.[7] A few weeks later, the War Department confirmed his appointment and unit of assignment.[8] However, so much did Byrnes wish to stay with the Cavalry, he tried to swap assignments with Second Lieutenant Reuben C. Winslow of the 5th Cavalry, who, in turn, wished to join the 17th Infantry. Colonel Innis Palmer, then commander of the 5th Cavalry, endorsed the idea: "Lieutenant Byrnes has always served with cavalry, and he is a good cavalry officer, and knows

[4] The War of the Rebellion: A Compilation of the Official Records of the Union and Confederate Armies (Washington, Government Printing Office) (hereafter: OR), Series I, Volume II, 382-405.
[5] Ibid.
[6] Ibid.
[7] Letter, Richard Byrnes to Adjutant General Lorenzo Thomas, 10 July 1861, Adjutant General's Office, Letters Received, Microfilm Roll #M619, Roll 7, NARA.
[8] War Department General Order 65, August 23, 1861.

nothing of infantry."[9] Major General George B. McClellan agreed to the exchange, and Byrnes received a transfer to the 5th Cavalry in September, 1861, ranked directly below Second Lieutenant George A. Custer.[10]

Byrnes' new officer's uniform hardly had time to get dirty before the Governor of Pennsylvania, Andrew G. Curtin, offered him the colonelcy of a cavalry regiment of volunteers. Honored, but unsure of such a career move, Byrnes asked the advice of the 5th Cavalry commander, George H. Thomas (later to be known as the "Rock of Chickamauga"). Thomas had just been promoted to brigadier general, and had to leave the newly-created 5th Cavalry for brigade command duties. Fearing an exodus of all the regular officers from the regiment just when they were needed the most, Thomas earnestly solicited Byrnes to stay with the 5th until it was organized and in the field. He agreed to Thomas' request, knowing that such an opportunity would not likely present itself again. He declined Curtin's generous offer.[11]

During that time of organization, men were attached almost willy-nilly to various units as the need arose. Richard Byrnes was no exception, and he found himself temporarily assigned to the 1st Pennsylvania Cavalry, led by his former commander and buffalo hunting friend, Colonel George D. Bayard. On November 26, 1861, this unit went to Dranesville, Virginia, to drive out Rebel pickets. The following morning, after successfully clearing the town, the weary troops were heading back to camp with their prisoners in tow. Suddenly, the head of the column came under attack from forces hiding in a nearby woods. Without hesitating, Byrnes and others rode forward, dismounted, and, taking their carbines, entered into the forest. Within minutes, the Union troops killed two men and captured four others. Colonel Bayard praised Byrnes in his official report by saying: "The fine manner in which . . . Byrnes (second lieutenant, Fifth Cavalry) . . . acted cannot be too highly commended or appreciated."[12] This was the first time Byrnes would be mentioned in dispatches, and it would not be the last.

---

[9] Letter, Richard Byrnes to Adjutant General Townsend, Adjutant General's Office, Letters Received, Microfilm Roll #M619, Roll 6, NARA. It was a good thing Colonel Palmer's endorsement did not reach the officers of the 28th Regiment Massachusetts Infantry Volunteers a year later, when Byrnes was appointed over them as an infantry commander.

[10] War Department General Order 106, 5 December 1861; Endorsement, on Letter, Richard Byrnes to Adjutant General Townsend, Adjutant General's Office, Letters Received, Microfilm Roll #M619, Roll 6, NARA.

[11] Letter, Major General John Sedgwick, VI Corps commander, to Governor John A. Andrew, 8 January 1864, Executive Incoming Correspondence, MMHRC&M.

[12] OR, Series I, Volume V, 449.

THE MASSACHUSETTS 28TH---FAG AN BEALAC---REGIMENT.

The Pilot, on January 18, 1862, ran this woodcut showing the Massachusetts 28th first flag. (Sergeant Kirkland's Museum and Historical Society.)

On March 18, 1862, Ellen Byrnes delivered their second daughter, Margaret Esther, at Graniteville, Staten Island.[13] After visiting with his wife and his two daughters, Richard Byrnes returned to his beloved cavalry, and fought in the Peninsula Campaign with, as the Boston newspaper *The Pilot* noted, "distinguished bravery."[14] On April 4, a skirmish broke out at two points: Warwick Court House and Howard's Mill. Byrnes established communications between the two for coordinated attacks and received General George McClellan's compliments for a job well-done.[15] Byrnes saw action at Williamsburg on May 6, 1862, and helped gather in enemy stragglers on the 7th. On May 21, he led a reconnaissance party from Harrison's Landing to Bottom's Bridge. With his forty-two men, Byrnes ran up against an advanced Confederate guard, routed and pursued them, killed seven, wounded nine and captured thirty-five, without any loss to his own force.[16]

A week later, he and the rest of Company C, 5th Cavalry, pursued a party of the enemy's rear guard just past Hanover Court House. Coming up on them, Byrnes and his unit cut off seventy-three of the enemy in a wheat field, while the balance of the Rebels made its escape through a thick wood. Four officers and sixty-nine enlisted men were captured.[17] That action won Byrnes the praise of Brigadier General Fitz-John Porter.[18]

On June 13, Confederate General James E. B. Stuart sent a force of cavalry and artillery that breached the thinly-held Union lines at its right flank, and drove in Lieutenant Byrnes' squadron at Old Church. The Fifth Cavalry unit was camped about a mile from the bridge on the Hanover Court House Road, at Old Church, when a corporal rode in from the pickets, yelling, "The Rebels are advancing, and they're only a mile and a half away!" Captain William B. Royall (another veteran of Indian battles on the plains before the war) ordered Company C (the only company in camp) to saddle up; he gave command to Lieutenant Byrnes while he went forward to the pickets.[19]

---

[13] Byrnes Pension File, NARA.

[14] "Flag Presentation." and Remarks found in a Roster of Commissioned Officers in the 28th Mass., NARA, 28th Mass Regimental Books, Record Group 94, Stack Area 9W3, Row 7, Compartment 33, Shelf D, Washington DC. (hereafter: 28th Rgt. Books, NARA).

[15] Letter, Colonel Richard Byrnes to Colonel Delos B. Sackett, Inspector General, 18 March 1863, Commission Branch, Letters Received, Microfilm Roll #M1964, Roll 4, NARA.

[16] "Flag Presentation."

[17] OR, Series I, Volume XI, Part 1, p.689, 692; and Major General George B. McClellan, *Report on the Organization and Campaigns of the Army of the Potomac to which is added an account of the Campaign in Western Virginia, with Plans of Battle-Fields* (New York: Sheldon & Company), 1864.

[18] Letter, Colonel Richard Byrnes to Colonel Delos B. Sackett, Inspector General, 18 March 1863, Commission Branch, Letters Received, Microfilm Roll #M1964, Roll 4, NARA.

[19] OR, Series I, Volume XI, 1023-1024.

It was not long before Byrnes and Company C were ordered to the front lines, which, at that point, were at the bridge. Together with Captain Royall and the force of pickets, the whole company advanced. The head of the column sighted the enemy and drew sabers. Royall ordered Byrnes to bring his forces up and this he did by moving to the right, into an open field, to flank the Confederate forces he assumed to be nearby. However, as Byrnes and his men rode into the field, musket fire commenced from a tree line to their front. It was quickly followed by shouting Confederates coming out of the woods in their effort to cut Company C off from Captain Royall and his picket force. "Charge" was sounded and Byrnes moved rapidly to the front toward the bridge, in time to see the rest of the Union force retreating. In his report of the affair, Byrnes recalled:

My company being cut off from the road I found it impossible to join Captain Royall, and immediately proceeded across an open field, leaping the fence into another open field, where I drew up in line along the fence and delivered a fire. Finding that the enemy were trying to get between my company and the woods I at once retreated to the woods, and reaching it before the Confederates, took a circuitous route and reached a point on the Hanovertown Ferry road about three hundred yards from the Richmond road opposite our camp at Old Church.[20]

While withdrawing to his camp, Byrnes saw the head of a column of infantry advancing on the road, leading into the Hanovertown Ferry Road. At first, he thought they were Union cavalry videttes, but, by their direction of march, he decided they had to be Confederates.[21] Seeing the danger, Byrnes immediately dispatched a rider to Brigadier General William H. Emory's Headquarters with the news.[22] His message reached Emory as well as Brigadier General Philip St. George Cook, the commander of the Cavalry Reserve, who was with Emory at the time.[23] This bit of news made the situation even more grave, further clouding the decision as to where to send forces to stop Stuart's men.[24] Meanwhile, Byrnes and his company rejoined other elements of the Fifth Cavalry, and made a line at the edge of the woods. Pickets were sent down the Richmond and Hanovertown Ferry Roads, which were driven back by enemy forces twenty minutes later. Byrnes afterwards wrote:

---

[20] Ibid.

[21] OR, Series I, Volume XI, 1007.

[22] General Emory was the First Brigade, Cavalry Reserve commander.

[23] OR, Series I, Volume XI, 1004-1031.

[24] Ibid.

When they [the Confederates] arrived within sight of us [we were given] the command to retreat on the Cold Harbor road... The enemy followed us about a mile on this road and then abandoned their pursuit... Throughout the whole affair I felt the want of carbines greatly.[25]

As it turned out, Confederate infantry had not participated in the raid, and Byrnes' report sent Union infantry down the wrong roads, in search of a foe that did not exist. Stuart's forces, consequently, were able to get away, after burning some railroad cars filled with supplies."[26] Although the damage was not great, Stuart's prestige increased, and the reputation of Union cavalry decreased.

The Union cavalrymen (including Byrnes) blamed their lack of defensive success on the recent withdrawal of their carbines. Without them, long-range engagements were next to impossible; the enemy could not be fought except in close quarters. Their complaints were heeded. Within a month, all were re-equipped with carbines; with the carbines came better results. The 5th Cavalry defended the withdrawal of the Army of the Potomac from Mechanicsville, on June 26, 1862. The very next day, Byrnes and the 5th Cavalry defended the left flank of the Army at Gaines' Mills, even to the point of staging a charge into advancing Confederates, resulting in severe losses for both.[27]

On July 16, during a reconnaissance from Westover, down the Richmond Road, two squadrons of the Fifth Cavalry (including Byrnes) ran into twenty-five Confederate cavalry pickets and two companies of infantry. After a slight carbine skirmish, the Federals successfully drove them back into their main lines. Looking for further game, the Union cavalrymen found a skirmish between a squadron of the Fourth Pennsylvania and one hundred rebel cavalry held up in a barn. While Byrnes took a platoon and engaged the Confederates at short range with a brisk fire, the rest of the unit proceeded to cut off the Rebels by getting behind them. Seeing that the game was up, the Southern troopers hastily mounted and fell back in a disorderly route, chased by the Federals for three miles.[28] On the very next day, July 17, 1862, Byrnes was promoted to first lieutenant.[29]

Before leaving the Peninsula, Richard Byrnes teamed up with Captain George A. Custer, in a cavalry screen to White Oak Swamp Bridge,

[25] OR, Series I, Volume XI, 1024.
[26] OR, Series I, Volume XI, 1004-1031.
[27] McClellan.
[28] OR, Series I, Volume XI, Part II, 931.
[29] 28th Rgt. Books, NARA.

while other Union forces reoccupied Malvern Hill on August 5. Upon arriving near the bridge, Lieutenant Byrnes led Company C, 5th Cavalry, as the advance guard (accompanied by Custer) and found thirty members of the 10th Virginia Cavalry acting as pickets. Quickly, Byrnes split the guard into two sections. He sent one straight for the bridge, and the other, his section, approached under cover of the woods, leaving the road and hugging close to the swamp until it was within a short distance of the bridge. Byrnes' plan worked magnificently. The Confederates were watching the bridge assault, but were taken by surprise when Byrnes attacked their left flank. The Confederates not captured in this initial assault retreated to the other side of the bridge and there tried to make a stand. Unfortunately for them, their guns, having been exposed to twenty-four hour picket duty and also having bad percussion caps, failed to fire. Byrnes shouted, "Custer, you take the right. I'll take the left;" and the rest of their men thundered through the resistance and chased, shot, and captured all the pickets they could find. [30] Custer gunned down one Rebel officer who did not heed the commands to surrender:

> Owing to the confusion and excitement I was not able to see the officer after he fell from his horse, but Lieutenant Byrnes told me that he saw the officer after he fell, and that he rose to his feet, turned around, threw up his hands and fell to the ground with a stream of blood gushing from his mouth. I had either shot him in the neck or body. In either case the wound must have been mortal. It was his own fault; I told him twice to surrender, but he compelled me to shoot him.[31]

In all, three of the enemy were killed and twenty-two were captured, with their horses, arms, and equipment.[32]

Byrnes withdrew from the Peninsula with the rest of the Army of the Potomac, just in time to participate in the battles of South Mountain and Antietam. The first of many weeks' skirmishing took place at Boonsboro, Maryland. The two enemies had sparred against each other for days, and the Union Army had caught up with Confederate forces at South Mountain at Turner's Gap on September 14, and forced them to retreat. Byrnes participated in the pursuit of these Confederates, catching up to their rear guard when they entered Boonsboro, early on the morning of September

---

[30] Jay Monaghan, *Custer. the Life of General George Armstrong Custer*, (Lincoln: Univ. of Nebraska Press), 1959, 87-89.

[31] Ibid.

[32] OR, Series I, Volume XI, Part II, 950-967.

15. Although outnumbered three to one, Byrnes and the rest of the cavalry charged the Southerners repeatedly, and drove them some two miles beyond the town. With the help of some Federal cannons, the Confederates broke and scattered, leaving behind two pieces of artillery, thirty dead on the field, fifty wounded, and several hundred stragglers.[33] The next day, September 16, Byrnes participated in reconnaissances, escorts, and supported artillery batteries.[34]

The Battle of Antietam, September 17, started off for Byrnes at about 10 a.m. when, under Brigadier General Alfred Pleasonton, he advanced down the turnpike toward Sharpsburg. Pleasonton's horse artillery and their infantry supports crossed the middle bridge and obtained clear shots against Rebel positions in "Bloody Lane." Late in the afternoon, all of Pleasonton's cavalry acted as supports and couriers. Advancing a little further towards Sharpsburg, Pleasonton's men were connected with Brigadier Edwin V. Sumner's soldiers on the right, and with Major General Ambrose E. Burnside on the left. With Burnside's men approaching Sharpsburg, Pleasonton requested more infantry support from General Porter and advanced with them. Unfortunately, Porter had no more men at his disposal, and Confederate General A. P. Hill's appearance stopped Burnside's advance. Byrnes held his position until 7 p.m., when all of Pleasonton's men were withdrawn to Keedysville. Byrnes spent the next day collecting stragglers and feeling out the enemy on different roads. On September 19, Pleasonton's cavalry pursued the enemy, capturing 167 prisoners, one cannon, and one flag. The Battle of Antietam fizzled out as the rest of the Confederate army crossed back into Virginia across the Potomac River.[35]

As part of the slow pursuit of Confederate forces, Byrnes crossed the Potomac with the rest of Pleasonton's forces on October 1, and drove the enemy's pickets out of Shepherdstown, Virginia (now West Virginia), and continued into Martinsburg, arriving at 2 p.m. Byrnes and the rest of Pleasonton's cavalry forced the Confederates to leave the town, much to the delight of the local population, who then rebuilt bridges so that Federal forces could use them. Staying in Martinsburg until 5 p.m., Pleasonton's forces withdrew, baiting the returning Rebel forces, drawing them

---

[33] OR, Series I, Volume XIX, Part 1, 208-213; and Letter, Richard Byrnes to Lieutenant W.G. Mitchell, Acting Assistant Adjutant General, Hancock's Division, February 27, 1863, Commission Branch, Letters Received, Microfilm Roll #M1964, Roll 4, NARA.

[34] See note above.

[35] OR, Series I, Volume XIX, Part 1, 208-212.

out, and capturing them in piecemeal fashion. Nine enemy cavalrymen and ten horses were thus captured.[36]

By coincidence, Byrnes had been in very close proximity to the 28th Massachusetts Volunteer Regiment during the assault across Antietam Creek and the drive towards Sharpsburg. Little did he know at the time how much each would depend on the other in the very near future.

At the same time, Colonel Harrison Ritchie, a member of the Governor of Massachusetts' staff, was visiting the Army, hoping to find a candidate for a particularly troubled regiment. The 28th Massachusetts Regiment, a predominantly Irish unit, was in sore need of a new colonel. The original colonel, after embarrassing, drunken incidents, had been forced to resign. The lieutenant colonel had also resigned; the major, George W. Cartwright, had been wounded twice at the Battle of Second Bull Run and was recovering at Alexandria, Virginia; the adjutant was absent without leave; and the remains of the regiment was commanded by a captain.[37]

Supporters of the regiment back in Boston, most notably Patrick Donahoe, the owner-editor of the Boston newspaper, *The Pilot*, submitted a petition to Governor John A. Andrew of Massachusetts. In it, he lionized the exploits of Major Cartwright at Second Bull Run, and recommended to the Governor that Cartwright be promoted to colonel and take command of the 28th Massachusetts.[38]

However, assuming that Mr. Donahoe really supported Cartwright's rise to the colonelcy of the 28th Regiment is a mistake. In a confidential note to the Governor, Donahoe made it clear that Irish politics forced him to play a role he did not really believe in. Donahoe wrote, "I signed a paper to have Major Cartwright appointed Col., but you must exercise your own judgment in this matter. . .I desire to withdraw my signature if you know of more competent persons."[39] Donahoe believed the rank and file troops of the 28th were as good as any Massachusetts unit,

> ...but the field officers -- God forgive me for favoring any of them. But I depended too much on others -- not being a military man myself. But do appoint some competent man no matter of

[36] OR, Series I, Volume XIX, Part 2, 10-12.

[37] "Flag Presentation;" "The 28th Massachusetts Volunteers," *The Irish American* Newspaper, New York, circa Oct. 1862; and Adjutant General of Massachusetts, *Massachusetts Soldiers, Sailors. and Marines in the Civil War*, Volume III (Norwood, Mass.), 1932 (hereafter: MSS&M).

[38] Petition, Patrick Donahoe, et al to Governor John A. Andrew of Massachusetts, circa September 1862, Executive Incoming Correspondence, Military History Research Center and Museum, Natick, Mass. (hereafter MMHRC&M).

[39] Letter, Patrick Donahoe to Governor John A. Andrew, 13 September 1862, Governor's Office Executive Letters Incoming, Massachusetts State Archives (hereafter: MSA).

what creed or nationality, provided he is an *educated* military man.[40]

Donahoe was not the only person to express a view on who should be the colonel of the 28th Massachusetts. Colonel Benjamin C. Christ, the commander of the 1st Brigade, 1st Division, IX Army Corps, submitted his nominees. Christ also suggested that Cartwright be made the colonel, that Captain Andrew P. Caraher, of Company A, be the lieutenant colonel, and that the regiment's adjutant, 1st Lieutenant Charles H. Sanborn, be major.[41] However, Sanborn, who had no such ambitions, said he would decline the appointment.[42]

With Irish politics in mind, Colonel Ritchie set out to find himself a colonel for the 28th Regiment. When he approached Brigadier General William W. Averell, the commander of the 1st Brigade, Cavalry Division, Averell recalled Byrnes' exploits. Grabbing Ritchie by the arm, Averell pointed to Byrnes and cried, "That's your man -- take him and you will not regret the choice!"[43]

Ritchie suggested Byrnes to the Governor, and it did not take long for the rumor to sweep through the 28th Regiment camp, where it was still licking its wounds from the recent battle. Lieutenant Jeremiah W. Coveney, of Company A, greeted the news with enthusiasm. "…the immediate appointment of Lieut. Byrne would have the effect of restoring order and discipline to the Regt. which it now lacks."[44] However, Lieutenant Coveney's enthusiasm did not make him naive to the politics within the regiment. "Vigorous efforts will no doubt be made to offset Lieut. Byrnes to the aggrandizement of other parties, but Sir I hope they will all fail."[45] The in-fighting of the unit's officers to promote themselves to the position of colonel absorbed all of their interests, leaving dull, routine matters to fall into a state of chaos. Coveney noted:

> Many things are now neglected that go to serve the organization or that would tend to benefit the Regiment, and all this seems to grow worse. I hope Sir that soon either Major Cartwright or Lieut Byrne will come here and straten out matters as they ought

---

[40] Ibid.

[41] Letter, Colonel Benjamin C. Christ to Governor John A. Andrew, 18 September 1862. Governor's Office, Executive Letters Incoming, MSA.

[42] Ibid.

[43] "Flag Presentation;" and "Irish American Soldiers' Obituary, Col. Byrnes, 28th Mass. Vols.--Acting Brigadier General of the Irish Brigade," *The Irish American*, New York, NY, June 25, 1864.

[44] Letter, Lieutenant Jeremiah W. Coveney to Adjutant General William Schouler, Massachusetts Adjutant General, September 30, 1862, Governor's Office, Executive Letters Incoming, MSA.

[45] Ibid.

to be, keeping every body at their duties and thus end at once all anxiety in relation to a Colonel."[46]

Coveney's understanding of the situation was accurate. The officers of the 28th Massachusetts Regiment were appalled that one of them was not chosen to become the new colonel. On September 29, 1862, Byrnes was mustered in as a colonel of the 28th. He had passed up one promotion to colonel by refusing Governor Curtin's offer; he would not make the same mistake again, even though it was an infantry regiment and not his esteemed cavalry. However, he did not report to his new regiment until he had received his commissioning paperwork from Governor Andrew, which arrived on October 17. He arrived at the camp of the 28th at the Antietam Iron Works, Maryland, on October 18.[47]

During the intervening weeks between Byrnes' muster and his taking command, the officers of the 28th began their campaign to rid themselves of him. A petition, sent to Governor Andrew of Massachusetts, and signed by seven of the nine remaining officers left on duty with the 28th Regiment, expressed outrage that one of their own was not picked to be the new colonel. They pleaded with the Governor to revoke the appointment of Byrnes, and based their argument on the fact "That he [Byrnes] has not the advantage of a military education; that the experience of an enlisted man in the ranks of any army does not qualify him for the important and responsible position of Col. of a Regiment."[48]

Unknowingly, the signers of the petition expressed the Governor's very reason for appointing Byrnes: "That the appointment of an officer of his rank over us, seems to us to be an avowal of the lack of the necessary Military and Administrative talent in our Regt. to command a Regiment."[49] That was exactly the reason, and to back it up, these seven officers vowed that Byrnes' appointment ". . . would cause the resignation of many, if not *all* of the Commissioned Officers of the Regiment."[50] It is noteworthy that the two officers who did not sign the petition were

---

[46] Ibid.

[47] Individual Military Records of Colonel Richard Byrnes, 28th Massachusetts Regiment, NARA, Washington, D.C. (hereafter: Byrnes IMR]. Byrnes received his commission from Governor Andrew while in camp near Knoxville, Md., on October 17. He penned a short letter to the Governor stating: "Whilst I thank you Governor most heartily for the honor done me, I trust the occasion may never occur to give you cause to regret the appointment." Letter, Byrnes to Governor Andrew, October 17, 1862, Executive Correspondence, Incoming, MMHRC&M

[48] Petition, Officers of the 28th Massachusetts Regiment to Governor John A. Andrew, October 1, 1862, Executive Correspondence, Incoming, MMHRC&M.

[49] Ibid.

· [50] Ibid.

Coveney (who would later be accused of leading a campaign against Byrnes) and the Captain of Company A, Andrew P. Caraher.[51]

As it turned out, the threat was a rather hollow one, with only one officer actually resigning.[52] However, Augustus Annand, a former sergeant with Company E who had recently been promoted to second lieutenant and acting adjutant, noted that Colonel Byrnes ". . . frequently held officer's resignations some time before forwarding, and placed them in my custody."[53] Evidently, Byrnes hoped the petitioners would change their minds after seeing how the regiment improved under his leadership, before giving up hope of reaching an understanding and forwarding their resignations to higher headquarters. Most of the petitioners did not resign until forced to do so by the severity of their wounds.[54] Those who did resign during the first few months of Byrnes' command were usually absent on sick leave. It is, therefore, doubtful that they acted on any moral outrage over the new colonel's appointment.[55]

---

[51] Ibid.

[52] The seven officers were: Captains John H. Brennan (resigning on 10 Mar 1863, which he attributed to wounds received during the Antietam battle); Charles H. Sanborn (resigning 3 June 1863, which he attributed to wounds received during the Fredericksburg battle), James Magner; (who was later killed 18 May 1864 at the battle of Spotsylvania); James O'Keefe (who did resign on 11 May 1863); Lieutenants William Mitchell (who followed through on his threat and resigned on 14 November 1862, a mere month after Colonel Byrnes reported to the unit); Josiah F. Kennison (who resigned on 12 October 1863); and Edmund H. Fitzpatrick (who resigned on 1 March 1864). Only William Mitchell resigned in protest, the others, if they did offer resignations, withdrew them, for a time, after Byrnes showed his flair for organization and discipline.

[53] Affidavit, Augustus Annand, 14 September 1885, in Captain James O'Keefe Pension File, NARA.

[54] MSS&M.

[55] Muster Rolls, 28th Massachusetts, Record Group 94, Stack Area 8W3, Boxes 1808, 1809, NARA (hereafter: 28th Muster Rolls, NARA).

Lieutenant Colonel George W. Cartwright, 28th Massachusetts, Dublin-born. Cartwright was promoted to major and was in command at James Island in June, 1862. He was badly wounded at Second Bull Run and served until discharged on December 20, 1864. (U.S. Army Military History Institute)

As a new colonel, Richard Byrnes had a mandate to fix a broken outfit. The few officers not attached to other units, on furlough, absent, sick, prisoner of war, or absent without leave were surly towards him. All routine regimental paperwork was ignored. Numerous men of the 28th were assigned to menial tasks throughout the Army, reducing the available for duty roster down to slightly over four hundred men -- less than half of a fully-manned regiment of 1,000. Byrnes had to act decisively and without tolerance toward anyone who would not do his duty or who stood in the way of rebuilding the unit. A flurry of messages and orders poured out of Colonel Byrnes' tent. Those men conducting additional duties throughout the Army of the Potomac received orders to return to the 28th Regiment. The sergeant major was relieved of duty and Byrnes appointed a new one. The Regimental Quartermaster was reduced to the ranks for inefficiency; drums were ordered for the Regimental Drum Corps (who, unbelievably, had none); details of men to clean up the campsite were created; NCOs were ordered to wear the chevrons of their rank, and new NCOs were appointed.[56]

In addition, the new colonel requested that Governor Andrew fill his ranks with an additional four hundred men. Byrnes wrote he would send an officer up to get the recruits so they would not go ". . . straggling about the countryside in whatever direction their inclination [would] lead them."[57] Unfortunately, there were no new recruits for the Governor to send them, so Byrnes had to work hard with the resources at hand, which was noticed immediately by the men of the regiment. Hiram T. Nason, of Company F, noted to his family: "On the 18th we had a new Colonel take command his name is Burns ... he seems to be very strict."[58] Concerning the new colonel, Peter Welsh, of Company K, wrote his wife "...I expect we will have what is much needed that is better order and discipline in the regiment."[59]

Byrnes wanted to bring back pride to the men in the unit; therefore, daily drill was instituted. Each company drilled for an hour in the morning; all companies drilled together for an hour in the afternoon, and, after Dress Parade for the brigade, company commanders inspected their

---

[56] 28th Massachusetts Regiment Special Orders, 28th Rgt. Books, NARA.
[57] Outgoing Message #37, Colonel Richard Byrnes to Governor John A. Andrew, 22 November 1862, 28th Rgt. Books, NARA.
[58] Letter, Hiram T. Nason, Company F, 28th Massachusetts, to his Father, Mother and Sister, 20 October 1862, Nason Pension File, NARA.
[59] Dr. Lawrence F. Kohl, editor, *Irish Green & Union Blue: The Civil War Letters of Peter Welsh* (New York: Fordham University Press), 1986, 25 (hereafter: *Irish Green and Union Blue*).

companies and Colonel Byrnes inspected the officers.[60] And so it went, as the 28th Regiment wound its way from Nolan's Ferry, Maryland, through Waterford, Waterloo, finally stopping at Falmouth, Virginia. Byrnes shuffled men around in the unit until he found those who did their jobs correctly. Pressure mounted on the young colonel; he had to mold the 28th back into an effective fighting force.

On November 23, a welcome organizational change took place. The 28th Massachusetts transferred from the IX Corps to Meagher's Irish Brigade in the II Corps.[61] The Irish 28th was originally raised for General Benjamin Butler's forces in 1861, but, when he refused it, they were offered to the Irish Brigade. Unfortunately, events in South Carolina in early 1862 required reinforcements and, because of its availability, the 28th was sent. When the regiment joined the Army of the Potomac in August, 1862, the 29th Massachusetts, a predominantly native-born Yankee outfit, had taken the 28th's place in the Irish Brigade. Gallant fighters that they were, the 29th stood apart from its fellow Irish Brigade units, and a mutually-agreeable trade was soon worked out. The 29th went to the IX Corps, and the 28th found a home in a prestigious unit. Byrnes undoubtedly found the arrangement satisfactory. The gallantry of the Irish Brigade was well-known to him, probably from first-hand experience, from its fights both on the Peninsula and from the fighting in Virginia and Maryland. Success breeds success, and the 28th had a role model to pattern itself after. The 28th had to become as good as the rest of the Brigade: it was then early December, and Fredericksburg lay right across the river.

Early on Thursday morning, December 11, 1862, Colonel Byrnes ordered the men of the 28th to assemble, ready to march. Joining the rest of the Brigade, they proceeded to the pontoon bridge across the Rappahannock, near Major General Sumner's headquarters. There they rested until the evening, while the bridges into Fredericksburg were secured, and Confederate pickets were cleared from the town. Drawing closer to the river, the 28th spent the night, shivering in the cold. At 8 o'clock the following morning, the Irish Brigade started across the river, and then along a road next to the river, ankle-deep in mud. Enemy cannons fired into the town near their position, and they awaited further orders. None came until dusk, and that made the troops even more miserable. No fires were permitted; therefore, no cooked rations were available. Byrnes and his men slept in the mud and frost that night, awaiting the terrible dawn.[62]

---

[60] 28th Regiment Special Order 25, 24 November 1862, 28th Rgt. Books, NARA.

[61] HQ, Right Grand Division, Special Order #25, 23 November 1862, 28th Rgt. Papers, NARA.

[62] OR, Series I, Volume XXI, 227-251.

Saturday morning came bright and clear, with the sounds of battle creating a constant background roar, but the Brigade did not move. Finally, at noon, the Irish Brigade began marching into position for what was destined to become one of the most famous assaults in the war. Looking around him, Richard Byrnes could see that his was the largest unit in the whole Brigade. Of the 1,200 men in the famed unit, the 28th accounted for over four hundred of them. The remaining eight hundred men were spread throughout the 63rd, 69th, 88th New York regiments and the 116th Pennsylvania. In addition, the 28th had the only green Irish flag that day. Although it was in tatters, it was in better shape than any of the New York colors. It did not surprise Byrnes, therefore, when the commander of the Irish Brigade, Brigadier General Thomas F. Meagher, ordered the 28th to the center of the battle line. General Meagher also ordered everyone in the Brigade to put sprigs of green boxwood in the bands of their hats. There would be no mistake as to who was Irish on that fateful day, despite the missing flags of the New York regiments.[63]

Moving through the streets of Fredericksburg, the Brigade wound its way, dodging shells and bricks blown off of nearby houses. Richard Byrnes wrote:

…we remained Lying on the ground for ten minutes, when the order was given to advance in line, and we marched to the crest of the hill, directly in front of grape, canister, and musketry. On arriving at the crest of the hill, the firing was so severe and concentrated that the men were compelled to take shelter by lying down and many endeavored to hold their position by piling wood, to form a barricade, in rear of a brick house on our right, behind which they did good execution….[64]

Peter Welsh, of the 28th's Company K, related:

…we had to cross that distance which is low and level with their batteries playing on us both in front and from right and left the storm of shell and grap and canister was terrible mowing whole gaps out of our ranks and we having to march over their dead and wounded bodies … but the storm of shot was then most galling and our ranks were soon thined our troops had to lay down to escape the raking fire … and we had but a poor chance at the enemy who was sheltered in his rifle pits and entrench-

---

[63] Ibid.
[64] Ibid. 246-247.

ments I seen some hot work at south mountain and Antietam in Maryland but they were not to be compared to this ...[65]

After enduring the slaughter for about forty-five minutes, the command of the 63rd New York fell to Captain P. J. Condon, the Captain of Company G. A sergeant of his command pointed over to the right -- the Green flag of the 28th was falling back. Condon, with all the men of his unit he could find, which numbered only nine, fell back, meeting the ten men clustered around the retreating flag. Colonel Byrnes, having been ordered to retire with the rest of the Brigade, was there. The two men looked each other solemnly in the eye, and shook hands. Byrnes looked around at the butchery, and remarked to Captain Condon, "The Brigade is gone."[66]

The rest of the day was spent trying to get the wounded away from the field of fire. The brick house quickly became a shelter for the wounded, and, at nightfall, Byrnes arranged to retrieve as many of his men from the building as possible. This was his first battle as a colonel, and his unit had lost 157 of the 426 men he had led into combat. Five days later, only 269 reported for duty.[67] General Meagher, however, was very pleased with his new colonel:

[Byrnes] eminently distinguished himself by the perfect fearlessness of his conduct, his gallant bearing, and his devotion to the orders he had received -- leading his men up within pistol-range of the enemy's first line of advance, and there holding his ground until the rest of the Brigade being hopelessly reduced, and his own command left without support whilst it was considerably weakened, he brought the 28th with honor from the field.[68]

---

[65] *Irish Green & Union Blue*, 42-43.
[66] Ibid. 250.
[67] Ibid.; and Consolidated Morning Reports of the 28th Massachusetts extracted from the Adjutant General of Massachusetts Record Group, 308FF, 37 3, 457X, MSA (hereafter: Morning Reports, MSA).
[68] Letter, Brigadier General Thomas F. Meagher, Irish Brigade Commander, to Assistant Adjutant General W.G. Mitchell, Hancock's Division, 28 February 1863, Adjutant General's Office, Letters Received, Microfilm Roll #M619, Roll 6, NARA.

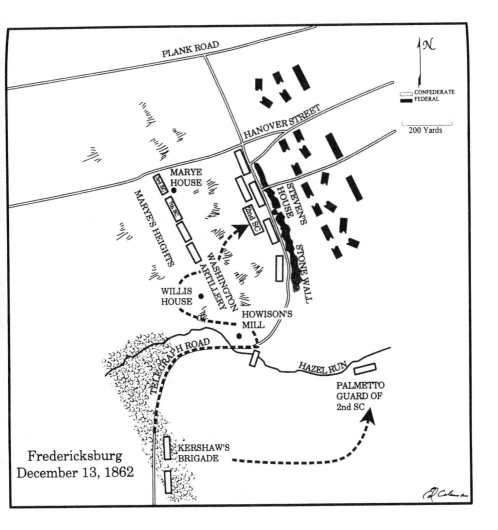

Map of Fredericksburg from Mac Wyckoff's *A History of the 2nd South Carolina Infantry*. The Irish brigade faced Kershaw's and Cobb's men behind its stone wall defense. (Sergeant Kirkland's Museum and Historical Society)

On the next day (December 14), the 28th occupied a portion of the town to defend against an expected enemy counterattack, and stayed there until the night of December 15. In the dark, the 28th returned to the camp it had left on December 11. Richard Byrnes realized quick action was needed to keep the regiment from falling into shock and paralysis. Drawing on his thirteen years of regular army experience, Byrnes immediately acted. He chose the paths of discipline, rooted out incompetence, drilled, and fought for more men and supplies. Throughout the rest of December and early January, corporals and sergeants were reduced to the ranks for incompetence, inefficiency, or neglect of duty. Promotions to replace them and those killed in the recent battle were quickly made. Byrnes made it quite clear that everyone was expected to produce quality results. One officer who absented himself from the regiment just before the Battle of Fredericksburg was forced to resign. Officers who had not reported back from sick leave were also asked to resign. The colonel needed men who were on the scene and ready to do their duty.[69] Peter Welsh wrote: "[O]ur Colonel is the right kind of man for that he is bound to make every man under his command do his duty or he will know for what."[70]

This "right kind of man" also needed more men. Byrnes heard a rumor that another Massachusetts unit would soon be disbanded and its men sent to other units. The colonel quickly wrote to Governor Andrew and put in his bid for some of these men.[71] He was not successful. Even in the area of supplies, Byrnes ran into obstacles. The lack of clothing and ordnance irritated him immensely. Some of his men were barefoot, and the sight of them at drill on a cold snowy ground grieved him mightily. Numerous letters requesting assistance poured forth from the colonel's pen.[72]

Being a professional soldier, Byrnes relied on drill to instill a sense of pride in his fellow Irishmen. Company drill took place for an hour in the morning, then battalion drill for an hour-and-a-half in the afternoon. That was followed by a dress parade by the whole regiment at sunset. "[A]t dress parade the regiment is drawn up in line in front of the camp and the

[69] Special Orders, General Orders, and Outgoing Messages in the 28th Rgt. Books, December 1862 and January 1863, NARA; December 1862 and January 1863 28th Muster Rolls, NARA.

[70] *Irish Green and Union Blue*, 45.

[71] Letter, Colonel Richard Byrnes, 28th Massachusetts, to Governor John A. Andrew, 17 December 1862, Executive Incoming Correspondence, MMHRC&M.

[72] Special Orders, General Orders, and Outgoing Messages in the 28th Rgt. Books, December 1862 and January 1863 NARA; December 1862 and January 1863, 28th Muster Rolls. NARA.

Colonel put us through the manual of arms," Welsh recalled.[73] Byrnes seemed to be everywhere at once. No function of the regiment escaped his notice, and, because of his low tolerance of incompetence, he provoked the ire of some, while this same tenacity of his provided much needed supplies for everyone.

Welsh related:

> their is a good many of our regiment who hate our Colonel because he is a man of decipline he is the right kind of an officer to have command he will allow neither Officers nor men to shirk their duty there is no partiality shown to any he also looks out for the rights of his regiment if there is any cause of complaint he makes it his business to look after it immediately we have clothing in abundance now we got woolen gloves and legans since Christmas . . .[74]

Joseph E. Sheedy, of Company E, wrote his parents: "We are like the Zouaves now we have got those White Legging and have to war them every day if [we] omit putting them on we are to be punished. we have got a very Strict Colonel."[75]

All of Richard's efforts paid off, and a feeling of pride and discipline infused the regiment's officers and men. Lieutenant Colonel George W. Cartwright, fully recovered from his wounds suffered at Second Bull Run, was back and supported the new colonel. The men were well-equipped, and competent officers and non-commissioned officers filled the ranks.[76]

The colonel's success and military bearing soon caught the attention of the 1st Division Commander, Brigadier General Winfield S. Hancock. Since Byrnes was an able officer with combat experience, Hancock chose him to inspect the newly-arrived Austrian rifle musket and the bayonets of the 27th Connecticut Regiment. Byrnes found the muskets to be of a "very inferior quality," and not to be relied upon.[77] Primer caps would not fire when the gun's hammer struck them; ramrods were inches too short; the stocks were made of soft wood and did not fit well to the metal parts of the musket. "The bayonets are so inferior, that they can be bent with bare hands. I stuck one into a log and twisted it as it were a piece of nail rod," related the disgusted colonel.[78] In the final analysis, Byrnes be-

---

[73] *Irish Green and Union Blue*, 51.
[74] Ibid.
[75] Letter, Joseph E. Sheedy to his parents, 20 January 1863, Sheedy Pension File, NARA.
[76] 28th Muster Rolls, NARA.
[77] Outgoing Message #76, Colonel Richard Byrnes to Captain W.J. Nagle, Headquarters, Irish Brigade, 2 January 1863, 28th Rgt. Books, NARA.
[78] Ibid.

lieved ". . . both guns and bayonets are unserviceable, and calculated to make cowards of good soldiers, in the face of the enemy. They cannot be depended on."[79] Having done his duty, Byrnes could then turn his attention to a more personal matter.

When Byrnes was stationed at Fort Leavenworth, Kansas, he fulfilled the American dream of owning his own property. Then, the War of Rebellion came along and he was transferred back East, along with his wife and children. Coupled with his absence and the irregular Army pay practices, pieces of Byrnes' land were sold off to pay overdue taxes. The colonel requested a leave of absence of twenty-five days to:

> . . . go to Kansas for the purpose of settling my business I
> have no Agent, nor any other person there to attend to my af-
> fairs and consequently my immediate presence in that State is
> absolutely necessary . . . . being a poor man, I cannot afford to
> lose what property I have left.[80]

Since it was the first time he had asked for leave since the War began, and his regiment was in a satisfactory condition, the leave was granted. Byrnes left for Kansas on January 24, but he also visited his wife, Ellen, in New Jersey.[81]

Because of this side trip to New Jersey, Byrnes got back to camp on February 23 -- five days late. He was surprised at what he found. Byrnes' strictness had made a deep impression on the officers and men of the 28th Massachusetts. As soon as the colonel had left, the lieutenant colonel had tried and punished thirteen men.[82] A week after that, he court-martialed five more men.[83] Most of the crimes were of a minor nature, so Byrnes canceled all of the punishments and fines imposed on the offenders.[84] It appears his disdain for volunteers may have played a part in his decision. He may have hoped to win the confidence of the men by showing them he would not be petty, but it also undermined his officers' trust. They probably believed the colonel had no confidence in their abilities and judgments, since they were volunteers and not regular army officers. On the other hand, Byrnes himself had to explain to higher authorities why

---

[79] Ibid.

[80] Letter, Colonel Richard Byrnes to Colonel Patrick Kelly, Commanding Irish Brigade, 10 January 1863, 28th Massachusetts Regimental Papers, Record Group 94, Stack Area 8W3, Row 9, Compartment 1, Shelf B, Boxes 1805 through 1807 (hereafter: 28th Rgt. Papers), NARA.

[81] Right Grand Division, II Corps, Special Order 51, 24 January 1863, 28th Rgt. Papers, NARA. Ellen, his wife, became pregnant this month (February) with their last child.

[82] 28th Regiment Special Order unnumbered, 24 January 1863, 28th Rgt. Books, NARA.

[83] 28th Regiment Special Order 121, 2 February 1863, 28th Rgt. Books, NARA.

[84] 28th Regiment Special Order 126, 23 February 1863, 28th Rgt. Books, NARA.

he had overstayed his leave by five days, and, taking the lesson taught in the Parable of the Unmerciful Servant (Matthew 18:23-35), he dispensed grace to his own men.[85] As an interim measure, until a court of inquiry looked into the matter, he was barred from receiving any pay. The court found Byrnes innocent of wrongdoing; the Secretary of War approved the court's verdict on April 27.[86]

As sticky as that situation proved, to be another problem soon reared its head, going as far as the War Department in Washington. General Hancock appointed Byrnes as the official mustering officer for the entire Division. Anyone in the Division who was promoted within or into officer ranks had to visit Colonel Byrnes. In this way, their names could be recorded to assure they would be officially recognized at their new rank, and be paid accordingly. Byrnes held this position for only a month-and-a-half, but he mustered over two hundred officers. Unfortunately, the War Department was not notified, and did not recognize Byrnes as an official mustering officer. Therefore, the II Corps' Commissary of Musters was notified to ignore any paperwork with Byrnes' signature. He wrote, imploringly, to the Division commander:

> I ... insured the instructions ...were followed. I also followed closely other instructions issued from time to time. Therefore, none but officers belonging to the regular army were selected for this duty ... I have carried out all instructions I have received on this subject; carried out as a 1st Lieutenant in the 5th U.S. Cavalry, qualifying me for this duty. I cannot understand why this course should have been resorted to.[87]

---

[85] Letter, William Mitchell, Assistant Adjutant to Brigadier General Hancock, to Brigadier General Thomas F. Meagher, requesting explanation as to why Colonel Richard Byrnes overstayed his leave. 26 February 1863. 28th Rgt. Papers, NARA.

[86] Letter, Thomas W. Vincent, Assistant Adjutant General, War Department, to Commanding Officer, 88th New York Volunteers, Headquarters, II Corps, Army of the Potomac, 27 April 1863, 28th Rgt. Papers, NARA.

[87] Outgoing Message #99, Colonel Richard Bymes to Captain John Hancock, Assistant Adjutant General for General Hancock's Division, II Army Corps, 6 April 1863, 28th Rgt. Books, NARA.

First Lieutenant Addison Augustus Hosmer, 28th Massachusetts, 1st Lt.,
Oct. 24, 1861; transferred Mass. 1st Artillery, Jan 28, 1862; Captain
March 1863; Major judge-advocate Nov. 24, 1863; Bvt. Lt. Col. and Col.
of vols., July 6, 1865, for meritorious service in the bureau of Military
Justice; Muster out, Nov. 28, 1865; [died Feb. 1, 1902.] (USAMHI)

The confusion resulting from this miscommunication hurt numerous individuals throughout the whole Division. A newly-promoted captain, braving battle in that position, would not be paid for it. Upon notification, sometimes months later, he would reapply to the new mustering officer and find his time as captain not officially recognized. Finally, this misunderstanding with the War Department was resolved. But, typical of the Army, there was someone who didn't get the news. That "someone" was the II Corps Commissary of Musters, and he continued to disregard the men Byrnes had mustered, which forced Colonel Byrnes to request help from Lorenzo Thomas, the Adjutant General of the Army in Washington.

> He refuses to recognize the mustering made by me. By doing so, he
> refuses to fill vacancies caused by officers mustered out by me. He
> also refused to muster officers mustered by me back to the date of
> previous muster, but only from the time they make their application
> to him to be mustered. This creates loss and injustice to officers now
> absent due to sickness or recruiting service, having no opportunity to
> be mustered. They do not know their muster is not legal.[88]

Thomas stepped in and the problem was fixed, but only after eight months of haggling.

While the mustering problem was sorting itself out, Byrnes realized that a number of officers who had been absent for months, due to sickness, had failed to return. It became apparent to him they would not reappear, so he requested William Schouler (the Massachusetts adjutant general) to dismiss them and promote men from within the unit to fill their positions. Byrnes, a man of high standards, found only three sergeants in the 28th Regiment who warranted his recommendation to Schouler to be made officers. Therefore, the colonel asked the Governor of Massachusetts to fill the other five spots with ". . . young men from Boston, preferably men who have been tried."[89] The Governor quickly responded and picked four sergeants and one private from other Massachusetts regiments to be commissioned in the 28th.[90] Byrnes, a pragmatic

---

[88] Outgoing Message #129, Colonel Richard Byrnes to Lorenzo Thomas, 9 September 1863, 28th Rgt. Books, NARA.

[89] Outgoing Message #105, Colonel Richard Byrnes to Adjutant General William Schouler, 21 March 1863, 28th Rgt. Books, NARA.

[90] Letter, Lieutenant Colonel Harrison Ritchie to Colonel Richard Byrnes, 1 April 1863, Executive Outgoing Correspondence, MMHRC&M. The three recommended men made officers in the 28th were: Private John B. Noyes, Company B, 13th Mass. Regiment; Sergeant William F. Cochrane, Company A, 1st Mass. Regiment; and Sergeant Walter Scott Bailey, Company A, 2nd Mass. Regiment. Noyes and Bailey served their allotted time until mustered out on 8 December 1864. Cochrane died of wounds he received at the Battle of Spotsylvania, 20 May 1864.

man, believed he was doing the best for the unit. Unfortunately, when the officers and sergeants of the 28th Regiment found out, they were incensed. Importing officers had almost caused a mutiny when Richard had been given command, and now it boiled up into open contempt. Peter Welsh, of Company K, wrote his wife:

> [This] is the meanest act I have heard of any commanding officer doing in this army and especially as his motives are purely selfish. . .the Colonel would lose command of [the 28th, due to its small size] as the law provides that such . . . shall be commanded by no higher officer then a major so in order to keep his own fat birth he has done a great injustice to the men a great many of whom are much more competent to hold commissions then the strangers he brought in all the officers of the regiment protested against it when they heard of it and he put two captains under arrest. . . those two were the leaders of the opposition to his scheme so he tried to wreak his wrath on them he had them court marshaled but made nothing of it.[91]

Byrnes had arrested three captains: Charles H. Sanborn, of Welsh's company; John H. McDonnell, of Company H; and Jeremiah W. Coveney, of Company F who had been so vocal in supporting Byrnes back when he had first become the 28th's colonel."[92] The honeymoon was over, and the battleground over who actually controlled the 28th -- Byrnes, a regular army officer, or the volunteer officers who had recruited a number of the men in the unit -- began. The officers and men approved of the way Byrnes had recreated the Regiment. He had defended the unit in the areas of supplies and extra duty, and brought pride back into them with fair discipline and drill. The 28th Regiment had become a very solid, successful outfit, and the officers and men wanted to have a prestigious part. But his judgment of their character, and his declaring it wanting, was another matter. Col. Richard Byrnes had re-molded the 28th Massachusetts into his image, and those who bridled were about to find life under their colonel very difficult.

He was, above all else, totally dedicated to the Army. As a "regular" who had gone from the rank of private to colonel, Byrnes had seen his share of good and evil men and officers. He had also seen how forthright action brought about a change of attitude for those who did not comply with orders. He had survived Indian attacks out west and Confederate

---

[91] *Irish Green and Union Blue,* 95 and 96.
[92] 28th Muster Rolls, April 1863, NARA.

assaults back east by being decisive. And now, with every indication that the Army would soon move against the Confederates again, it is no wonder the colonel brought the three captains up on charges before a General Court Martial on April 20, 1863. They had protested about bringing in strangers from other units and commissioning them. Unfortunately, their protests occurred in front of the men and Byrnes could not ignore it. "Mutinous and seditious conduct" is what the colonel called it. The court found one man innocent and the other two guilty of lesser offenses. These two were publicly reprimanded in a general order; however, the tempering of the court's decision probably rested on the fact that these men had been volunteers."[93]

Byrnes suffered a moral defeat with that verdict. Regular Army officers, like Byrnes, looked askance at the volunteers. Their conduct would not have been tolerated in the peacetime Army -- but that was not peacetime, and the Army could ill-afford to lose officers unless it was in the best interest of all concerned. A degree of tolerance of the volunteers' attitude had to be instituted. It was a hard lesson for Byrnes, and it took some time for him to get used to it Meanwhile, the commander of the Irish Brigade, Thomas F. Meagher, went on leave, so Colonel Byrnes assumed command. Drill for the entire brigade became routine.[94]

At this time, Byrnes had the pleasure of seeing an old friend from his days on the Plains: Percival G. Lowe, who had since left the army to pursue a business career. Out East to visit his brother, Professor Thaddeus Lowe (commander of the balloon corps), Percival Lowe and Byrnes renewed their acquaintance with stories of the old days and by catching up on the news about mutual friends.[95] It rankled Byrnes, as he recounted his war exploits to Lowe, that so many of his peers in the regular cavalry had been brevetted to a high rank.

> ...almost all of my fellow officers in the 5th ... Cavalry have been brevetted for meritorious conduct during the Battles on the Peninsula...but not I. I deserve a Captaincy. I find some officers Brevetted, who, I think, have done far less towards meriting such Brevet than I have.[96]

General Hancock agreed with Byrnes, noting that, "The conduct of Col. Byrnes at Fredericksburg was excellent: the loss of officers and men

---

[93] Court Martial Records, NARA; Letter, Colonel Richard Byrnes to Lieutenant Mitchell, Assistant Adjutant General, Irish Brigade, 18 April 1863, 28th Rgt. Papers, NARA.
[94] Circular, Headquarters, Irish Brigade, II Corps.13 April 1863, 28th Rgt. Papers, NARA.
[95] *Five Years a Dragoon*, 399.
[96] Letter, Colonel Richard Byrnes to Colonel Delos B. Sackett, Inspector General, 18 March 1863, Commission Branch, Letters Received, Microfilm Roll #1964, Roll 4, NARA.

in his Regt. was quite great. I think him entitled to a Brevet for that action. Col. Byrnes has a fine, disciplined regiment."[97] Byrnes had even written a letter to an old friend and former commander in the Inspector General's Office, requesting a brevet to captain in the regular army. Although his request was endorsed by numerous generals, no promotion ensued.[98]

Meanwhile, the Army exhibited signs of a new movement on the enemy, and Byrnes wanted the Irish Brigade ready when Meagher returned.[99] The Battle of Chancellorsville was less than two weeks away.

Major General Joseph Hooker, commander of the Army of the Potomac, planned a grand strategy to outflank Confederate General Robert E. Lee's Army of Northern Virginia, and to surprise them from behind. This necessitated a move across the Rappahannock River across Kelly's Ford. Probably due to its small size, the Irish Brigade was relegated primarily to guard and skirmish duties during most of the battle.

On April 27, the Irish Brigade was split; the 63rd and 88th New York Regiments, under the command of Colonel Patrick Kelly, went to Banks' Ford (just a little west of Fredericksburg), where they conducted a show of force with the object of deceiving the Confederates. Meanwhile, the 69th New York, 116th Pennsylvania, and 28th Massachusetts, under the command of Richard Byrnes, moved toward another river crossing, known as United States Ford or more simply, U.S. Ford. Before arriving, Byrnes and the 28th were ordered to guard the road running between Banks' Ford and U.S. Ford. Byrnes chose Hartwood Church as his headquarters. From there, he watched the rest of the Brigade (the 69th New York and the 116th Pennsylvania) march off to U.S. Ford. The 28th spent the night at Hartwood Church and greeted the arrival of General Meagher, who then took command of the Brigade. On the next day, 28 April, the regiment moved to U.S. Ford, where the whole Brigade received orders to march back to Banks' Ford.[100] That night was spent at Banks' Ford, but not without the men getting lost and marching five miles more than needed.[101]

[97] Endorsement, General Winfield S. Hancock, to Letter, Colonel Richard Byrnes to Colonel Delos B. Sackett, Inspector General, Commission Branch, Letters Received, Microfilm Roll #1964, Roll 4, NARA.

[98] Letter, Colonel Richard Byrnes to Colonel Delos B. Sackett, Inspector General, Commission Branch, Letters Received, Microfilm Roll #1964, Roll 4, NARA. Sackett had served with Byrnes in the 1st Dragoons and the 1st Cavalry. Bymes wrote: "There are but few men that I would thus address, or ask such a favor from, as I do from you have known me as long, and perhaps longer, than any officer I have ever served under." Sackett endorsed the request: "From my own knowledge of Lieut. Byrnes' services while on duty with his regiment, he is fully as much entitled to be Brevetted as any officer of the 5th & 6th Cavalry."

[99] Letter, Allen Landis, 116th Regiment Pennsylvania Volunteers, Irish Brigade Inspector General's Office clerk, to his brother William Landis, Landis Papers, Manuscript Division, Library of Congress.

[100] OR Series I, Volume XXV, 311-329.

[101] Letter, Hiram T. Nason to W. W. Sanborn, his brother, 2 May 1863, Nason Pension File, NARA.

The dawn of April 29 brought orders to march the Irish Brigade back, yet again, toward U.S. Ford. The whole of Hancock's Division (of which the Irish Brigade was a part) settled into a camp one-and-a-half miles away from the now-familiar ford. On the next day, April 30, after all the bridges had finally been completed, the Brigade moved across the Rappahannock and into enemy territory. General Meagher was temporarily absent, so Byrnes again assumed command of the Irish Brigade. Almost immediately after getting across, Major General Darius N. Couch, the II Corps commander, ordered Colonel Byrnes to take the Brigade, except the 88th New York, and guard the road leading to Banks' Ford at a place named Scott's Mill.[102]

At Scott's Mill, Hiram T. Nason, of Company F, 28th Massachusetts, observed, in a letter to his brother:

> Our brigade is so small we are on the reserve we are I believe to hold this please against any cavalry raid which might try to cut off and capture our train to day they are digging trenches and planting there Guards there . . . I believe that we will whip them at last . . as a cat would a mouse.[103]

It was, however, not to be. The Brigade, now commanded again by General Meagher, stayed for most of the battle of Chancellorsville, listening to the crash of musketry and cannon rising in tempo. On the morning of May 2, the attack of Confederate General Thomas J. "Stonewall" Jackson's troops (now commanded by Major General James E. B. Stuart -- Jackson having been being wounded) on the XI Corps forced a panic. Federal soldiers were streaming back toward the Irish Brigade at an alarming rate. Meagher threw a line across the road and into the woods, and had the men bring their bayonets to bear. The runaways, finding their retreat cut off by men more dreaded as antagonists than as the enemy, came to a halt, about-faced, and rejoined the army.[104]

Early the next morning, May 3, the Confederates renewed their attacks, and the Army of the Potomac started withdrawing into fortifications. However, they needed time to do so. Hancock's Corps provided the answer, as did the Irish Brigade. At about eight in the morning, General Meagher advanced the Brigade to the front, and was posted, two hours later, at the opening of the wood commanding the plain towards Chancellorsville. The 5th Maine Battery had come to support Hancock's men,

---

[102] OR, Series I, Volume XXV, 311-329.

[103] Letter, Hiram T. Nason to W. W. Sanborn, his brother, 2 May 1863, Nason Pension File, NARA.

[104] Michael Cavanagh, *Memoirs of Gen. Thomas Francis Meagher* (Worcester, Mass.: The Messenger Press), 1892, 483 (hereafter: *Memoirs of Gen. Thomas Francis Meagher*).

and were furiously shelling the advancing Rebels. The Confederate guns found the Maine cannons immediately, and delivered pounding blows until only two enlisted men were left, who fired their last shot. At that time, Hancock finally got the message that he could fall back into the fortified lines. His Corps had bought the time necessary for the rest of the Army. But, before he could leave, the cannons of the 5th Maine Battery had to be saved from capture by the then-advancing enemy. The Battery had lost all its officers, cannoneers, and horses for the guns; therefore, a detail of infantry from the Irish Brigade, men of the 116th Pennsylvania, grabbed ropes and pulled. The cannons didn't budge. Stuck in stiff, yellow clay, and under a galling fire of the enemy which killed or wounded four or five of the men, the remaining soldiers strained under the load of five different guns. Slowly, the clay released the cannons, all of which were pulled from the field.[105]

As the Brigade reached the plain with the rescued guns, General Hancock rode up to General Meagher and, very emphatically, called out, "General Meagher! You command the retreat!"[106] The Irish Brigade occupied the front line of battle in the new position, fending off Confederate sniper fire and awaiting an attack that never came. Positioned in that manner until May 6, the Brigade left its fortifications before the sun rose, and returned via U.S. Ford back to its original camp, near Falmouth, arriving at 2 p.m.[107] The Battle of Chancellorsville was over. Byrnes' command had lost eleven enlisted men who had been wounded; five were missing.[108]

Just a few days later, on May 7, 1863, President Abraham Lincoln visited the Army of the Potomac. The Irish Brigade passed in review, as did the rest of the Army. Samuel Chapman, of Company I, 28th Massachusetts, noted that Lincoln ". . .is a slim dark complected man he looks very careworn from his work."[109] Byrnes was also "careworn." Although the battle with the enemy was over, the infighting with his officers was still on. Just before marching into the Battle of Chancellorsville, Byrnes had tried to put Captains Charles H. Sanborn and Jeremiah W. Coveney back in charge of their companies. However, as the Captains arrived, the men in the ranks began to cheer them. As a test of wills, Byrnes would not

---

[105] OR, Series I, Volume XXV, 314; 328.
[106] *Memoirs of Gen. Thomas Francis Meagher*
[107] OR, Series I, Volume XXV, 315.
[108] OR, Series I, Volume XXV, Part 1, 176.
[109] Letter, Samuel Augustine Chapman to his mother and sister (Sarah), 10 May 1863, Chapman Pension File, NARA.

back down to this affront to his authority. Both men were placed back under arrest.[110]

While bringing normalcy and regular army routine back to the 28th Regiment during the next two months, Byrnes applied pressure to remove all of the officers who didn't toe the line. This included those who, although commissioned for his regiment, had not reported to the unit; those who had been on sick leave for months and apparently had no intention of returning. In May and June 1863, four company officers and the Chaplain resigned from the 28th Massachusetts. One of those who resigned was Captain Sanborn. Captain Coveney, originally a supporter of Byrnes and now one of the trouble-makers in the colonel's eyes, remained with the unit until he was wounded during the Battle of the Wilderness.[111]

Byrnes probably believed the troublemakers in his officer staff had been removed. For the most part, he was right. But the strain was telling on him and he spent numerous days in May and June staying in his tent, sick.[112]

Nevertheless, because of his high rank and being an officer in the regular army, he was part of the court-martial board presiding over the trial of Colonel T. W. Hudson, the commander of the 82nd New York Volunteers.[113] Byrnes also was called away to Washington for a few days in May to account for ordnance items he had signed for when he was in the 5th Cavalry.[114] In addition, he discovered the 28th Regiment had been shortchanged in the post fund, and worked hard to clear up unfounded debts and succeeded in bringing $96.00 back into the unit's account.[115]

The unit appeared to be in as about as good a shape as it was going to get. At the end of June, the number of available men totaled 274 officers and men.[116] Indications of another march and another battle were abundant, so Byrnes started preparing for the inevitable in early June. First, he made sure every man in the unit had good shoes and necessary clothing.[117] Next, he conducted target practice on Tuesdays and Fridays and cleaned out the Guard House of 28th soldiers placed there for minor

---

[110] *Irish Green and Union Blue*, 95-96.
[111] 28th Muster Rolls, NARA.
[112] Byrnes IMR, NARA.
[113] II Army Corps Special Order 106, 8 May 1863, 28th Rgt. Papers, NARA.
[114] Letter, Colonel Richard Byrnes to Captain M.H. Wall, Assistant Adjutant General, II Corps, May 12, 1863, 28th Rgt. Papers, NARA.
[115] Letter, Colonel Richard Byrnes to HQ 2nd Brigade (Irish Brigade), 5 June 1863, 28th Rgt. Papers, NARA.
[116] 28th Muster Rolls, NARA.
[117] 28th Regiment Special Order 149, June 7, 1863, 28th Rgt. Books, NARA.

infractions.[118] He needed them for the next battle, which he sensed was on the horizon.[119] He also made it very clear to his soldiers that no one would be allowed to leave the ranks for any reason, without written permission, during the march. To prevent any straggling, he placed an officer at the head and tail of each company during the march.[120]

Byrnes' men started trudging north on June 14, pushing further into Northern territory until they arrived in the vicinity of Gettysburg, Pennsylvania, late on July 1. There, they camped about three miles behind the town. At daylight, on July 2, the march resumed, and the Irish Brigade, with the rest of the II Corps, took its position facing the Emmitsburg Road. Placed in position, in columns of regiments by brigades, the 116th Pennsylvania formed the first line, the 28th Massachusetts the second, and the rest of the Brigade consolidated to form the last line.[121] Although the battle raged elsewhere on the field, little action took place where the II Corps was positioned, until early in the afternoon. Portions of the Corps became engaged with the Confederates near the Emmitsburg Road at about 3 p.m., and the Irish Brigade moved forward to support its comrades. However, a column of the V Corps appeared to assist the II Corps, and the Irish were ordered back to their original position. While they waited, the sounds of a furious battle erupted on their left. A little while later, between four and five o'clock, the entire First Division (which included the Irish Brigade) was ordered to help the III Corps.[122]

Just as they were about to leave, Chaplain William Corby proposed to give a general absolution to all the men before they would go into the fight. Addressing the men, he explained that each one could receive the benefit of the absolution by making a sincere Act of Contrition and firmly resolving to embrace the first opportunity of confessing his sins. He urged them to do their duty, and reminded them of the high and sacred nature of their trust as soldiers. As he finished speaking, every man fell on his knees with his head bowed. Father Corby stretched his right hand out towards them, and pronounced the words of the absolution. Father Corby noted that, "Even Major General Hancock [watching nearby] removed his hat ... [and] bowed in reverential devotion."[123]

---

[118] Outgoing Message #115, Colonel Richard Byrnes to Captain W.M. Wall, Acting Assistant Adjutant General, June 4, 1863, 28th Rgt. Books, NARA.

[119] Outgoing Message #118, Colonel Richard Byrnes to Captain M.W. Wall, Acting Assistant Adjutant General, June 8, 1863, 28th Rgt. Books, NARA.

[120] 28th Regiment General Order 27, June 13, 1863, 28th Rgt. Books, NARA.

[121] OR, Series I, Volume XXVII, Part I, 366-393. See also OR Series I, Volume XXVII, Part III, 1087 for a diagram of the disposition of units along the Emmitsburg Road.

[122] Ibid.

[123] Memoirs of Chaplain Life, 385.

The absolution being over, the men moved to their left at the double-quick, and the Irish were placed in a position to stop Rebel forces from advancing through a wheat field. Colonel Patrick Kelly, commanding the Irish Brigade that day, recounted that, while the Irish advanced, the enemy "...poured into us a brisk fire . . . . We, however, drove them a considerable distance, and sent a great many prisoners to the rear."[124] The Irish Brigade would load, fire, charge, take prisoners, reload, fire, charge, and take more prisoners all the way across the field and into some woods where they fired while advancing. Colonel Byrnes found that the Confederates ". . .were posted in an advantageous position on the crest of a rocky hill."[125] Without hesitating, the Brigade began to ascend the hill, despite the large boulders impeding its progress, and returned fire. Standing shoulder to shoulder, the men of the Irish Brigade gave and received volleys of lead for ten minutes. Kelly gave the order, and the Irishmen advanced up the hill, taking hundreds of prisoners who laid down their arms and went meekly to the rear.[126] Byrnes wrote afterward:

> We forced them to retire from this eminence, and advanced over the top and almost to the bottom of the other side of the hill, being all the time exposed to a very severe fire of musketry, and losing many men in killed and wounded.[127]

The 28th had been fighting for almost an hour-and-a-half, holding that rocky hill, when Byrnes noticed the rest of the Irish Brigade retreating. Looking around, he spied a large, Confederate battle line formed on both of his flanks, firing with deadly precision into his ranks. The Rebels had moved a sizable force, unobserved, and had outflanked the First Division. General John C. Caldwell, commanding, had just inspected his left flank and was riding over to do the same for his right. He saw all his troops fleeing to the rear in great confusion. "As soon as they broke, and before I could change front, the enemy in great numbers came in upon my right flank and even my rear, compelling me to fall back or have my command taken prisoners."[128] Caldwell had no choice; he ordered his entire division to fall back and reform at a stone wall at the other end of the wheat field. Unfortunately, no one told Colonel Byrnes. Finding himself almost surrounded, he ordered his men to withdraw, but to continue to shoot. "I brought my command from the field, losing many men from the

[124] OR, Series I, Volume XXVII. Part 1, 386.
[125] Ibid., 387.
[126] Ibid., 392.
[127] Ibid., 387.
[128] Ibid., 380.

concentrated fire of the rebels. Our loss in this action was one hundred in killed, wounded, and missing, out of 224 taken into the engagement."[129] The 28th narrowly escaped being captured. Byrnes reformed the regiment at the stone wall, and rejoined the rest of the Brigade near the Second Division Hospital at dusk. The unit didn't stay there long, for General Hancock ordered Caldwell's division back to the place they had started the day, facing the Emmitsburg Road.[130] The men fell, exhausted, and slept on their muskets. The second day of the Battle of Gettysburg was over.

The sky was clear the next morning, July 3, and the rising sun brought with it random shots from the Confederate cannons aimed at the men of the Irish Brigade. Hancock passed along the men early in the day. He moved the line a little forward, in order that the Irish would have a better range, and that their fire would be more effective, should the Rebels choose to attack them. During the whole of the morning, the men of the 28th busied themselves with building breastworks made of fence rails and earth. There they remained, awaiting an attack. Finally, the ominous stillness ended at about noon when the Confederate artillery began the heaviest fire anyone had ever seen. The air was filled with projectiles, and the Federal troops had no irregularity of ground to afford protection. Soon, the plain behind the 28th was swept of everything movable. Hancock noted with satisfaction that his ". . . troops maintained their position with great steadiness, covering themselves as best they might by the temporary but trifling defenses they had erected . . ."[131]

After about an hour and forty-five minutes of cannonading, the guns fell silent and more than 12,000 Confederate soldiers stepped out from their cover and started their march towards the Federal lines, over a mile away. Although the inevitable clash between the majority of opposing forces did not take place where Byrnes and his men were located, the 28th did manage to fire volley after volley into the enemy as it drew within range. A small enemy brigade advanced into the First Division's immediate front, but, after having taken a terrible beating, they surrendered almost to a man.[132]

Further to the Division's right, the Confederates managed to breach the Federal line, but the hole was quickly plugged up. Suddenly, the Battle of Gettysburg was over. The remaining Rebel soldiers limped back to their lines, and the two hostile armies were content to stop the bloodlet-

[129] Ibid., 387.
[130] Ibid.
[131] Ibid., 373.
[132] Ibid., 393.

ting. The rest of the day passed without incident, and the 4th of July was celebrated by picking up arms and equipment from the battlefield, while watching for signs of another attack by the Southerners. Late that afternoon, it began to rain, and the enemy army left the next day, July 5. The Irish Brigade helped the wounded and buried the dead, before moving to the town of Two Taverns.[133] Leaving Two Taverns on July 7, Byrnes led his men back into Maryland, heading for Taneytown. It was during that march, wet, tired, and worn out from days of fighting, that Byrnes had another explosive disagreement with one of his officers.

Byrnes had explicit instructions for the placement of his officers during a march. An officer had to be at the head and tail of each company to prevent any soldiers from straggling. Second Lieutenant Charles V. Smith, of Company C, however, allowed his men to leave the ranks to take short-cuts through fields, and did not march at the end of his company as Byrnes ordered him to do. Byrnes ordered him to take his place a number of times, and became so exasperated that he put Smith under arrest and ordered him to march at the end of the entire regiment. Smith merely left the unit and found an ambulance to ride in.[134] This breach of discipline, in front of the men, would not be tolerated, and Byrnes brought court martial charges against Smith. A month later, when the trial was conducted, Smith pleaded "not guilty" of all charges, and the court agreed with him.[135]

That was the second time Byrnes had tried to discipline one of his officers with a court martial and had been forced to accept a "not guilty" verdict. The court-martial board, headed up by a colonel of a New York volunteer regiment, was not sympathetic to a regular army officer who was not willing to overlook what it felt was a minor offense. Byrnes finally must have realized this volunteer army would not be run like the old peacetime army. He never tried to have any of his officers court-martialed again.[136]

Slowly, the 28th Massachusetts wound its way south. Frederick and Crampton's Gap, in Maryland, went by, and, every time they stopped, the men built entrenchments. Finally, on July 14, the Irish Brigade bumped into a Rebel rear guard. Byrnes ordered a line of battle, and the 28th advanced under sporadic fire as the Confederates retreated. No battle actually developed, and the enemy crossed back into Virginia. Colonel Byrnes

---

[133] Ibid.

[134] "Charges and Specifications preferred by Col. R. Byrnes 28th Mass Vols. against 2nd Lieut. Chas. V. Smith, "Co. C" 28th Regt. Mass. Vols.," 28th Rgt. Papers, NARA.

[135] 1st Division, II Corps General Order 188, 4 August 1863, 28th Rgt. Papers, NARA.

[136] 28th Rgt. Papers; 28th Rgt. Muster Rolls, NARA.

led the 28[137] through Sandy Hook and Pleasant Valley, in Maryland, and crossed the Potomac at Harpers Ferry. Still marching at a leisurely pace, the regiment moved from town to town until stopping near Morrisville, Virginia, on July 30, where they stayed until early October.[137]

Byrnes was getting tired and he again took ill. Dysentery, a common ailment, crippled him, and prevented him from leaving his tent. The regimental surgeon, Peter Hubon, recommended a twenty-day sick leave. Byrnes applied for it, but he was granted only a fifteen-day absence.[138]

Byrnes took his fifteen days, and asked for another fifteen-day extension, which was granted. Although his whereabouts during his thirty day leave is not known for certain, he probably spent most of the time with his very pregnant wife, Ellen, in New Jersey. Ellen gave birth to their third and last child, Catherine, on November 13, 1863.[139]

Byrnes returned to the field on September 10, 1863, to find 175 draftees had joined, bringing the strength of the 28th Massachusetts up to three hundred men for duty.[140] Life was very quiet for the month of September. The unit moved to new campgrounds near Rapidan Station, then moved again in early October, to an area near Culpeper Court House. It was during that time that Captain Andrew J. Lawler, of Company D, was found to be drunk on duty. Byrnes knew a court martial would not give the results he wanted; however, Lawler had just been picked to become the 28th's new major. Therefore, Byrnes only threatened Lawler with a trial. The colonel told the major-to-be that he would not press charges if Lawler would sign a written oath not to indulge in alcohol again. Lawler, knowing he could lose his promotion with a court martial, quickly agreed and pledged not to be ". . . under the influence of liquor from this time forward as long as I am in anyway connected with this Regt."[141] If he broke his pledge, the charges of drunkenness would be pressed. Byrnes thus found a way to maintain order, and still keep a good man. Within a few days, Lawler was mustered in as the unit's major. He remained with the unit, and was true to his pledge until he was killed during the Battle of Spotsylvania.[142]

---

[137] 28th Muster Rolls, NARA.

[138] Letter, Colonel Richard Byrnes to Lieutenant H. Bailey, Assistant Adjutant General, 6 August 1863; Certificate of disability for leave, Peter Hubon, Surgeon, 28th Massachusetts Volunteers; II Corps Special Order 183, 8 August 1863, 28th Rgt. Papers, NARA.

[139] Byrnes Pension File, NARA.

[140] Morning Reports, MSA.

[141] Pledge, Captain Andrew J. Lawler, Company D, 28th Mass, to Colonel Richard Byrnes, 3 October 1863, 28th Rgt. Papers, NARA.

[142] MSS&M.

Colonel Byrnes also filled a vacant lieutenant's position with the 28th's sergeant major, Edward F. O'Brien, to replace a man who had resigned. Byrnes confided in William Schouler, the Massachusetts Adjutant General, that he had two more lieutenant positions, but, "I will reserve them as rewards for meritorious conduct."[143]

Meanwhile, Confederate General Robert E. Lee learned that Federal commander Major General George G. Meade had lost two of his Corps by transfer to the Western Theater of the war. Lee then took the offensive, hoping to turn the Federal positions from the west. Lee forced Meade's retreat, but failed to cut him off. Along with the rest of the Federal Army, the Irish Brigade spent an indecisive period of marching and counter-marching, but never actually had a fight. The II Corps acted as a rear guard, and marched day and night to keep the Confederates at bay while still staying with the rest of the Union army concentrated at Centreville, Virginia. Late on the night of October 13, the unit reached Auburn. Early the next morning, wrapped in a thick fog, the unit crossed Cedar Run, a small creek, and climbed to the top of a nearby hill to provide support to a battery of cannons. Expecting the Rebels from the Northeast, the men and cannons were posted looking in that direction. Little did they know a contingent of Confederate cavalry and artillery lay directly behind them. The Battles of Auburn and Bristoe Station were about to begin.[144]

The men had marched for days without any opportunity to eat or drink anything hot. The cold morning of October 14 presented a few minutes for the soldiers to get some hot food or drink. Fires blazed for breakfast and coffee. A small force of Confederate artillery and cavalry, caught in between the retreating Federal corps, saw the campfires, and could not pass up the clear, well-lit hilltop filled with Union soldiers. They fired, one of their shells killing seven soldiers. Quickly, the brigades moved to the other side of what would always thereafter be known to II Corps veterans as "Coffee Hill." The coolness of the new recruits impressed Brigadier General John C. Caldwell, commander of the division to which Byrnes and his men belonged:

Notwithstanding the unexpectedness of the fire in the rear and their unprepared state, the men showed but little confusion, and kept their ranks while moving around the hill, the conscripts moving nearly as steady as old soldiers.[145]

[143] Outgoing Message #140, Colonel Richard Byrnes to William Schouler, 3 November 1863, 28th Rgt. Books, NARA
[144]. OR, Series I, Volume XXIX, Part 1, 235-265.
[145] Ibid., 238.

This remnant of Confederates that fired upon the Union troops was quickly displaced by others in the II Corps, and the Rebels slipped away. The fog burned off, and Byrnes clearly could see the advancing enemy. Again the Union soldiers moved around the hill, and, as the rest of the II Corps moved toward Bristoe Station in retreat, the men of the Irish Brigade acted as rear guards. The last to leave Auburn, the Irish Brigade delayed the enemy as planned. As the II Corps moved along the road, the Irish Brigade's division kept reforming and contesting any advance by the enemy.[146] As they moved towards Bristoe Station, via Catlett's Station, Byrnes' men were used as skirmishers and guards for the wagons. The men had been marching for days with very little sleep or rest. Major General Gouverneur K. Warren, the commander of the II Corps, saw officers on foot carrying the muskets of weary soldiers.[147]

Early in the afternoon, about a mile from Bristoe Station, cannon and musket fire could be heard. Immediately, the Irish Brigade, trotting at the double-quick found the enemy charging the other divisions in the II Corps, which were positioned behind a railroad embankment. The embankment provided perfect cover, and they easily repulsed the enemy. Byrnes and his men lay behind the embankment for several hours, part of the time under the fire of enemy cannons, but the 28th suffered no casualties.[148] Once in a while, the Massachusetts troops could hear the Confederates. Recalled Company F's Hiram T. Nason:

> At Bristoe Station we lay behind the rail road we could hear every word they said and see our artillery kill there men thare officers were trying to get them to chance upon us you could here them say Forward there or I blow your Brains out but they did not come and lucky it was for them they did not for if they did come half would never would live to fight again.[149]

Despite the good defensive position the II Corps was in, it was alone, and needed to get back to the rest of the Federal army. The Confederates did not attack, and the whole II Corps quietly slipped away as soon as it was dark, meeting up with the rest of the army at Centreville.[150]

On November 26, at about the same time Byrnes heard that Ellen had presented him with another daughter, Catherine, General Meade took the initiative, and attempted to maneuver General Lee out of his position on

---

[146] OR, Series I, Volume XXIX, Part 1, 254.
[147] Ibid., 244.
[148] Ibid., 262.
[149] Letter, Hiram T. Nason, Company F, 28th Massachusetts, to his Father and Mother, 14 November 1863, Nason Pension File, NARA.
[150] OR, Series I, Volume XXIX, Part 1, 235-265.

the Rapidan River.[151] Marching up to Germanna Ford, Byrnes and the 28th Massachusetts were one of the first to cross, scattering a handful of Confederate sentinels, who offered no resistance. Halting only momentarily in the empty enemy earthworks, Byrne and his men then continued to march another four miles into Confederate territory before stopping for the night. On the next day, November 27, the men marched to Robertson's Tavern, arriving at 11 a.m. They remained there until 4:30 p.m., before moving even further forward and spending the night in line of battle. At daybreak, November 28, the entire I, II, and VI Corps advanced in line of battle, only to find more abandoned works and a trail of discarded debris leading in the direction of Mine Run. With the II Corps in the lead, the pursuit continued, in a heavy rain. Two miles further, they found the enemy in a strong fortification on the west bank of Mine Run, about two miles from Robertson's Tavern. They stopped for the night, which was very dark and stormy. There, the II Corps commander, General Warren, received permission from General Meade to try to outflank the Rebels on their extreme right.[152]

Early the next day, November 29, the men counter-marched back to Robertson's Tavern, and found their way to the thinly-held enemy earthworks. Colonel Byrnes, in charge of the skirmishers (composed of the 28th Massachusetts and other men of the Irish Brigade), immediately engaged the enemy's skirmishers, whom he forced back, under a heavy fire of musketry. Byrnes continued the advance until he reached the crest of a hill, a half-mile ahead of the rest of the II Corps. He caught a glimpse of the enemy he was pursuing, ducking into more earthworks. Daylight failing, the rest of the division could not organize itself for an assault before dark. Byrnes and his men had been engaged for forty-five minutes, pushing the Rebels back, with the loss of only five men wounded.[153] During that engagement, Corporal Charles Wheeler Lovell Hayward, Company G of the 28th Massachusetts, managed to capture two Confederates, the only prisoners taken by the unit that day.[154]

Expecting a grand assault the next day, Byrnes eyed the enemy earthworks unenthusiastically. The slaughter at Fredericksburg kept playing on his mind and he now had a wife and three daughters to concern him. The next day brought renewed worries, as he saw that the breastworks had been reinforced with more material and enemy troops

---

[151] Catherine Byrnes was born in Jersey City on 13 November 1863, Byrnes Pension File, NARA; OR, Series I, Volume XXIX, Part 1, 235-265.

[152] See note above.

[153] Ibid., 694-714.

[154] "Home News," Newspaper unknown, circa 1900, Hayward Pension File, NARA.

during the night. Remaining on picket duty until 3:30 p.m., Byrnes and everyone slated for the assault breathed a sigh of relief when the commanding general called off the attack. Byrnes was ordered to take his men and guard the ammunition wagons while the entire Union Army withdrew across the Rapidan River. By December 2, everyone was encamped near Brandy Station, moving once more on December 5 to Stevensburg.[155] The Mine Run Campaign was over, and the two contending armies went into winter quarters. Major operations in the East did not start again until Ulysses S. Grant arrived and launched the Wilderness Campaign the following May.

After everyone was safely installed into winter quarters, Byrnes again asked to be allowed to have thirty days leave, so he could go to Fort Riley, Kansas, for ". . .the purpose of settling up some Real Estate that is now, and has been in an unsettled condition, owing to my absence."[156] Granted a fifteen-day leave, it is unknown where he spent it.[157] However, he was back with the 28th again right after Christmas, and was allowed to take leave again, starting on January 1, 1864. By January 6, he was back with the 28th Regiment with some exciting news: Massachusetts had begun to raise a new regiment of cavalry, and a colonel was needed to lead it.[158]

Through the army grapevine, Byrnes had heard of the plans to create new cavalry units from Massachusetts, and to combine a new battalion of veteran cavalrymen, which had been raised in Massachusetts during the winter, with the Independent Battalion, Massachusetts Volunteer Cavalry, already in the field. The new organization was destined to be the 4th Regiment Massachusetts Volunteer Cavalry.[159] With barely 320 men available for duty in the 28th, justifying a colonel's position was not such a sure thing.[160] The idea of getting back to his first love, cavalry, motivated Byrnes to write a letter on January 6 to Colonel Harrison Ritchie, the man who had invited him to be the 28th's colonel back in 1862:

> I am induced to solicit your opinion as to whether it would be advisable for me to make application to his Excellency. . . for the command of one of these Regiments. I am very desirous of ob-

---

[155] OR, Series I, Volume XXIX, Part 1, 694-707.

[156] Letter, Colonel Richard Byrnes to Lieutenant Miles McOmah, Acting Assistant Adjutant General, 11 December 1863, 28th Rgt. Papers.

[157] Evidently the men in the unit thought he had gone up north to New York (he actually called New Jersey his home, and his wife was living there), and not to Kansas. See *Irish Green and Union Blue*, 137.

[158] 28th Muster Rolls, NARA; and Morning Reports, MSA.

[159] MSS&M, Volume VI, 421.

[160] 28th Muster Rolls, NARA.

taining command of one of these Regiments, and would esteem it a very great favor if you would inform me as early as is practicable whether my application would be likely to prove successful.[161]

Before Ritchie had time to reply, Byrnes obtained letters of recommendation. Major General John Sedgwick, VI Corps commander, wrote:

Col. Byrnes . . . is in my opinion one of the best cavalry officers in the service. His age, habits, zeal and ability eminently fit him to command a Cavalry Regiment. I cannot believe there is a better officer to prepare a regiment for the field and to command it when there, than Col. Byrnes.[162]

Major General Alfred Pleasonton, the Army of the Potomac's commander of the Cavalry Corps, endorsed Byrnes by stating:

I make this recommendation in consequence of the high qualities as a cavalry commander of Col. Byrnes -- and there is no position more difficult to fill than that of Colonel to a Cavalry Regiment. Colonel Byrnes' reputation as a brave and gallant officer must already be well known to you, but it is his peculiar qualifications for cavalry with which he has been long connected . . . .[163]

Brigadier General Alexander S. Webb, the commander of the Second Division, II Corps, recommended Byrnes to Governor Andrew, noting that he would ". . . be a credit to the State and would be advantageous to the Regiment of Cavalry."[164] Believing he had a strong case, Byrnes decided to ask for twelve days' leave to go to Boston so he could present his case to Governor Andrew personally. Approval was given the same day he asked, January 9, and he sped to Massachusetts as quickly as he could.[165] It is not known exactly what happened in Boston, but it is known that Byrnes was back in camp with the 28th near Stevensburg, Virginia, by January 15.[166] A week later, Governor Andrew announced that

[161] Letter, Colonel Richard Byrnes to Colonel Harrison Ritchie, 6 January 1864, Executive Incoming Correspondence, MMHRC&M.

[162] Letter, Major General John Sedgwick, VI Army Corps commander, to Governor John A. Andrew, 8 January 1864, Executive Incoming Correspondence, MMHRC&M.

[163] Letter, Major General Alfred Pleasonton, Cavalry Corps commander, to Governor John A. Andrew, 8 January 1864, Executive Incoming Correspondence, MMHRC&M.

[164] Letter, Brigadier General Alexander S. Webb, Second Division, II Army Corps commander, to Governor John A. Andrew, 9 January 1864, Executive Incoming Correspondence, MMHRC&M.

[165] Letter, Colonel Richard Byrnes to Lieutenant A. Watts, Acting Assistant Adjutant General, II Army Corps, 9 January 1864; II Corps Special Order #9, 9 January 1864, both in 28th Rgt. Papers, NARA.

[166] Morning Reports, MSA.

Arnold A. Rand had been chosen to be the colonel of the 4th Massachusetts Cavalry.[167]

Strong evidence points to a scenario in which Byrnes was told Rand would get command of the 4th Cavalry, but the Governor would ask the War Department to send officers of the 28th back to Boston to recruit for the unit. In this way Richard's rank and position would be secure. The first day of his return, January 15, II Corps headquarters wanted to know how many of his men were on recruiting duty. Byrnes responded that he had no one, but suggested some men whom he would be willing to send. He did not recommend himself for this duty.[168]

However, nothing appeared to change due to his response, and routine army life took over again. On February 1, 1864, Byrnes became the Irish Brigade commander while the regular commander, Colonel Thomas A. Smyth, went on leave.[169] As brigade commander, Byrnes used his influence to procure needed clothing for his men. They ". . . are in a suffering and wretched condition, because they need clothing . . . ." he wrote his superiors. "They are now almost naked, please furnish clothes to this command."[170] In addition, Byrnes was appointed the Superintendent of Recruiting, which required him to report directly to Washington the number of veterans who volunteered to reenlist for another three years or 'til the end of the war, whichever came first.[171]

On the same day, February 5, word finally came from Governor Andrew. The Massachusetts chief executive had contacted Major General Winfield Scott Hancock, II Corps commander, and told him ". . . that great success may be expected to attend active efforts to fill up the 28th Regiment . . ."[172] Andrew added that officers from the 28th might be spared to take part in the work of recruiting.[173] General Hancock responded with his usual rapidity. On February 11, Colonel Byrnes and

---

[167] MSS & M, Volume VI, 421.

[168] Outgoing Message #164, Colonel Richard Byrnes to Lieutenant A. Watts, II Army Corps Acting Assistant Adjutant General, 15 January 1864, 28th Rgt. Books, NARA.

[169] Outgoing Message #177, Colonel Richard Byrnes to Major L. Breck, Assistant Adjutant General, Washington D.C., 1 February 1864, 28th Rgt. Books, NARA.

[170] Outgoing Message #182, Colonel Richard Byrnes, 2nd Brigade commander, to Lieutenant R. Watts, Acting Assistant General II Army Corps, 5 February 1864, 28th Rgt. Books, NARA.

[171] Outgoing Messages #184 and #187, Colonel Richard Byrnes to Brigadier General Lorenzo Thomas, Adjutant General, United States Army, Washington D.C., 8 and 9 February 1864, respectively, 28th Rgt. Books, NARA.

[172] Letter, Lieutenant Colonel L. A. Walker, Assistant Adjutant General, II Army Corps, to Brigadier General John C. Caldwell, 1st Division commander, 5 February 1864, 28th Rgt. Papers, NARA.

[173] Ibid.

four other officers of the 28th were ordered to Boston to recruit, and they left for Massachusetts on February 14.[174]

Upon arriving in Boston, Byrnes set up his recruiting office at Faneuil Hall, while he roomed at the Parker House Hotel on School Street. His officers were scattered across the eastern side of the state. One officer went to New Bedford, another to Lowell, and a third to Milford. A few recruits were gathered, but the colonel believed the best results could be obtained if the main recruiting drive took place in Boston. On March 4, he brought all of his officers into Boston and led an intense enlistment drive.[175] The results were impressive.

In all of 1863, even with a few officers of the 28th Regiment detailed for recruiting duty, the unit received a total of 189 men. Of these 189, 182 were draftees, leaving only a grand total of seven volunteer recruits. In January and February 1864, thirty-eight men voluntarily joined the 28th Massachusetts. In March, with the colonel and his men in place, another eighty-four joined.[176] By late March, Byrnes and his officers were considered so successful that the War Department decided to extend their stay in Boston indefinitely.[177]

Byrnes received badly-needed help from Irish community leaders. Patrick Donahoe (editor of the weekly newspaper, *The Pilot*, and founder of the 28th Regiment) and Martin Griffin assisted in the enlistment drive.[178] Together, another 133 men were recruited in April, and an additional seventy-one in May. This brought the total for the three months of active recruiting to 288 approved enlistments. Another 149 men tried to join, but were rejected by the army doctors as being unfit for service.[179]

Despite his success, Byrnes again found himself embroiled in the same old controversy that had plagued him throughout his association with the 28th Massachusetts. Instead of elevating sergeants into the officer ranks, he chose outsiders to be commissioned. Henry Martin Binney and Patrick W. Black had both been in other Massachusetts regiments and were highly thought of by their former comrades. On March 18, Binney had come to Faneuil Hall to enlist in a regiment. An officer who knew

---

[174] II Army Corps Special Order 43, 11 February 1864, 28th Rgt. Papers, NARA; and Morning Reports, MSA.

[175] Letter, Colonel Richard Byrnes to Major T. P. Clarke, Superintendent of Recruiting, 4 March 1864, 28th Rgt. Papers, NARA. It is probable that Byrnes visited his wife, Ellen, in New Jersey from time to time while he was on duty in Boston.

[176] 28th Muster Rolls, NARA; and Morning Reports, MSA.

[177] War Department Special Order 126, 24 March 1864.

[178] D. P. Conyngham, *The Irish Brigade and its Campaigns*, (New York: William McSorley & Co.,) 1867, 442

[179] 28th Muster Rolls, NARA; Morning Reports, MSA; and "Rejected Recruits -- Descriptive Rolls," for the 28th Massachusetts Regiment, March through May 1864, 434X, MSA.

him pointed out the man to Byrnes and recommended him. After meeting Binney, Richard did a background check on his record and found him a good candidate for commissioning. He therefore offered Binney the commission, which was accepted. Binney enlisted on March 18, mustered in as an officer on March 22, and was commissioned on March 23. Unfortunately, the muster rolls showed him receiving the state bounty money, meant for enlisted soldiers only, on March 31. This "fact" was brought to Governor Andrew's attention and he forcefully told Byrnes to cancel Binney's commission [180]

It was very much the same story with Black. He enlisted as a private soldier on March 29, was commissioned on March 30, and paid state bounty money on April 5.[181] Byrnes recalled Black's commission until he could investigate the charges, but Binney had already arrived at the camp of the 28th Regiment in Virginia. Binney had undoubtedly discussed the charges against him with fellow 28th officers, because the rumor mill in camp started up. Peter Welsh recorded:

> That mean scoundrel of a Colonel of ours is sending out a lot
> more strange officers to the regiment it is generally believed here
> that he has been selling commissions in Boston some of them are
> men who were dismissed from the service in other regiments.[182]

After careful investigation, it turned out that neither man had ever been paid any state bounty money. Byrnes sent Black's commission to the Governor's office with affidavits stating that fact and similar testimonials for Binney. Byrnes requested that both men be allowed to keep their commissions.[183] Andrew agreed that a disservice had been done to the men and upheld their commissions.[184] The governor's trust was not misplaced. Binney stayed in the hottest part of the fight with the 28th Regiment. He was wounded at the Wilderness, Spotsylvania, and at Reams Station before being discharged. Black remained with the unit, rising to the rank of captain by the end of the war. Both men proved to be good officers.[185]

---

[180] Letter, Colonel Richard Byrnes to Governor John A. Andrew, 14 April 1864, Executive Incoming Correspondence, MMHRC&M; and Draft Letter, Governor John A. Andrew to Colonel Richard Byrnes, 18 April 1864, unsigned and not sent, Executive Outgoing Correspondence, MMHRC&M.
[181] Ibid.
[182] Irish Green and Union Blue, 150.
[183] Letter, Colonel Richard Byrnes to Governor John A. Andrew, 26 April 1864, Executive Incoming Correspondence, MMHRC & M.
[184] MSS & M.
[185] Ibid.

Meanwhile, back in Virginia, spring had arrived and plans were formulated to put the Army of the Potomac back on the offensive. Men on detached duty, like Byrnes, were ordered back to the army.[186] Before he left, Martin Griffin and Patrick Donahoe presented a new regimental flag to the colonel in a ceremony at the Parker House Hotel on the evening of May 5. Griffin made a speech, and spoke of the new green flag as a token of the respect in which both Byrnes and the 28th were held by the Irish citizens in Boston. In typical prose of the time. Griffin said:

> The green flag of Erin is dear to every chivalrous heart, and the gilt is in keeping of brave men. Though Ireland is buried as a nation, yet its flag is still honored by all her sons, and it is no disloyalty to the Stars and Stripes, for the two banners should float together.[187]

Richard replied with his own speech, emphasizing his Irish background, befitting the occasion:

> Sir, In behalf of my fellow-soldiers I thank you, and, through you, the kind friends who have presented us this beautiful flag. It will be dearly cherished; and, in their name, I promise it shall be gallantly defended. I can promise no more, sir, than to assure you that it will be a fresh incentive to the brave men who are periling their lives in defense of that flag which typifies union and liberty, and beneath which the shamrock has ever bloomed. In a few days, sir, that flag will throw its emerald folds to the breeze, and the smoke of battle will encircle it; its freshness and beauty may be tarnished, but while there is an Irish arm to strike in its defense, its honor shall never, never be sullied nor impaired. I can only point to the past history of my regiment to vouch for the future. Neither Massachusetts nor the historic fame of our race need to blush for such a regiment. And, sir, your kindness tonight has imposed new obligations upon us. We shall endeavor to merit the one and uphold the other. Again, sir, I thank you for the flag, and trust that one day we shall return it to the care of Massachusetts, crowned with the laurel of victory of union and liberty forever.[188]

---

[186] Letter, Assistant Adjutant General Thomas M. Vincent, Adjutant General's Office, War Department, to Major F. W. Clarke, 5th U.S. Artillery, Recruiting Officer for Boston, Massachusetts, 26 April 1864, 28th Rgt. Papers, NARA.

[187] Flag Presentation.

[188] Ibid.

Richard received his orders to return to the army on April 28, but it took until May 6 before he could wrap up his affairs in Boston.[189] He probably visited his wife, Ellen, and continued his journey south, back to the 28th Regiment. Stopping off in Washington, and having been recently paid, the colonel decided to buy a horse for his own use, instead of relying on government-procured steeds. Choosing a fine-looking animal, he continued south. The spring campaign had started without him when the 28th Regiment left Stevensburg on May 3. While Byrnes was traveling, the Army of the Potomac had fought in the Wilderness, at Todd's Tavern, had crossed the Po river, and had struggled over the "Salient" in the Battle of Spotsylvania by the time he arrived, about May 15. Tired from his ride to rejoin the 28th, he removed the saddle from his new horse. As he pulled the saddle blanket off, he was horrified to see the brand "US" underneath. Obviously the mount belonged to the government, and could not be legally sold as private property. Byrnes had been deceived, but there was nothing he could do about it at that moment. He would turn the stolen property back to the Quartermaster and accept the loss of his money later. Right then, he needed to sleep.[190]

Byrnes found out quickly how badly the 28th had been mauled. His lieutenant colonel, George W. Cartwright, had led the unit of twenty officers and 485 men across the Rapidan River and had been wounded in the left shoulder in the battle in the Wilderness. Two other captains of the regiment had been killed in the same battle, and a captain and one lieutenant had also been wounded at the same time. The 28th had lost a total of thirty-four killed, 133 wounded, and twenty-three missing. The unit had only 315 men left.[191]

The rain which had started May 12, had stopped, and the roads looked like they could be passable the next day, May 17. The Irish Brigade commander, Colonel Thomas A. Smyth, formerly of the 1st Delaware Volunteer Infantry Regiment, greeted Byrnes with the news that since he was the senior colonel in the Irish Brigade, he would take his place as brigade commander. Smyth was reassigned as the commander for the 3rd Brigade, 2nd Division, II Corps, the next day."[192]

[189] Ibid., endorsement to above noted letter.

[190] *Memoirs of Chaplain Life*, 238; 28th Rgt Muster Rolls, NARA; Francis A. Walker, *History of the Second Army Corps*, (New York: Charles Scribner's Sons 1887) (hereafter: *History of the Second Army Corps*).

[191] Report of Casualties, 28th Massachusetts Regiment, May 1864, 28th Rgt. Papers, NARA; *OR*, Series I, Volume XXXVI, Part 1, 388-389; *Annual Report of the Adjutant General of the Commonwealth of Massachusetts, for the Year Ending December 31, 1864*, (Wright & Potter, State Printers, Boston, MA) 1865, 704 (hereafter: *Adjutant General Report. 1864*).

[192] Frederick H. Dyer, *A Compendium of the War of the Rebellion*, (The National Historical Society, Dayton, Ohio) 1979; Byrnes IMR, NARA.

Colonel Richard Byrnes awoke early on May 17, and contemplated the chances of staying alive under Lieutenant General Ulysses S. Grant's continuous, pounding style of warfare. The more he thought of it, the more he became convinced that his chances were not very good. He wrote out a note to be sent to his wife, Ellen, in case he was killed, and visited the brigade chaplain, Father William Corby. On the way over to the priest, he thought of his new horse. Byrnes not only gave Corby the letter for Ellen, but he left instructions to make sure that, after he (Byrnes) was killed, the steed would be returned to the quartermaster, where it belonged. Leaving Chaplain Corby, Byrnes took over the duties of brigade commander and prepared his men for another assault against the Confederates.[193]

No attack took place on May 17; however, the II Corps was ordered back to the battlefield of the "Salient" (also known as the "Mule Shoe") of May 12, and prepared for another rush against the Confederate earthworks. Federal generals hoped that the enemy had weakened this position in order to follow the movements of the V and VI Corps. The commanders hoped the II Corps could advance through the Salient, and cut off the remaining Confederates.[194]

During the night, the Irish Brigade moved to the Landron House, nearby the "Salient." On moving forward, at daybreak, May 18, the enemy was found strongly posted in rifle-pits, its front completely covered by heavy abatis, a tangle of tree limbs placed in front of the breastworks, while a powerful artillery promptly opened upon the column.[195] Rushing through the shrieking shells, the Union troops crossed the open field to the Rebel fortifications where they had fought on May 12. Major W.G. Mitchell, General Hancock's aide-de-camp noted:

> . . . as but a portion of the dead. . . had been buried, the stench which arose from them was so sickening and terrible that many of the men and officers became deathly sick from it. The appearance of the dead who had been exposed to the sun so long, was horrible in the extreme as we marched past and over them -- a sight never to be forgotten by those who witnessed it.[196]

Only part of the assault gained the entrenchments, the Irish Brigade being part of that success by carrying the enemy's first line. However, support was not available and the brigade had to hold the left of the en-

---

[193] *Memoirs of Chaplain Life*, 237-239.
[194] *History of the Second Army Corps*, 484-486.
[195] OR, Series I, Volume XXXVI, Part 1, 361-362.
[196] Ibid., 361.

emy's line all day, exposed to an enfilading fire of grape and canister from the enemy's battery. The cost was appalling. The 28th lost its acting commander, Major Andrew J. Lawler, and a number of its officers and men, a total of fifty-six.[197]

Byrnes and his Irish Brigade slugged it out, but, after viewing the battle, Major General Hancock advised a discontinuance of the assault, and General Meade agreed. At 10 a.m., General Meade ordered the assault stopped. Extracting the men proved difficult; Byrnes lost many of his best officers and men in the withdrawal. Finally, the brigade was reformed at the earthworks captured May 12, and remained there until 9 that evening. At that time, the brigade was moved two-and-a-half miles away from the battlefield and allowed to rest in a cornfield, near Anderson's Mill, on the Ny River, for the night.[198]

Battle for the Wilderness

[197] Ibid., 389.
[198] Ibid., 361-362, 389, and 398; *Adjutant General's Report.1864*, 705.

Colonel Richard Byrnes to Ellen Byrnes, May 17, 1864. (The Papers of William Corby, C.S.C., Province Archives Center, Priests of Holy Cross, Indiana Providence, Notre Dame, Indiana.)

On May 19, fighting took place in other parts. Byrnes and the Irish Brigade moved to support, but were called back to their campgrounds, since their services were not needed. The brigade stayed in place until May 21, when the whole II Corps marched across the Mattapony River over a wooden bridge, easily dislodging the few Confederate defenders. General Grant watched the crossing with approval. Taking possession of the high ground about a mile from the river, a line of battle was formed with the Irish Brigade on the Union right, while earthworks were erected. However, no enemy counterattack materialized, and the day passed quietly, as did the next.[199]

Frustrated with the failed attacks at Spotsylvania, General Grant planned another turning movement to the south. Using General Hancock's II Corps as bait, Grant ordered it to move along the Richmond, Fredericksburg, and Potomac Railroad toward Hanover Junction. The Federal general hoped the Confederates would attack this corps, and that the rest of the Union army would then hit the Rebels before they could entrench.[200]

The trip was full of weariness, hunger, and thirst for the men of the Irish Brigade. Water was scarce, and the air above the roads hung heavy with dust kicked up by the marching troops. While the rest of the First Division crossed over to the south side of the North Anna River on 23 May, and entered into a fight against some Rebels behind their fortifications, most of the Irish Brigade were detailed as guards for the brigade's wagons or as pickets. On the next day, May 24, Byrnes brought the brigade over to the south side of the North Anna, and was ordered to keep his soldiers available for action, if necessary, while the fighting was renewed. First Lieutenant Martin Binney, the 28th's adjutant, noted the "Very heavy cannonading along the line. The regiment lay all day in an open field exposed to the blistering sun, without shelter. Third Division storm enemy's works and meet with success; the enemy falls back."[201]

That night, the brigade was forced to sleep on its muskets, in a drenching rain. The men suffered much, having had no rest for the previous three days, and their rations having run short, due to the long marches and constant combat. The officers were no better off, and shared in the fatigue, exposure, and short rations. Although there were no

---

[199] See note above, 362-363.
[200] *Civil War Dictionary.*
[201] Ibid.; and *Adjutant General's Report*, 705. Although Captain James Fleming is credited for writing the 28th Regiment's report in the OR, he had been wounded on 18 May and was absent from the unit at the time in question. In fact, there were only seven officers, all first lieutenants, left in the unit. Lieutenant West was the senior officer and commanded the unit, while Binney was the acting adjutant.

movements conducted on the following day, May 25 was spent in destroying the Richmond and Fredericksburg railroad track and bridge. Members of the brigade tore up the track and cut up the embankment for miles. This destruction continued most of May 26 also, at Chesterfield. Finally, rations were issued at 8 p.m. that night. Two hours later, the order came to fall back and recross the North Anna. Grant had decided that a frontal assault against the entrenched Confederates would not accomplish anything, so another flanking movement was tried.[202]

With only short halts, Byrnes and his Irish Brigade marched all night, all the next day, through the following night, and until noon on May 28. There the exhausted men camped on the banks of the Pamunkey River. The Pamunkey, a tributary of the York River, lay just miles away from Richmond. Unfortunately, the Rebels were able to beat the Union army to the area and got between Richmond and the Federal troops, and built fortifications in time to stop any further Union advance.[203]

On the next day, May 29, the brigade moved again to conduct reconnaissance of the Totopotomoy. Along the way the men passed dead Confederate cavalrymen, left unburied, from the previous day's battle. Their dress elicited much speculation as to whether or not they were from Richmond, since their clean, white shirts and new, gray uniforms seemed so "city-like."[204]

At the junctions of the Cold Harbor and Hanover Court House Roads, some enemy cavalry disputed the passage, but were speedily dispersed. On Swift Creek, a tributary of the Totopotomoy, Confederate breastworks were found to be well-manned. Cannons were brought up, and the Irish Brigade supported a battery to protect the artillery's flank.[205]

On the following day, May 30, another brigade of the First Division felt out the enemy breastworks, with the Irish Brigade ready to support them, and found them to be very strong. A long-range artillery duel took up most of the day; however, at 7 p.m., the V Corps was attacked and the II Corps was ordered to attack the enemy in its front to take pressure off the V Corps. Byrnes got his men ready; in fact, another brigade had succeeded in capturing some enemy entrenchments, but the attack was called off by General Meade due to the oncoming darkness. The attack was resumed on the following day, May 31, and the Irish Brigade pushed close up to the enemy's works at all points; but the position was too

---

[202] Ibid., 369-399.
[203] Ibid.
[204] Ibid.
[205] Ibid.; and *History of the Second Corps*, 500-502.

strong to afford a reasonable prospect of success. The remainder of the day was spent skirmishing.[206]

Meanwhile, Union reinforcements were arriving from Major General Benjamin Butler's army at White House, fifteen miles from the Pamunkey River. To stop any of these troops from cutting his army off from Richmond, General Lee moved his troops toward a crossroads named Cold Harbor, three miles from where Grant's left flank ended.[207] Grant, detecting the move, ordered the Union army to converge on Cold Harbor.

While other army corps moved toward Cold Harbor, the II Corps stayed in camp. During a short quiet spell, Colonel Byrnes was able to issue a commendation from Brigadier General Francis C. Barlow, First Division commander, to two officers of the Irish Brigade who had distinguished themselves during the battle of May 18. In the stuffy language of the time, and of the regular army, Byrnes endorsed the communiqué: "It is with great satisfaction that the Colonel commanding the brigade communicates the above to the command, and he hopes that for the creditable manner in which those officers have conducted themselves, they may be duly rewarded whenever an occasion may present itself."[208] This is the last surviving document written by Richard Byrnes.

With opposing forces rapidly concentrating near Cold Harbor, the II Corps was ordered to join the rest of the Federal army as soon as possible. After dark, Byrnes withdrew the Irish Brigade from the line of the Totopotomoy and began marching for Cold Harbor. One division tried to take a shortcut and ended up having to backtrack, delaying the whole II Corps. Consequently, the II Corps did not arrive at Cold Harbor until the early morning of June 2.[209] Martin Binney, the acting adjutant for the 28th Massachusetts, wrote: "[We] started at 10:30 p.m.; had a long, weary, rapid march; the dust lay very heavy. This was the most severe march of the campaign, marching ten and a half hours."[210] So worn out were the men, that the scheduled attack was postponed until 4:30 a.m. the next day (Friday, June 3). In fact, many of the men didn't know where they were exactly. Many thought they were at "Coal Harbor."[211]

The II Corps occupied the Union Army's left flank, and was directed to assault the Confederate works in front of it. Richmond was only eleven

---

[206] Ibid.

[207] Noah Andre Trudeau, *Bloody Roads South*, (Little, Brown and Company) 1989, 259

[208] St. Clair A. Mulholland, *The Story of the 116th Regiment Pennsylvania Volunteers*, (Philadelphia: F. McManus, Jr. & Company, 1903) 225 (hereafter: *The Story of the 116th PA*).

[209] OR, Series I, Volume XXXVI, Part 1, 344-399.

[210] Ibid., 390.

[211] Ibid.

miles away. When day broke that Friday morning, June 3, the II Corps formed up in columns of assault. The First Division, Barlow's, was in front, with Miles' and Brooke's brigades comprising the first line, with Byrnes' and McDougall's brigades making up the second line. The first line advanced, driving the enemy posted in a sunken road, and followed the Rebels up a gentle hill, and into their works. Approximately three hundred Confederates were taken prisoner, along with one set of regimental colors and three cannons. Unfortunately, Colonel Byrnes did not advance his Irish Brigade in a timely manner. This was apparent enough to him and he was very harsh with Captain Frank R. Lieb, the commander of the 116th Pennsylvania Volunteer Regiment, in urging him to move faster. The initial success of Miles and Brooke was soon cut short as the southern defenders were able to bring other cannon and musketry to bear on the Federal attackers. Despite the enfilading, the first line held on, while Byrnes brought his men up. The 28th Massachusetts' Binney later recorded, in his report:[212]

> We formed in line and charged the enemy over the earthworks, and our men fell in heaps. Forward we went to the second hill, which was reached and held until nearly dark, when we fell back to the old position, badly used.[213]

Many of the Irish Brigade members succeeded in gaining the main works and joining the rest of the division, already fighting over their newly won entrenchments. The enfilading fire proved too much, and Byrnes ordered a retreat. Falling back a short distance, the Irish Brigade halted about seventy-five yards away and dug rifle pits for themselves. These were only short-term measures, as everyone was still exposed to direct and raking fire.[214]

It is believed that, at about that time, while trying to extract his men from this murderous enfilading fire, Richard Byrnes was wounded. A Confederate minié ball hit him in the middle of the back and lodged near his spine. According to one newspaper account, the ball had first passed through the breast and arm of his aide, Captain James D. Brady of the 63rd New York Volunteer Regiment.[215] Byrnes was quickly removed to the rear, where a field hospital was set up. Everyone who looked at the wound knew that it was mortal.

---

[212] Ibid., 344-399.
[213] Ibid., 390.
[214] *The Story of the 116th PA*, 254-255.
[215] *New York Times*, June 8, 1864, 1.

As he lay upon the makeshift cot, Byrnes overheard that the commander of the 116th Pennsylvania had also been wounded and was in the same hospital. Feeling contrite for his harsh words earlier in the day, he ". . . had himself carried to where Captain Lieb was lying, and the dying colonel apologized in the most courteous manner for anything rude that he might have said."[216]

At 4 p.m. on June 3, Byrnes was moved from the hospital and sent in an ambulance to White House Landing, where the wounded were collected to be shipped to Washington. The journey was tortuous and slow; the landing was not reached until 8 a.m. the next morning, June 4. While waiting for transportation, which did not arrive until June 5, Byrnes spied one of his own soldiers from the 28th Massachusetts, Private Amos A. Loring, Company B, who had been detailed to move the wounded from the hospital to White House Landing. The Colonel immediately made Loring his orderly and therefore had someone familiar to look after his needs. As Byrnes was allowed to be loaded on the boat, his desire to keep Loring nearby intensified.

> ...he got ready to start and he says come I want you and I said that I could not get by the . . . guard and he said you take my saber and revolver and I will pass you as my servant so when we got to the boat and took him out on a stretcher and carried him on board the boat and I followed him and the guard stopped me I says I am not an enlisted he said I could not go I told him that I wanted to see the col. out he told me to go but come right back again when I got up I would not go back.[217]

It didn't take long for the news of Byrnes' wounding to be announced. Charles A. Dana, the Assistant Secretary of War, and personal observer at Grant's headquarters for the administration, sent a telegraph, on June 3, to Washington remarking that Byrnes' wound was probably mortal.[218] Major General Hancock noted in his reports that Byrnes was one of a select group of ". . . most promising young officers,"[219] who had never failed to distinguish themselves in battle ". . . all tried and excellent officers."[220] Major Mitchell, Hancock's Aide, wrote that Byrnes was one of

[216] *The Story of the 116th PA*, 256.
[217] Letter, Private Amos A. Loring, 28th Massachusetts. to his Mother and Father, 19 June 1864, in his pension file, NARA.
[218] OR, Series I, Volume XXXVI, Part 1, 88.
[219] Ibid., 345.
[220] Ibid., 367.

the "...most tried and gallant soldiers, unequaled for courage and all high soldierly qualities."[221]

Byrnes arrived, late in the evening of June 6, 1864, at Armory Square General Hospital, Washington, where the doctors could only try to make him as comfortable as possible. Chaplain Corby later wrote, "He lived, I was told, to be transported to Washington, where his loving, faithful, and weeping wife and children met him and embraced him before he departed for the unknown future."[222] That "unknown future" came to Byrnes on June 12, 1864. The record of death and interment, filled out at Armory Square, noted that his body was "delivered to friends."[223] The same day that Byrnes had passed away, Mr. Tufts, the Massachusetts State Agent who looked out for the welfare of his state's soldiers, telegraphed a short note to Governor John A. Andrew, informing him of the sad news.[224]

On Sunday, June 19, a funeral was held at the Byrnes' residence at 399 Grove Street, Jersey City, New Jersey, and was attended by a number of respectable citizens and comrades in arms. Among those present were the Irish Brigade's last commander, Colonel Robert Nugent, then commanding the 69th New York Regiment, and Lieutenant Colonel George Cartwright of the 28th Massachusetts, who was recovering from his wound from the Wilderness battle. The pallbearers were Colonel Nugent, Lieutenant Colonel Cartwright, Colonel John O'Mahony of the Phoenix Regiment, and Captain Cartwright of the 63rd New York Volunteer Regiment. The 69th Regiment, New York State National Guard, under the command of Colonel James Bagley, escorted the casket through the streets en route to Calvary Cemetery, in Long Island City, New York.[225] There Richard Byrnes was placed to rest, later to be followed by his second daughter, Margaret, in 1900; his wife, Ellen, in 1911; and, finally, his third daughter, Catherine, in 1913.[226]

---

[221] Hospital bed card, Byrnes Pension File, NARA.

[222] *Memoirs of Chaplain Life*, 239.

[223] Record of Death and Interment, Byrnes Pension File, NARA.

[224] Telegram, Mr. Tufts, Massachusetts State Agent, to Governor John A. Andrew, 13 June 1864 (received), Executive Incoming Correspondence, MMHRC&M.

[225] "Irish American Soldiers' Obituary, Col. Byrnes, 28th Mass. Vols.- Acting Brigadier General of the Irish Brigade," *The Irish American*, New York, N. Y., 25 June 1864.

[226] Calvary and Allied Cemetery records, 1011 First Avenue, New York, N.Y. 10022.

Officers of the 28th Massachusetts, c.1865, standing left to right: 1st Lt. Michael E. Powderly, 1st Lt. Thomas Cook, 1st Lt. John Knight, Mr. McParland, a civilian, 2nd Lt. George W. Beattie, 1st Lt. John H. Minor, 2nd Lt. William H. McCarthy, Assistant Surgeon Albert A. Chase, 2nd Lt. John McGlim, Seated left to right: Captain John Miles, Captain Patrick W. Black, Lt. Col. James Fleming, Captain Patrick H. Bird, Captain John Connor. (Mass/MOLLUS/USAMHI)

Ellen Toy Byrnes never remarried, and lived her life first in Jersey City, then in Bensonhurst, Brooklyn. She operated a boarding house, where her three daughters lived with her, as did various boarders she took on. For the last few years of her life, after her second daughter, Margaret, died, Ellen resided with her oldest daughter, Mary Louise Byrnes, who ran the boarding house in Brooklyn. In the latter part of 1910, fifty year-old Mary married a man named John Power. He moved into the boarding house.[227]

Ellen suffered from heart disease and required constant care and attention starting in 1900, coinciding with the death of Margaret. Ellen's last illness came in October, 1910, shortly after Mary's wedding, when Ellen caught pneumonia. Living until January 12, 1911, Ellen was buried with Richard.[228]

On April 15, 1874, a Washington lawyer, named John Pope Hodnett, contacted the War Department in an effort to find the descendants of Colonel Byrnes. "It is only a simple act of charity," he wrote, after the staff refused to help him. It seemed that some property in Kansas belonging to the heirs of Richard Byrnes had been sold by the local sheriff, due to overdue taxes, and Hodnett wanted to make sure the family received its share of the proceeds, now that the taxes were paid. It is not known if he ever found Ellen or not.[229]

Richard Byrnes came to the United States at a very turbulent time. Indian wars plagued the West, and sectional tensions were to soon erupt in civil war. In the midst of this cauldron of sweeping change, Byrnes would find much of America generally hostile to Irishmen. Perhaps because of this prejudice or, perhaps, in spite of it, he went out West to seek his destiny. He established it with the army, and the army acquired in him a man who adapted to its ways. St. Clair Mulholland, a Medal of Honor recipient, a member of the Irish Brigade, and, at one time the commander of the 116th Pennsylvania Regiment, remembered Byrnes as:

> Strict, reserved and reticent, and one who did not know him, would think him severe, but he was a man who did his full duty and expected everyone else to come up to the full measure of all demands. To those who knew him best, he was kindly and lovable.[230]

---

[227] Byrnes Penison File, NARA.
[228] Ibid.
[229] Notes by Brian Pohanka while researching at the NARA.
[230] *The Story of the 116th PA*, 256.

Francis A. Walker, the II Corps historian, remembered Colonel Byrnes as, ". . . a good disciplinarian in camp; cool and resolute in action; mingling, in just proportion, impetuosity with sound judgment."[231] Considering his strict regular army training, Byrnes would have found these glowing words indeed, an eloquent summary of his colorful military career.

THE REGIMENTAL
COLOR OF THE 28TH
MASSACHUSETTS
VOLUNTEER
INFANTRY.
PRESERVED IN THE
STATE HOUSE,
BOSTON,
MASSACHUSETTS.

---

[231] *History of the Second Corps*, 512.

Chapter VI

WEAPONS
OF THE
IRISH BRIGADE

by Joseph G. Bilby

The droves of new recruits flocking to Federal and Confederate colors at the outbreak of the Civil War clamored for Model 1855 or 1861 *.58* caliber, muzzle-loading rifle muskets, the most modern infantry arms then available. Supplies of these guns were, however, quite limited. Of the 503,000 shoulder arms held in Federal and Northern state arsenals at the outbreak of the war, 400,000 were *.69* caliber smoothbores, and 100,000 of the 135,000 small arms either seized or held by Southern states were smoothbores as well. By August of 1861, when Thomas Francis Meagher kicked off the Irish Brigade recruiting drive at Jones' Wood, Brigadier General James W. Ripley, Union Chief of Ordnance, had exhausted his reserve supply of rifle muskets.

The men of the 69th New York Volunteers brought a mix of imported Prussian smoothbores and Enfield rifled muskets to Virginia with them, but were re-equipped with U. S. Model 1842, *.69* caliber smoothbore muskets. The preferred load for these weapons was a *.64* or *.65* diameter round ball and three buckshot, encased, along with a powder charge, in paper. The soldier would bite off the end of the paper cartridge to expose the powder, ram the cartridge down the muzzle of his musket, then affix a cap on the nipple or "cone" underneath the hammer. When the trigger released the cocked hammer, it hit the explosive cap and ignited the charge in the gun.

Although Company K, Zouaves carried rifled *.69* caliber muskets, conversions of older smoothbores using the hollow based "minie ball," General Meagher preferred smoothbores for all his regiments because he thought much of the Irish Brigade's fighting "...would be at very close quarters." William O' Grady, of the 88th New York recalled afterward, however, that "...sometimes our short range weapons were a disadvantage." O' Grady was one of the men who "found" rifled muskets to silence Confederate skirmishers on the brigade front at Antietam.[1]

Many army officers, assuming that most fights would take place at seventy-five yards or less, agreed with Meagher's small arms choice. As late as 1863, Colonel George L. Willard, of the 125th New York, flatly stated that, for most military purposes, the smoothbore musket was actually better than its rifled relative. Although he conceded the rifled musket's accuracy over longer ranges, Willard asserted that the necessity to change sight settings during the course of combat, especially when infantrymen faced a fast-closing cavalry charge, was too confusing for average troops. He believed infantrymen would do better to hold their fire until the horsemen were close and then deliver a withering volley of buck and ball. According to Willard, "...decisive victories cannot be gained by firing at long ranges; at short ranges the buck and ball cartridge is certainly more effective."[2]

In fact, throughout the Civil War, cavalrymen were, generally very reluctant to charge infantry armed with anything, but Meagher's and Willard's general philosophy might not have been too far off the mark, at least in the war's early years. British military historian Paddy Griffith has asserted that the types of small arms used by opponents in Civil War battles mattered little because the tactics (or lack of same) employed by officers on both sides led to essentially short-range fire-fights in which the accuracy of the individual or his weapon was largely irrelevant. If this is true, then the .69 caliber smoothbore may have had an advantage over the rifled musket in most fights, as a buck and ball load gave the shooter four chances to kill or disable his enemy. Most authorities thought buck and ball effective up to one hundred yards, which Griffith states was the average distance of a firefight during the first two years of the war.

In a test conducted in Texas in 1855, soldiers firing .69 caliber buck and ball rounds at a six feet-by-eighteen-inch target one hundred yards away scored as many hits with their Model 1842 smoothbore muskets as a company armed with .54 caliber Model 1841 rifles firing patched round balls when each group fired a specified number of rounds. Although

[1] O'Grady, "88th Regiment," 511.
[2] Willard, Rifled and Smooth Bored Arms, 13. Interestingly, when Willard was killed at Gettysburg commanding the Third Brigade of the Third Division of the Third Corps, all of his regiments, including the 125th New York, were armed with rifle muskets.

buckshot's lethality at that distance can be fairly questioned, a wound does not have to be fatal, or even serious, to be tactically effective. In most cases, a wounded man will quickly leave the immediate scene of battle, and may require one or more other men to help him off. Due to a lack of surgical antisepsis, minor wounds during the Civil War often proved fatal or disabling far out of proportion to their initial damage.

By mid 1862, many soldiers who had clamored for rifled muskets had modified their previously dim view of smoothbores. Colonel Robert McAllister, commander of the 11th New Jersey, was not unhappy when eight of his ten companies traded in their Austrian rifles for smoothbore muskets. McAllister wrote that "…it is now thought that the musket with buck and ball is after all the best arm in the service." The 12th Rhode Island and 12th New Hampshire, raised, like the 11th New Jersey, in 1862, received the same mix of imported rifles and native smoothbores.[3]

The companies armed with rifles in these regiments were the "flank" companies. Longer range guns were considered desirable for men who could protect a regiment or brigade's vulnerable flanks by delivering accurate long range fire on an attacking force. The flank companies were also used as skirmishers, for whom individual marksmanship against specific targets was highly valued. Marksmanship was stressed, at least theoretically, for soldiers serving in flank companies.

The 28th Massachusetts, which joined the Irish Brigade just before Fredericksburg, was armed with Enfield rifled muskets. The Bay State men retained their Enfields and were often detailed as brigade skirmishers or flankers, so much so, in fact, that a Massachusetts officer complained of the "arduous" duty. The remainder of the brigade's regiments, the 63rd, 69th and 88th New York and the 116th Pennsylvania, retained smoothbore muskets far beyond the end of the Meagher era. These Irish Brigade outfits were among the twenty-six, or 10½ percent of Federal regiments in the Army of the Potomac, still armed in whole, or in part, with smoothbore muskets at the battle of Gettysburg.

When infusions of large numbers of recruits led to the formation of new companies for the New York and Pennsylvania regiments over the winter of 1863-1864, the new men were issued smoothbores, at a time when rifled muskets were again in good supply. The only rationale for such a peculiarity would be that the tactical doctrine symbolized by the smoothbore musket was still ascendant in the brigade. The rest of the army, however, was beginning to realize the potential of the rifled mus-

---

[3] McAllister to wife, September 19, 1862, in Robertson, ed. McAllister Letters, 209.

ket, and, for the first time in the Army of the Potomac, an organized program of target practice was established in the spring of 1864.

With the notable exception of the 28th Massachusetts, smoothbores remained standard issue in the Irish Brigade until the brigade was temporarily broken up in June of 1864. Although sorry to leave their Irish comrades, the Pennsylvanians of the 116th were delighted to finally turn in their smoothbores for rifled muskets. In the course of Grant's overland campaign, fighting distances had stretched out so, that opponents were often firing at each other at ranges of up to two hundred yards, which was, by the standards of the day, "long range."

Surviving ordnance reports indicate that the brigade's New York regiments exchanged their smoothbores for rifled muskets at around the same time the Pennsylvanians did. The switch probably coincided with the creation of the "Consolidated Brigade." Unlike the men of the 116th, the New Yorkers left no record of whether or not they approved the change. There were, however, no complaints registered, either.

The following ordnance reports for the Irish Brigade's core regiments, the 28th, 63rd, 69th, 88th and 116th, were abstracted, from the Union army's compiled ordnance reports on file in the National Archives, by William C. Goble. Each company commander in the army was responsible for issuing in a quarterly ordnance report to his regimental commander, who, in turn, submitted in a regimental return.

The existing records are incomplete, for various reasons. Records were often not turned in, during the immediate wake of a disastrous battle. For example, only one company of the 69th New York Infantry, a regiment which lost all of its officers who had been either killed or wounded at Fredericksburg, handed in an ordnance return for the fourth quarter of 1862.

Other records may well not be accurate because the officer or clerk filling the form out checked the wrong column. The 69th New York is listed as having Model 1842 smoothbores in one quarter, then older model flintlock smoothbores converted to percussion in the next quarter, then Model 1842s the following quarter. It is more likely that the wrong column was checked rather than that the regiment was issued different weapons in successive quarters. Other quarters were simply not turned in by deceased or careless officers, or were lost somewhere between the field and the War Department in the 130 years that have intervened. For similar reasons, the reports of individual companies are often missing. It should be remembered, however, that the 116th and the three New York regiments were consolidated in 1863, then expanded again in 1864. The

28th Massachusetts was consolidated following the discharge of veterans who had not re-enlisted in late 1864.

A careful perusal suggests that certain peculiarities existed at times in different regiments. The 28th Massachusetts, for example, reports a sole "U.S. Rifle with Sword Bayonet" (a modified Model 1841 or a Model 1855) in most companies for the first quarter of 1863. Company A continued to report one of these arms throughout the year. Similarly, Springfield .58 caliber rifled muskets, which showed up here and there were, no doubt, battlefield pickups to replace damaged arms or to supply more adequate rifled weapons for skirmishing duties.

With all their inherent defects, however, the records buttress the testimony of the brigade's soldiers that, for a longer period in time than in any other outfit in the Army of the Potomac, save perhaps the 12th New Jersey Infantry, the majority of the men of the Irish Brigade carried smoothbore muskets into battle.

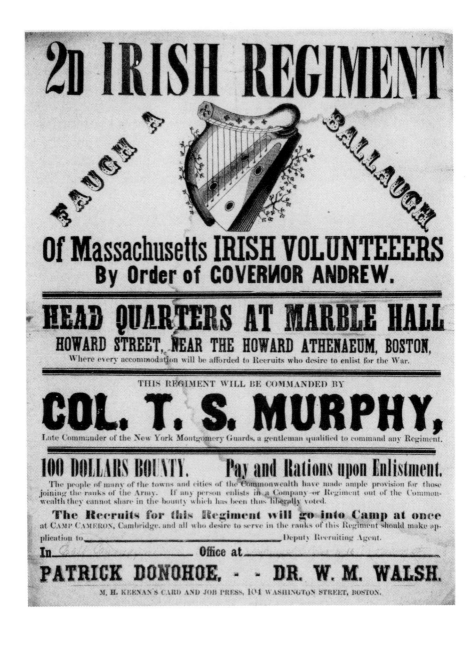

Chapter VII

THE GREEN FLAGS OF THE IRISH BRIGADE

by Barney Kelly

INTRODUCTION

In 1989, the Veteran Corps, 69th Regiment, instituted a restoration project of all Regimental artifacts and memorabilia, to include paintings, sculptures, photographs, and books, which are housed in the armory; and this collection includes the paintings in the Mural Room and the Historic Flag Collection. We hope to correct some of the errors and misconceptions that have existed for a great many years about the Regiment's Irish Colors of the Civil War.[1]

Incorrect data on the flags of the 69th New York State Militia and 59th New York State Volunteers were originally made by Conyngham in his *Irish Brigade and Its Campaigns*, in 1867, and by Cavanagh in his *Memoirs of General Thomas F. Meagher*, in 1893. These errors and discrepancies have been given credence by various authors since. These authors, to name a few, include Jones in his *Irish Brigade*, Hayes-McCoy in his *History of Irish Flags*, and, most recently, by Warren in his *Flags and Uniforms of the 69th New York State Militia and the Irish Brigade 1854-1865* for the Federal Data Series No. 3 [Confederate society] in 1988.

None of these later authors contacted the source, namely the 69th Regiment of New York and its Veteran corps. If they did, as in the case of Hayes-Mc Coy, they did not view the colors nor ask what they looked like, nor what was embroidered on them. Most authors talk about the surviving colors of the 69th and 63rd Regiments of the Irish Brigade, but do

---

[1] Records and Proceedings, Veteran Corps, 69th Regiment, 1989 to present.

not know that some of the colors of the 88th Regiment exist and are in our possession. We had some colors of the 69th and 88th Regiments photographed on Friday, February 8, 1991 and had a replica made of the 69th New York State Volunteer's flag, the first Irish color made for the St. Patrick's Day Parade of 1991, the 130th Anniversary of the Formation of the Irish Brigade. Other Irish Colors photographed were the 69th New York State Militia - Prince of Wales Color, the 69th New York State Volunteers - 1st Irish Color, the 69th New York State Volunteers - 2nd Irish Color, and the Corcoran Legion Headquarters Flag.

Also, during 1991, the graduating Class of the United States Army War College, at Carlisle, Pennsylvania, commissioned a painting by Civil War artist Mort Kunstler. It featured General Thomas F. Meagher and the 1st Irish Color of the 69th New York State Volunteers, at the Battle of Antietam (Sharpsburg), Maryland, on September 17, 1862. We visited Mr. Kunstler at his home in Cove Neck, New York, and noted he was using misleading data concerning the flag and gave him the correct data, for which he was most grateful.[2] Thus, a historically accurate painting was produced.

During the course of the general flag restoration project, additional information was discovered on the colors of Michael Corcoran, and we have made them known to various artists and historians, who have an interest in this area. The forty-five Civil War flags in our collection are in very delicate condition and most can not be handled. We have sought professional conservativeship and have raised some monies to start the restoration and conservation project.

The first course of action was to take the colors from their cases and examine, measure, and record all pertinent data and photograph them. Because of the fragility of the colors, it was decided to make replicas of each flag. This was done so that scholars, artists, and historians who sought information and wanted to view them, would be able to do so. In 1991, the 69th New York State Volunteer's 1st Irish Color was replicated. It was paraded with the Regiment in the St. Patrick's Day Parade in New York City and it was blessed by John Cardinal O'Connor. The 69th New York State Volunteer's 2nd Irish Color was completed in June, 1993, and was shown for the first time at a museum exhibit, *The 69th Regiment In The Civil War*, at the New York State Convention of the Ancient Order of Hibernians, at the Wind Watch Hotel, Haupauge, New York, from July 15-16, 1993. (The cost of these replicas has, so far, exceeded $ 8,000.00)

---

[2] Kunstler, Mort: 1991 *Raise The Colors and Follow Me: The Irish Brigade at Antietam, September 17, 1862.*

In the course of this project, we have contacted many professional conservators, restorers, researchers, museums, etc. We have searched for money by contacting the United States Government, the New York State Division of Military and Naval Affairs, the National Guard Bureau, SUNY at Buffalo, NYU, the Pennsylvania and Michigan Historic Flags Restorations, various grants, private institutions and government agencies. After four years, we are starting to achieve some results, e.g. The Mural Room, which measures thirty by fifty feet; its walls are covered by paintings on canvas depicting the Regiments' history, which were done as a W.P.A. project, in 1937, by the artist, Earl Lonsbury. The original cost to restore these paintings was quoted at $250,000.[00], but it will done in conjunction with the Arts Commission of the City of New York and the Art Students' League for $9,000.[00]. Our search still continues.

It is our fervent hope that the following discourse will be the definitive work on these Irish Colors and will end, once and for all, speculation on this subject. The following colors will be dealt with: the 69th New York State Militia's Prince of Wales Color, the 69th New York State Volunteers' 1st Irish Color, and the 69th New York State Volunteers' 2nd Irish Color. This essay will give the historical background and known data for each color as compiled to date.

THE PRINCE OF WALES FLAG
69TH REGIMENT NEW YORK STATE MILITIA

The 69th Regiment New York State Militia was formed from the Second of the Irish Regiment Volunteers and accepted into the New York State Militia on October 12, 1851. It had been formed for the express purpose of organizing a body of troops, who would use its military training for the liberation of Ireland from British rule. In 1860, in its tenth year of turbulent existence, the 69th Regiment New York State Militia had survived many intrigues, plots, counter-plots from Irish revolutionary leaders and societies, the Know Nothing Party, Native Americans, politicians, the New York State Militia and the Catholic Church to remain the sole Irish regiment in the New York State Militia. It had a renewed confidence, which was marked by successful recruiting and military skills, and it was enjoying a rise in public opinion.[3]

In August, 1859, Michael Corcoran was elected Colonel of the Regiment.[4] He was a native of Carrowkeel, County Sligo; he had attended the local school and was taught the standard curriculum. Although there is no documentation to prove it, the learning he displayed in later life makes it likely that he completed secondary school.[5] In 1845, just after his eighteenth birthday and just as the potato blight struck Ireland, Michael Corcoran received an appointment to the Revenue Police.[6] After basic training -- including infantry tactics -- at Dublin Headquarters, he reported to the depot in Creeslough, County Donegal, in March, 1846, where he hunted moonshiners, plunged into an artificial famine.[7] In 1848, he broke his oath to the Crown and the Revenue Police. Driven by the suffering of the Irish, he joined a guerrilla band called the Ribbonmen and became a double agent.[8] He led a precarious double life until he was found out, whereupon he resigned and fled to America,[9] arriving in New York aboard the *Dromahair*, on October 1, 1849.[10]

---

[3] O'Flaherty, D. P.: *The History of the 69th Regiment NYSM 1851-1861*; Ann Arbor: University Microfilms, 1964.

[4] *The Irish American*: NY, June 22, 1861, 1

[5] Lane, Phyllis: Michael Corcoran - Notes Toward A Life, *The Recorder - Journal of the American Irish Historical Society* Vol. 3, No. 3, Summer 1990.

[6] Constabulary List and Directory; Containing a List of the Constabulary Departments, Resident Magistrates, Dublin Metropolitan Police, Coast Guards, & Revenue Police No.10 , Dublin, 1846) 157; No. 25 (Dublin, 1854) 147 Garda Siochana Archives Headquarters.

[7] Lane: 42.

[8] Ribbonmen were the Ancient Order of Hibernians.

[9] Revenue Police in Ireland Records; London Public Records Office reference CUST 111/9 f 87.

[10] *The Irish American*; January 2, 1864.

Concorn secured a position as clerk in the Hibernian House at 42 Prince Street. In addition to his duties as clerk, he tended bar and acted as a bouncer. He later became manager and then proprietor of this establishment. Hibernian House was a site used by the local Irish charitable and political societies, as well as the Democratic Party District Polling Place.[11] In 1851, he joined the Second Irish Regiment of Volunteers, which was to become the 69th Regiment New York Volunteers, as a private soldier.[12] By 1854, he had become a Captain in the Regiment and an American citizen.[13]

By that time, the Irish revolutionary struggle had shifted its base from Ireland to New York. Many of the leaders of the abortive young Irelander Rebellion, including Michael Doheny, John Mitchell, Richard O'Gorman, Thomas F. Meagher, John O'Mahoney and John Savage were present in New York, and Michael Corcoran had befriended them and helped in the fund-raising efforts for the Irish Societies. [14] Corcoran was committed to a free Ireland, devoted to the 69th, and was involved in Tammany Hall politics. He was instrumental in winning ward elections for the Democrats, which meant jobs for the Irish, and, in October, 1859, was elected to the five man Tammany Judiciary Committee for his ward.[15] In 1861, he was elected a member of the Tammany Delegation to the Democratic State Convention in Albany, New York The others were August Belmont, Samuel Tilden, William 'Boss' Tweed, Peter Sweeney, and Richard Connally.[16]

Militarily, Corcoran was just as successful. He had received an outstanding commendation for his leadership in the Staten Island and Quarantine Riots and he was cited by the Brigade Inspector "as the best," if not the very best, infantry officer in the 4th Brigade NYSN;[17] on August 26, 1859, he was elected Colonel of the 69th Regiment.[18] In April, 1859, he was one of the first Americans to be inducted into the Fenian Brotherhood,[19] and was soon to become its military commander and number two man in the organization.[20] Under his leadership, the Regiment's training intensi-

---

[11] *New York Herald*: October 1, 1849, 4.

[12] Lane: op cit. 43.

[13] *The Irish American*: August 9, 1851.

[14] Naturalization Records: Court of Common Pleas for City and County of New York, Federal Achieves & Record Center, bundle 131, rec. 164.

[15] Lane, 43.

[16] Tammany Scrapbooks: 1857-1868, Vol 2, NYPL (NY 1927) 328.

[17] Brummer, Sidney D. *Political History of New York During the Period of the Civil War* (New York: Columbia, UP, 1991) 114-115.

[18] New York State: Adjutant General Office Annual Report 1858 (Assem. No 184) Albany, 1855, 40.

[19] New York State: Adjutant General Office Annual Report 1859 (Assem. No 1793) Albany, 1860, 145.

[20] *The Irish American*, November, 29 1862.

fied and it was hailed by the press as a "...splendid regiment of Irishmen."[21] The Regiment seemed to have achieved a place of respectability in the New York community.[22] Then, in October 1860, an incident occurred that threatened this newly-won and deserved position. Prince Albert Edward, the Prince of Wales (later King Edward VII) of Great Britain was on a grand tour of North America. President Buchanan, who had previously been the Ambassador to the Court of Saint James, invited the prince to visit the United States. Upon leaving Canada, the prince traveled, incognito, as Baron Renfrew.[23]

With so many exiles of famine and oppression in New York City, the prince's visit was hardly popular with the Irish. But there was no shortage of Anglophiles, and they decided to honor the prince with a grand military parade and ball. They called out the local militia regiments, including the Irish 69th to march in this parade. Colonel Corcoran felt it an insult to entertain the great grandson of George III and to pay homage to the offspring of Queen Victoria. He issued a statement that he "...could not in good conscience order out a regiment of Irish born citizens to parade in honor of a sovereign, under whose reign Ireland was made a desert and her sons forced into exile." Corcoran and the 69th refused to parade for the little prince and, as a result, Corcoran was arrested and held for court martial. This action of Corcoran, of course, endeared him and the Regiment to the New York Irish.[24] Corcoran also wrote a letter to a B. Fields, who was the coordinator of the grand ball, refusing admission tickets.

---

[21] *New York Herald*, February, 23 1860.
[22] O'Flaherty, 204.
[23] Morris, Lloyd: *Incredible New York.*
[24] Ridge, John T: *The St. Patrick's Day Parade In New York*, Brooklyn: AOH Pub., 1988.

NATIONAL CADETS.

HEAD QUARTERS, 69th REGIMENT, N. Y. S. M.

New York, October 6th 1860

W. B. Field Esq.

Sir

I beg to acknowledge the receipt of an Invitation to attend the Ball to be given in Honor of the Prince of Wales. As I am not desirous of joining in the Festivity it will be unnecessary for you to send me admission tickets.

Your Obt. Servant

Michael Corcoran

Colonel 69th Regiment

Letter of Colonel Michael Corcoran, of the 69th New York, refusing admission tickets to the Prince of Wales' Ball. (Lt. Col. Kenneth H. Powers Collection)

This action created a sensation locally and nationally. There was bitter denunciation of his actions and equally bitter support of it. Men often came to blows in arguments about the right or wrong of Corcoran's course. Letters and telegrams from many parts of the country, approving Corcoran's actions, poured into New York. Echoes of anti-Irish and anti-Catholic bigotry swept the country. Many suspected the Irish of being so independent and authority-resistant as to make poor soldiers. Some feared the Irish would not do battle under commanders whose lineage they did not like.[25] There was talk of disbanding the 69th; *Harper's Weekly* sourly referred to Irish militiamen as "not infrequently an absolute nuisance."[26] The court martial dragged on into 1861 with no end in sight.

Corcoran received many gifts from the Irish throughout the country - - a palmetto cane from South Carolina, a three-inch gold medal from San Francisco, and a beautiful sword from the New York Irish.[27] On March 16, 1861, the grateful Irish citizens of New York presented, to the 69th Regiment, a beautiful green color in recognition of its part in the Prince of Wales fiasco.[28]

The description of the flag is as follows: The color was hand-embroidered and was one-sided. It measured five feet and six inches on the staff and six feet and eight inches on the fly; its field was green with red ribbons (scrolls) and gold edging, lettering, sunburst and fringe. The cords and tassels were of gold, also. The top scroll read *PRESENTED TO THE 69TH REGIMENT* and the bottom scroll read *IN COMMEMORATION OF THE 11TH OCT. 1860.* Between the two scrolls was a golden sunburst (a Fenian symbol).[29] The scrolls and sunburst were embroidered separately and then were sewn onto the flag as appliqués. The reverse side showed only the outline of the scrolls and the sunburst.

---

[25] Concannon, John: *Colorful and Gallant Gen. Michael Corcoran,* 1990 Unveiling of Monument to M. Corcoran-Calvary Cemetery, April 29, 1990.

[26] Bilby, Jos. G: "Remember Fontenoy, 69th NYSM & Irish Brigade in the Civil War," *Military Images* March-April 1983, 16.

[27] *The Irish American,* March 16, 1861.

[28] Ibid., March 23, 1861.

[29] Chaplan & Todd: 69th Regt. NYSM At The First Battle of Bull Run, June 21, 1861.

The recently restored "Prince of Wales Color" presented to the 69 New York Militia following Colonel Corcoran's snub of the heir to the British throne. (Veterans Corps, 69th New York)

On April 12, 1861, the Confederates fired on Fort Sumter and the Civil War was on. President Abraham Lincoln called for 75,000 militia volunteers for ninety days to defend Washington, D.C., and to fight the rebels. Corcoran immediately asked the 69th not to consider his own suspended status when it voted on whether or not to volunteer for service. The 69th voted to serve! The following day, the court martial was summarily dissolved, the charges dismissed, and Corcoran was returned to the 69th as its colonel.

On April 23rd, just twelve days after the firing on Fort Sumter, the 69th marched off to war. Amid deafening cheers, they left their armory, and marched down Prince Street, past Hibernian Hall (in tribute to the Ancient Order of Hibernians and the Fenian Brotherhood).[30] They marched behind a banner with the motto "Sixty Ninth – Remember Fontenoy." The banner recalled the triumph of French Marshal Maurice de Saxe over the British in 1745, a victory made possible by the unstoppable bayonet charge of the Irish Brigade of the French Army.[31] The 69th paraded down Broadway to Pier 4 and boarded the Steamer *Adger* for the trip south. They answered, once and for all time, the question of whether the Irish Militia in New York City was loyal to the United States.[32]

The regiment landed at Annapolis, Maryland and marched to Georgetown College with the band playing *"Garry Owen."*[33] At the college, the unit honed its military skills in preparation for its call to destiny. It moved across the Potomac and built Fort Corcoran, protecting Arlington Heights, Virginia. The Regiment proved its mettle at Bull Run, rallying 'round its distinctive flag, beating back the 3rd and 4th Alabama Regiments and forcing them and the famed Black Horse Cavalry of Virginia, as well as the Louisiana Tigers, to retire;[34] they earned for themselves the title of *Dread noughts*.[35] They formed a square, protecting their brigade commander, Colonel William T. Sherman, during what became a Union rout. The 69th left the field in an orderly and military fashion.[36]

During the ensuing retreat, Corcoran became separated from the Regiment and was taken prisoner. Two officers, nine men, and the National Color of the Regiment were captured with him.[37] He spent a year as

[30] Ridge, John T.: *Erie's Sons In America (The Ancient Order of Hibernians)* Brooklyn, AOH PUB 1986, 29.
[31] Bilby, 16.
[32] *NY Daily Tribune*: April 22-23, 1861; *The Irish American*, April 27, 1861.
[33] G. Flaherty 237.
[34] Souvenir Program: *John Mc Cormack Concert to the Gallant 69th*, September 30, 1917.
[35] Oral Tradition - 69th Regiment New York.
[36] Cavanagh M.: *Memoirs of General Thomas F. Meagher*, Worcester, Mass., 1892, 399.
[37] Official Records: Series I, II, 532, Report of Col. R. C. W. Radford, 13th Virginia Cavalry (hereafter O.R.).

a prisoner of war and was released on August 15, 1862. He returned to New York with the rank of Brigadier General of Volunteers, dated to the day of his capture, and promptly raised another Irish Brigade (The Corcoran Legion). This brigade fought through to the end of the war in 1865. Corcoran died while in service on Dec. 23, 1863. He was thirty-six years of age.[38]

The Regiment returned to New York to a tumultuous welcome. New York had fallen in love with its Irish regiment. A national color was borrowed from the 7th Regiment New York State Militia, which acted as escort for the parade. Along with this color, the Prince of Wales Color was carried triumphantly through the streets of old New York.[39]

The Prince of Wales Color was carried in nearly all parade and military functions in New York City during the Civil War, and was carried by the 69th New York State Militia. The Prince of Wales Colors was partially restored in the 1970s and it rests today in the color cases of the hallowed halls of the 69th Regiment Armory in New York City.

A note of irony: In November, 1943, the 69th landed on and captured Makin Atoll in the Gilbert Islands. Makin had been a British protectorate. In 1944, King George VI of Great Britain honored the Regiment by awarding the Distinguished Service Order to its Regimental Commander, Colonel Gerard Kelley, eighty-four years after the Prince of Wales incident.

---

[38] National Archive & Records Service: Rec. group 107, M 504, roll 128.
[39] *New York Daily Tribune*: August 3, 1861.

1ST IRISH COLOR
69TH NEW YORK STATE VOLUNTEERS

The 9th Regiment New York State Volunteers was authorized, on August 30, 1861, under the command of Colonel Robert Nugent, who had been the Lieutenant Colonel of the 60th New York State Militia at Bull Run.[40] So great was the response for enlistment in the 69th, that it was decided to form an Irish brigade. The 63rd New York State Volunteers, the Independent Regiment,[41] which had been partly organized, joined, and the 88th New York State Volunteers (Mrs. Meager's Own) quickly followed. [42] The Irish Brigade was envisioned as a multi-state organization, and in addition to the three New York regiments, it was to have consisted of two other infantry regiments, one from Boston, the 28th Massachusetts Volunteers,[43] and the other from Philadelphia, the 115th Pennsylvania Volunteers,[44] and of a combined artillery and cavalry regiment raised jointly between New York and Philadelphia.[45]

When the Irish Brigade left for the war, it was comprised of only the three New York regiments. Because of interstate rivalries, the 115th Pennsylvania Vols. was sent to the Third Corps area and never joined the Brigade.[46] The 28th Massachusetts Vols. was sent to Port Royal, North Carolina, in the Ninth Corps area. It finally joined the Brigade in November, 1862, just in time for the debacle at Fredericksburg.[47] The sixth regiment never passed the embryonic stage and was never fully organized.[48]

The Regimental Colors were presented to the New York regiments in November, 1861, at an elaborate ceremony in front of Archbishop Hughes' residence, on Madison Avenue at 37th Street. The archbishop was in France on a mission for President Lincoln, and the colors were blessed by the Very Reverend Doctor Starrs in the absence of the archbishop. The

[40] Conyngham, Capt. D. P.: *The Irish Brigade and Its Campaigns*, (New York, William Mc Sorley & Sons, 1867) (letter from Thomas A. Scott-Asst. Sec'y. of War to COL. T. F. Meagher) 50.
[41] O'Flaherty, Patrick D.: *The History of the Sixty-Ninth Regiment In The Irish Brigade*, Fordham Press NY, 1986, 9.
[42] Independent meant: independent of the Fenians.
[43] O'Flaherty, 9 (The designation of the numeral 88 was sought after and petitioned for: There had been an 88th Regiment in the French Irish Brigade and in the British Army, and the 88th Regiment of Foot was the storied 'Connaught Rangers').
[44] O'Flaherty: 11.
[45] O'Flaherty: 9.
[46] Ibid.
[47] Ibid.
[48] Ibid.

colors, six in number, had been hand-embroidered[49] by a committee of patriotic Irish ladies, were of the richest silk, and had been executed in Tiffany's best style.[50]

Each color was of a deep, rich green, and bore an embroidered design consisting of a harp surmounted by a sunburst, above a wreath of shamrocks; over this a scroll bore the regimental designation 1st REGT. IRISH BRIGADE[51] on the color of the 69th New York State Volunteers, the senior regiment of the Brigade; beneath, a second scroll bore the motto in Irish "RIAM NAR DRUID O SBAIRN LANN," (Who Never Retreated From The Clash of spears.)[52] The scrolls were pinkish crimson, shaded with a darker crimson, and had been inscribed and narrowly edged in gold; the cloud was beige shaded in light brown, and the sunburst yellow was similarly shaded; the harp was a golden yellow shaded in light and dark brown tones, and the shamrocks appeared in tones of green with dark shading. It was fringed with saffron yellow silk. The pike was tipped with a silver pikehead, and a streamer of saffron yellow silk was tied below the pikehead with the regimental designation 69th New York State Volunteers,[53] bearing a design of a string of nineteen shamrocks, all in tones of green with dark shading.[54] The streamer measured twelve feet from end-to-end, including the golden tassels. The flag was six feet, six inches on the fly, and six feet deep on the pike, which was the standard size of authorized infantry colors. The length of the pike was nine feet, ten inches, including pikehead and ferrule. The colors are embroidered on two sides, the reverse side showing a mirror (backwards) image.

---

[49] Embroidered flags were the exception and were highly prized. Most Civil War flags were painted.

[50] Conyngham: 55

[51] Conyngham's description was stated in a run-on sentence and was very ambiguous. Because of his description, most historians were using erroneous data. On examination of the 1st Irish Color, the scroll simply says — 1st REGT. IRISH BRIGADE.

[52] Cavanagh: 426, (The ancient Gaelic motto was furnished by the eminent Irish scholar and American leader of the Fenians, John O'Mahoney and was adapted from Oisin, the Fenian Bard.)

[53] On examination of the streamer, the shamrocks were 19 in number. The streamer of the 88th had 18 shamrocks.

[54] The streamer measured 12 feet including the tassels. It was embroidered and one-sided. The reverse side was covered by a layer of saffron silk.

The first Irish flag of the 69th New York Volunteers was carried through the Peninsula campaign, at Antietam, and also was on loan to the U.S.S. Antietam. (Lt. Col. Kenneth H. Powers)

The flag was full of Irish and Fenian symbolism:

- The harp is the Brian Boru Harp. He was the only king of a united Ireland and was killed at the Battle of Clontarf in 1014.
- The shamrocks are symbols of Ireland and her Christianity.
- The sunburst is a Fenian symbol and was found mostly in America. It was thought to represent the "Scal Ghreine"[55] which decorated the banners of antiquity -- Ireland's Gaelic past. ("Let the sunburst be unfurled" was the cry at Fenian meetings.)[56]
- The motto on the bottom scroll was taken from Oisin, the bard and the son of Fionn Mac Cumbal in the Fenian Cycle of Irish mythology. Oisin, as a blind old man, meets St. Patrick and has the famous debate (Agallamh) with the saint. The saint tried to convert him, but the bard would have none of it and he regaled the saint with tales of Fionn and the Fianna. Saint Patrick said, indignantly that was all well and good but, since they had worshipped the old, false gods and not the one, true God, they would all be condemned to hell. Oisin replied: Were Fionn and Mac an Loin with me – (Two who never retreated from the clash of spears;) despite the clerics, bells and thee, We'd hold -- where Satan domineers. (The pikehead recalls the weapon of choice of the Galloglach Eirinn in Ireland's military past.)

The colors were carried throughout most of 1862. Matches were issued during the Seven Days Campaign to be used in the event of capture.[57] At Antietam, the 69th's color was riddled, its staff broken by a bullet, and eight color bearers were shot down.[58] At Malvern Hill, a Confederate general was heard to remark, "Here comes that damned green flag again."[59] At Fair Oaks the 88th's color was ripped.[60] The colors of the New York regiments were returned to New York in November of 1862, for safekeeping at the Manhattanville home of New York City Chancellor,

---

[55] Hayes-Mc Coy, Gerard A.: *The History of Irish Flags*, (Dublin: Academy Press, 1979), 156.

[56] Ibid 50; *The Freeman's Journal*: March 5, 1867

[57] Conyngham: 305.

[58] Athearn, R. G.: *Thomas Francis Meagher: An Irish Revolutionary In America*, (University of Colorado Press, 1949), 11.

[59] Conyngham: 122; Cavanagh: 456

[60] Cavanagh: 445

Daniel Devlin.[61] There were six colors made, and four were issued. The
69th's and 88th's colors are in the 69th Regiment Armory. The 63rd's color is
at Notre Dame, and the 28th Massachusetts Volunteers' color hangs in the
State House in Boston, Massachusetts. Research has to be done on the
colors of the 5th and 6th regiments to determine whether or not they still
exist, and where they are located.

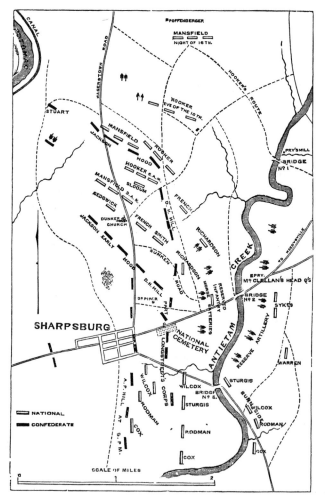

Battle of Antietam

[61] O'Flaherty 189; Conyngham: 330

2ND IRISH COLOR
69TH REGIMENT
NEW YORK STATE VOLUNTEERS

A battle flag of the 69th New York State Volunteers, used during the American Civil war, hangs in Leinster House, the parliament house of the Irish Republic in the City of Dublin. The flag was presented to the Irish people by President John F. Kennedy as a symbol of the friendship existing between the Irish Republic and the United States of America. The saga of that flag began more than ten years ago in the City of New York.[62]

The activity of the Irish in the Militia during the 1850's, and, the openly-expressed purpose of training men for a future Irish Revolution, aroused considerable suspicion on the part of native-born Americans. Many feared that Irish regiments commanded by Irish officers would do something which would involve the United States in difficulties with England.[63] Others worried, when they saw so many Catholics under arms in their uniforms of green, that they were planning a take-over by the Pope.

The splendid record of the 69th New York State Militia at Bull Run, and the bravery of the Irish Brigade during General McClellan's Peninsula Campaign and during the terrible battle of Antietam, inspired a group of American gentlemen, led by Henry F. Spaulding to make reparation for the discrimination against the Irish Militia during the middle 1850's, by presenting the Irish Brigade with a set of flags to replace those torn to pieces in battle. The old flags were brought from the camp of the Irish Brigade in Virginia and were entrusted to Daniel Devlin, Chancellor of the City of New York, and Chairman of the Executive Committee of the Irish Brigade, to be preserved at his home in Manhattanville.[64] The committee of Americans turned over the new flags to Captain James McGee

---

[62] *Dublin Times*: June 29, 1963; *New York Times*: June 29, 1963.

[63] O'Flaherty: 189 & footnote 203.

[64] Pickett, Raymond: Conversation with Mr. Pickett, who is the great grandnephew of Daniel Devlin on his mother's side reveals that Daniel Devlin was the Chairman of the Executive Committee of the Irish Brigade and owned one of the largest firms in the garment industry and outfitted the Irish Brigade with its uniforms. His estate in Manhattanville was called "Craigmoor" and was located on the North Hudson River from 137th to 145th Streets. Mr. Pickett has a great deal of Devlin memorabilia, including a signet ring with the Devlin crest. Inside is inscribed "To our dearest friend from the Officers of the Irish Brigade." On his father's side, Mr. Pickett is the great grandson of General George Pickett, who made the famous charge at Gettysburg.

of the 69th New York State Volunteers, as representative of General Thomas F. Meagher in a ceremony at Devlin's home.[65]

The soldiers of the Irish Brigade, in preparation for the presentation of the flags to the 69th, 88th and 63rd New York State Volunteers, had erected a large log building (125 x 30 feet) called the *Green House* at Falmouth, Virginia just opposite Fredericksburg, in which ceremonies were to take place during a dinner. Food and drink had been shipped in from Washington, and all things were ready for the festivities, which were planned for December 13, 1862.[66]

There was no celebration. General Burnside chose, that day, to hurl his army against the impregnable Confederate positions on the heights above Fredericksburg. The Irish Brigade, with the 28th Massachusetts Vols. showing the green flag, charged up Marye's Heights, where most of them fell dead or were wounded. The New York Regiments, having no green flags, wore sprigs of boxwood in their hats.[67]

Every officer and enlisted man in the Brigade was requested to put the evergreen on his hat or cap. Meagher himself set the standard, placing a sprig on the side of his cap. Every officer and man followed his example, recalled Major Mulholland of the 116th Pennsylvania Vols. Wreaths were hung from the tattered [U.S.] flags.[68] The chaplain of the 69th, Father Thomas Ouellett (Willett) asked Colonel Nugent if he could walk along the lines of the regiment and say a word to each man. "Although not a Catholic myself," Nugent wrote, "I was the first man to receive the good father's blessing." He then went along the lines blessing each man, Catholic and Protestant alike. After the chaplain finished his religious duties, Nugent placed a bunch of evergreen on the chaplain's hat, telling his men "He would make an Irishman out of the Father that day." The good Father was a French Canadian.[69]

The command, "Irish Brigade: Advance!" was heard and regimental officers shouted. "Right shoulder, shift arms, battalions forward, guide center, march!" Two long lines of bayonets, gleaming in the sunlight advanced on the rebel lines four hundred yards away.[70] Ironically, the Confederate troops on Marye's heights were mostly Irish -- Geor-

---

[65] *The Irish American:* December 13, 1862.

[66] Cavanagh: 471; O'Flaherty: 190; *The Irish American:* December 27, 1862 & January 10, 1863.

[67] *The Irish American:* December 27, 1862.

[68] Mulholland, St. Clair A. *The Story of the 116th Pennsylvania Volunteers In The War of the Rebellion,* Philadelphia 1903, 43-44.

[69] Nugent, Robert: *The Sixty-ninth Regiment at Fredericksburg,* in the *Journal of the American Irish Historical Society,* vol. 15, 195-196.

[70] *The Irish American:* January 3, 1863; Mulholland: 47.

gia's Cobb's Legion and Kershaw's 2nd South Carolinians, and they were formed behind a stone wall in a sunken road in several lines of muskets. [71]

Bombardment of Fredericksburg

[71] O.R. XXI, 608.

Major James Cavanagh, of the 69th New York Volunteers, was badly wounded at Fredericksburg and was, later, discharged only to return with the 69th Militia. (USAMHI)

Never before had General Robert E. Lee massed such firepower on such a narrow front.[72] The Rebel fire was so fierce that the Irishmen bowed their heads as if walking against a blizzard. Many of them staggered under the fire, seemingly blown off their feet.[73] Their faces and clothes were spattered with mud as bullets and canister struck the ground around them.[74]

The Irish Brigade had to cross two lines of fences, and it stalled under concentrated fire. Sergeant Peter Welsh, of the 28th Massachusetts reported seeing, "...some hot work at south mountain and Antietam [sic] in Maryland but they were not to be compared to this the old troops ... that they never were under such heavy fire in any battle."[75] Colonel Nugent was carried off the field with a bullet wound in his side, and the command devolved around Major James Cavanagh. They could go no farther and the officers then yelled, "Lie down and fire!" "Blaze away and stand to it; remember what they will say about us in Ireland," shouted Major Cavanagh, just before he fell wounded. Captain Leddy took his place, and he, too, was shot down. All was lost; only a couple of officers were left unhurt, but some of the men ploughed on until they were within twenty-five feet of the enemy, only to fall dead or wounded.[76] The 69th was given no order to fall back, so men sought shelter and continued to fire. The Irish went farther than any other units that day, but did so in vain.[77] With the dead, dying, and wounded scattered over the field, and with its survivors out of ammunition and pinned down by Rebel fire, the Irish brigade fell back in groups. At a fence line not far from the stone wall, where the remnants of the Brigade sought shelter, Colonel Richard Byrnes, of the 28th Massachusetts, and Colonel Patrick Kelly, of the 88th, agreed to collect what they could of their regiments and meet back in town. Captain Patrick Condon, of the 63rd, leading nine men of his regiment, met Colonel Bynes with ten men of his regiment. "We shook hands and he remarked that our 'Brigade was gone,' meaning cut up."[78]

---

[72] Freeman, Douglas *Lee's Lieutenants*, (New York: Charles Scribner, 1946) 304.

[73] Cory, Eugene A. *A Private's Recollections of Fredericksburg, in the Rhode Inland Soldiers and Sailors Historical Society, Personal Narratives of the Battles of the Rebellion* 3rd series, No. 4 Providence XI, 1883, 25.

[74] Hitchcock., Frederick L : *War From The Inside: The Story of the 132nd Penna. Vol. Infantry 1862-3*, Philadelphia, 1904, 121.

[75] (Welsh) Kohl, Lawrence F. & Richard, Margaret C. *Irish Green and Union Blue*, (New York, Fordham Press, 1986) 43.

[76] Junkin, D.K. & Norton, Frank H.: *The Life of Winfield Scott Hancock*, (New York, D. Appleton Co., 1880) 73.

[77] Owen, William M. "A Hot Day of Marye's Heights," *Battles and Leaders*, vol. III, 70; Letter of Colonel John Rutter Brooke to Colonel St. Clair A. Mulholland, January 1881; Letter of Bismuth Miller to the New York Sun 'Fredericksburg Deadline,' April 22, 1911.

[78] O.R.: XXI, 250.

Meagher led 1250 men on to the field on the morning of the battle, and on the following day, only 280 men answered the roll call at a muster formation. As the poet said, "...there were blossoms of blood on the sprigs of green."[79] The final count showed the Brigade had lost 545 men. The 69th suffered the most, with sixteen of its nineteen officers, and 160 men killed, or wounded. The battle was not renewed, and, on December 15, the Brigade took care of some important business, which was to present the new colors to its regimental commanders.[80]

THE DEATH FEAST

And the room seemed filled with whispers,
As we looked at the vacant seats.
And, with choking throats, we pushed aside,
The rich but untasted meats;
There in silence we brimmed our glasses
As we rose up JUST ELEVEN
And bowed as we drank to the loved and the dead,
Who had made us THIRTY SEVEN.

Gen. Charles G. Halpine

General Meagher, since all the supplies for the dinner had arrived, proposed to hold the presentations in the theater in Fredericksburg on December 15. The food was cooked in the neighboring houses and served in the theater to the officers, and to the representatives of the enlisted men and their guests, among whom were twenty-two generals. The sharp-eyed Confederates added spice to the occasion by turning a battery on that part of town. The banquet broke up when one of the soldiers brought in a canon ball which had struck the house next to the theater and served it to General Meagher. During the night, the Union Army recrossed the Rappahannock River and returned to its camp at Falmouth.[81]

---

[79] O.R.: XXI, 242-3, 250.
[80] O.R.: XXI, 129.
[81] Cavanagh: 471-3; *The Irish American*: November 29, 1862.

The 29th Massachusetts Volunteers had been brigaded with the three New York regiments since the spring of 1862. This regiment was neither Catholic nor Irish, but had fought bravely and had won the admiration of the Irish. Meagher was so pleased with the men's fighting ability that he proposed to make them honorary Irishmen, and, knowing that the Native Americans were about to present flags to the New York Regiments, he secured a fourth green flag which he proposed to give to the 29th Massachusetts. The 29th was sensible of the honor, but, not being Irish, Colonel Barnes did not want to be called Fenian. He informed General Meagher that they would not carry a green flag. General Meagher took the refusal in good humor, but some of the Irish officers did not understand, and, a short time later, the 29th was transferred out of the Irish Brigade to be replaced by the 28th Massachusetts Volunteers, an Irish regiment, which had been raised for the Irish Brigade but had been sent to Hilton Head, South Carolina. They were added to the Irish Brigade on November 23, 1862. They had their own Irish color, so General Meagher was left with an extra flag.[82]

In April, 1863, the Brigade was encamped near the 9th Massachusetts Volunteers, an Irish regiment, which had developed out of the Columbian Artillery, and was suppressed by the Know Nothing Governor, Henry J. Gardner, in the mid 1850's. Captain Thomas Cass, after surrendering the charter of the regiment on January 5, 1855, formed the Columbian Association for literary and military purposes. The Columbian Association formed the nucleus of the 9th Regiment of which Cass became Colonel. The 9th won great honors during the Peninsula Campaign, and but lost its Colonel, who was succeeded by Colonel Guiney.

Meagher decided to present the flag originally intended for the 29th Massachusetts Infantry Volunteers to the 9th Massachusetts Infantry Volunteers The "2" was removed from the "29" in the two places it was inscribed on the flag, and the flag was made ready for presentation to the 9th. The ceremony came as somewhat of a surprise to the rank and file, who did not know why they had been assembled until Colonel Guiney explained the reason for the gathering. Meagher made a brief speech touching on the splendid accomplishments of the 9th, and expressed the hope that they would be able to end the war to make their contribution to the freedom of Ireland.[83]

---

[82] Conyngham: 234; *The Evening Bulletin*, Philadelphia, July 2, 1963.
[83] McNamara, Daniel G. *The History of the Ninth Regiment Massachusetts Volunteer Infantry*, (Boston, MA, 1899) (in passim).

The flags were cherished by the New York Regiments, as an expression of American good will. They do not seem to have been carried in battle. They reposed in various places until 1963, when President John F. Kennedy, planning a visit to Ireland, desired something that would be an expression of the services rendered to the United States by the Irish emigrants in America. Msgr. Patrick D. O'Flaherty, a Historian of the 69th, was contacted and he suggested that, if a symbol of Irish American unity was wanted, there was nothing that would express it better than the Fredericksburg Color of the 69th. The permission of Colonel Alfred S. Byrne, the Commanding Officer, 1st Battle Group 165th Infantry having been secured, and the flag was given to the President, who, on June 28, 1963, presented it to the Irish Republic in the presence of the Executive, and Representatives of the Irish people in Leinster House in Dublin.

The Flag of the 69th is enshrined in Leinster House, while that of the 63rd is in the library of the University of Notre Dame, South Bend, Indiana. The Flag of the 88th is in the Armory of the 69th in New York City, and that of the 9th Massachusetts lies in the State House in Boston.

The Second Irish Colors, made by Tiffany's, were of rich green and measured the same as the first Irish Colors. They are six feet, six inches on the fly and six feet on the pike. There was no streamer attached. On the field of green the device of the original appears in the canton, a harp ensigned with a sunburst, with a wreath of shamrocks beneath it. On the scroll above the sunburst was the regimental designation: *69th REGIMENT, N.Y.S.V.* and on the scroll below is the inscription *IRISH BRIGADE.* On the lower, left-hand quarter the following inscription appears *Presented by the Citizens of New York to the 69th N.Y.V. (1st Regiment Irish Brigade) Brigadier Gen. Thomas F. Meagher Commanding. In grateful appreciation of their gallant and brilliant conduct on the Battlefields of Virginia and Maryland in the War to maintain the National Domain and the American Union. Nov. 1862.* The two quarters of the fly are now covered by a list of thirteen battles. The nine original battles were placed centrally on the fly between two wreaths, a wreath of laurels above, and a wreath of oak below. The battles are: Yorktown, Fair Oaks [Seven Pines], Gaines's Hill [Gaines's Mills], Allen's Farm, Savage's Station, White Oak Bridge [White Oak Swamp], Glendale [Fraser's Farm], Malvern Hills [Malvern Hill], and Antietam. Added at a later date were the following battles: Fredericksburg and Chancellorsville on the top, and Gettysburg and Bristoe's Station on the bottom.

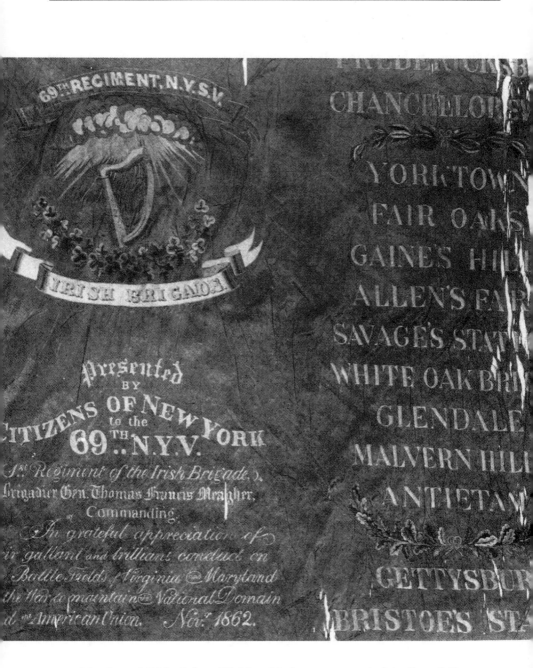

The Second Irish Color, 69th New York, was presented to them following the battle of Fredericksburg. This flag was restored and presented to the citizens of Ireland by President John F. Kennedy in 1963. This flag now hangs in the Irish Parliament building, Leinster House.

THE BALLAD OF THE SIXTY - NINTH

1861 - 1917

Clouds black with thunder o'er the Southern states;
　　North, East and West a sickening fear;
The Union on the dark laps of the Fates,
　　And nowhere sign the skies would clear.
Would hate haul down the flag we loved so well
　　The star-flag that at Yorktown flew?
For answer came the hurtling of a shell,
　　With the Union cleft in two!

Never since out of chaos the world
　　Sang such resolve as took us then:
"'Thro' blood and fire, with that brave flag unfurled
　　The Union shall be whole again."
At Lincoln's call men swarmed from towns and farms:
　　An ecstasy shook all the land.
Tramp! tramp! the people's bravest rose in arms
　　With them the Irish took their stand.

For here their slave rags had away been cast.
　　Freedom had met them at the door.
To share such empire lovelit, rich and vast
　　As never fronted man before.
Our great Republic! Shall the kings behold.
　　Neath slavery's thrust, its overthrow?
Loud, righteous, quick our regiment's answer rolled
　　The Irish Sixty-ninth says, "No!"

Tramp! Tramp! At Corcoran's command they've swung
　　Down Broadway's length a thousand strong.
Their flag of green by grand Old Glory flung.
　　Their steps like music to the cheering throng.
The great Archbishop, blessing rank and file,
　　Bends o'er them -- soldier, gun and blade.
On every face the bold-heart Irish smile
　　That looks in Death's eyes unafraid.

Mother of Irish regiments, march in pride;
    No idle presage in your tread!
The way is long; the battle ground is wide;
    High will be the roster of your dead.
Ever you'll find the battle's crest and front,
    Then march to seek new fighting ground:
Ever, when shattered in the battle brunt.
    Men for the gaps will still be found.

You'll be baptized in fire at Blackburn's Ford.
    Bull Run shall see two hundred fall --
You facing south when north the rout has poured:
    At Rappahannock like a wall:
You'll strike at Fair Oaks; clash at Gaines's Mill.
    And ramp like tigers over Malvern Hill:
Stand and be hammered at Chancellorsville:
    Antietam's corn shall redden at your name.
The while you deal the blow that stuns:
    At Marye's Heights your men shall feed on flame.
Up to the muzzles of the guns;
    At Gettysburg fire-dwindled on you'll press.
And then remanned again seek fight:
    All through the tangle of the Wilderness.
You'll battle day and night:
    At Petersburg you'll spring to the assault:
Only at Appomattox shall you halt!

Let Nugent, Meagher, Cavanagh be praised.
    MacMahon, Kelly, Haggerty, Clark.
But the thousands three that the regiment raised.
    As surely bore the hero-mark.
Fame's darling child, the Sixty-ninth shall shine
    Never in duty's hour to lag:
Forty-eight times in the battle line.
    Never, never to lose a flag.

    Tramp! tramp! you saw the Union split in twain
    Tramp! tramp! you saw the nation whole.
Your red blood flowed in torrents not in vain:
    It fed the great Republic's soul.
Your drums still roll: your serried ranks still form:
    From manhood's service no release:
Ready at call to ride the battle-storm,
    And, in God's time, the Guard of Peace.

JOSEPH I. C. CLARKE

Contributors' Biographies

Joseph G. Bilby was born in Newark, New Jersey. He received his BA and MA degrees from Seton Hall University, and served as a lieutenant with the First Infantry Division in Vietnam in 1966-1967. Mr. Bilby is employed by the New Jersey Department of Labor and has taught military history at Ocean County College. He is the author of *Remember Fontenoy! The 69th New York and the Irish Brigade in the Civil War*, *Three Rousing Cheers: A History of the Fifteenth New Jersey Infantry from Flemington to Appomattox*, and *Forgotten Warriors: New Jersey's African-American Civil War Soldiers*. He lives in New Jersey with his wife, three children, and labrador retriever.

Chris Garcia is a graduate student in American History at Scranton University, Pennsylvania. He is in the process of writing a detailed history of the 69th New York Infantry. He lives in Island Park, New York.

Barney Kelly is one of the Nation's leading historians of the 69th New York Infantry and the Irish Brigade. He has written several articles on the Irish Brigade and is a noted speaker. He lives in New York.

Phyllis Lane is currently writing a biography on Michael Corcoran. Phyllis is a well-respected authority on the Irish Brigade. She lives in Flushing, New York.

Kevin E. O'Brien has written several articles on the Irish Brigade and is considered a respected authority on the Irish Brigade. He lives in Scottsdale, Arizona.

Barry Lee Spink was born in Virginia. Barry has published several articles on the Irish Brigade and is a well-respected historian. He is in the process of writing a detailed history of the 28th Massachusetts Infantry. He is active with the Irish Brigade Association, Fort Schuyler, Throggs Neck, New York, and lives in Elmore, Alabama.

Phillip Thomas Tucker was born in Poplar Bluff, Missouri. He received his Ph.D. in History, from St. Louis University. He is the author of *Westerners in Gray, The South's Finest* and *The Confederacy's Fighting Chaplain*.

BIBLIOGRAPHY
Books, Pamphlets and Published Documents

Books

Alotta, Robert I. *Civil War Justice: Union Army Executions Under Lincoln.* Shippensburg, PA: White Mane, 1989.

Arner, Frederick B. *The Mutiny at Brandy Station: The Last Battle of the Hooker Brigade.* Kensington, MD: Bates & Blood Press, 1993.

Atlheam, Robert G. *Thomas Francis Meagher: An Irish Revolutionary in America.* Boulder, CO: University of Colorado Press, 1949.

Bates, Samuel P. *History of Pennsylvania Volunteers, 1861-1865,* Vol. III. Harrisburg PA: B. Singerly, 1870.

Beyer, W. F. & O. F. Keydal. *Deeds of Valor: How America's Civil War Heroes Won the Medal of Honor.* Detroit: Perrian-Keydal Co., 1903.

Bilby, Joseph G. *Three Rousing Cheers: A History of the Fifteenth New Jersey Infantry from Flemington to Appomattox.* Hightstown, NJ: Longstreet House, 1993.

Boatner, Mark M. III. *The Civil War Dictionary.* New York: David MacKay Company Inc., 1959.

Bredin, A. E. C. *A History of the Irish Soldier.* Belfast: Century Books, 1987.

Burton, William L. *Melting Pot Soldiers: The Union's Etimic Regiments.* Iowa State University Press, 1988.

Busey, John W. and Dr. David G. Martin. *Regimental Strengths at Gettysburg.* Baltimore: Gateway Press, 1982.

Busey, John W. *These Honored Dead. The Union Casualties at Gettysburg.* Hightstown, NJ: Longstreet House, 1988.

Cannan, John. *The Wilderness Campaign: May, 1864.* Conshohocken, PA: Combined Books, 1993.

Carter, Robert Goldtllwaite. *Four Brothers in Blue: Or Sunshine and Shadows of the War of the Rebellion: A Story of the Great Civil War from Bull Run to Appomattox.* Austin: University of Texas Press, 1978.

Corby, William, C.S.C. (Lawrence F. Kohl ed.) *Memoirs of Chaplain Life: Three Years With the Irish Brigade in the Army of the Potomac.* New York: Fordham University Press, 1992.

Collins, F., Battle of Bull Run dedicated to the 69th Regt. N.Y.S.M., New York: J. Wrigley, c 1861, (Broadside) 24 x 17cm.

Cooling, Benjamin Franklin and Walton H. Owen II. *Mr. Lincoln's Forts: A Guide to the Civil War Defenses of Washington.* Shippensburg, PA: White Mane, 1988.

Corcoran, Michael, *The Captivity of General Corcoran* Philadelphia: Barclay & Co., c.1865, reprinted, NY, AMS Press, 1973.

Cunliffe, Marcus. *Soldiers & Civilians: The Martial Spirit in America.* New York: The Free Press, 1973.

Daly, Robert W., ed. *Aboard the Monitor: 1862; The Letters of Acting Paymaster William Frederick Keeler, U. S. Navy to His Wife, Anna.* Annapolis: U. S. Naval Institute, 1964.

D'Arcy, William O.F.M. Conv. *The Fenian Movement in the United States: 1858-1886.* Washington: Catholic University Press, 1947.

Dungan, Myles. *Distant Drums: Irish Soldiers in Foreign Armies.* Belfast: Appletree Press, 1993.

Fox, William F. *Regimental Losses in the American Civil War, 1861-1865.* Albany: Brandow Printing Company, 1898.

Frassanito, William A. *Antietam: The Photographic Legacy of America's Bloodiest Day.* New York: Charles Scribner's Sons, 1978.

Gallagher, Gary W., ed. *The Second Day at Gettysburg: Essays on Confederate and Union Leadership.* Kent, OH: Kent State University Press, 1994.

Griffith, Paddy. *Battle Tactics of the Civil War.* New Haven: Yale University Press, 1989.

Hanchett, William. *Irish Charles G. Halphine in Civil War America,* Syracuse: Syracuse Univ. Press, 1970.

Halpine, Charles Graham. *Baked Meats of the Funeral, A Collection of Essays, Poems, Speeches, Histories and Banquets.* New York: Carleton, 1866.

Hayes-McCoy, Gerard A. *Irish Battles: A Military History of Ireland.* London: Longmans, Green & Co., Ltd., 1969.

_____. *The History of Irish Flags*. Dublin: Academy Press, 1979.

Headley, P. C. *Massachusetts in the Rebellion: A Record of the Historical Position of the Commonwealth and the Services of the Leading Statesmen, the Military, the Colleges, and the People, in the Civil War of 1861-1865*. Boston: Walker, Fuller, and Co., 1866.

Hernon, Joseph M. Jr. *Celts, Catholics & Copperheads: Ireland Views the American Civil War*. Columbus, OH: Ohio State University Press, 1968.

Johnson, Robert U. and Clarence C. Buel, eds. *Battles and Leaders of the Civil War*. New York: The Century Company, 1887.

Jones, Paul. *The Irish Brigade*. New York: Luce, 1969.

Jones, Terry I. *Lee's Tigers: The Louisiana Infantry in the Army of Northern Virginia*. Baton Rouge: LSU Press, 1987.

Kenny, Michael. *The Fenians: Photographs and Memorabilia from the National Museum of Ireland*. Dublin: Country House, 1994.

Kohl, Lawrence F. and Margaret Cosse Richard, eds. *Irish Green and Union Blue: The Civil War Letters of Peter Welsh*. New York: Fordham University Press, 1986.

Ladd, David L. and Audrey J. Ladd, eds. *The Bachelder Papers: Vol. I.* Dayton, OH: Morningside Press, 1994.

Lonn, Ella. *Foreigners in the Union Army and Navy*. Baton Rouge: LSU Press, 1951.

Lyons, W. F. *Brigadier General Thomas Francis Meagher: His Political and Military Career; With Selections From His Speeches and Writings*. New York: D. & J. Sadlier & Co., 1870.

Malone, Michael P. and Richard B. Roeder. *Montana: A History of Two Centuries*. Seattle: University of Washington Press, 1976.

Matter, William D. *If It Takes All Summer: The Battle of Spotsylvania*. Chapel Hill: UNC Press, 1988.

McLaughlin, Mark G. *The Wild Geese: The Irish Brigades of France and Spain* London: Osprey, 1980.

Meagher, Thomas Francis. *The Last Days of the Sixty Ninth in Virginia*. New York: Irish American, 1861.

Menge, W. Springer and J. August Shimrak, eds. *The Civil War Notebook of Daniel Chisholm [116th PA]*. New York: Ballentine, 1989.

Miller, Kerby A. *Emigrants and Exiles: Ireland and the Irish Exodus to North America*. New York: Oxford University Press, 1985.

Moody, T. W. and F. X. Martin, eds. *The Course of Irish History*. New York: Weybright and Talley, 1967.

Mulholland, St. Clair A. *The Story of the 116th Regiment, Pennsylvania Infantry: War of Secession, 1862-1865*. Gaithersburg, MD: Old Soldier Books, 1992. [reprint]

New York Monuments Commission for the Battlefields of Gettysburg and Chattanooga. *Final Report on the Battlefield of Gettysburg [New York at Gettysburg]* Three Vols. Albany: J. B. Lyon Co., 1900, 1902.

O'Faolain, Sean. *The Irish: A Character Study*. New York: Devin-Adair, 1956.

O'Flaherty, Very Rev. Patrick D. *History of the Sixty-Ninth Regiment in the Irish Brigade, 1861-1865*. Ann Arbor: University Microfilms, 1976.

Palfrey, F. W. *The Antietam and Fredericksburg*. New York: Charles Scribner's Sons, 1882.

Osborne, Seward, ed. *The Civil War Diaries of Col. Theodore B. Gates, 20th New York State Militia*. Heightstown, NJ: Longstreet House, 1991.

Pfanz, Harry W. *Gettysburg: The Second Day*. Chapel Hill: UNC Press, 1987.

Priest, John Michael. *Antietam: The Soldiers' Battle*. Shippensburg: White Mane, 1989.

Reynolds, Lawrence. *A Poetical Address, Delivered by Doctor Lawrence Reynolds, 63rd Regiment, N.Y.S.V.,* Albany: Weed, Parsons and Co., 1863.

Robertson, James I., ed. *The Civil War Letters of General Robert McAllister*. New Brunswick, NJ: Rutgers University Press, 1965.

Sears, Stephen W. *To the Gates of Richmond. The Peninsula Campaign*. New York: Ticknor & Fields, 1992.

Sparks, David S., ed. *Inside Lincoln 's Army: The Diary of Marsena Rudolph Patrick, Provost Marshal General, Army of the Potomac*. New York: Thomas Yoseloff, 1964.

Squier, E. G. ed. *Frank Leslie's Pictorial History of the American Civil War*, Vol. I. New York: Frank Leslie, 1862.

Taylor, Frank H. *Philadelphia in the Civil War, 1861-1865*. Philadelphia: City of Philadelphia, 1913.

Trudeau, Noah Andre. *Bloody Roads South: The Wilderness to Cold Harbor, May-June, 1864*. New York: Ballentine, 1989.

U. S. War Department. *The War of the Rebellion: A Compilation of the Official Records of the Union and Confederate Armies.* 128 Vols. Washington, D. C.: U. S. Government Printing Office, 1880-1901.

Walker, Francis A. *History of the Second Army Corps.* New York: Charles Scribner's & Sons, 1887.

White, Russell C., ed. *The Civil War Diary of Wyman S. White, First Sergeant, Company F, 2nd United States Sharp Shooters.* Baltimore: Butternut and Blue Press, 1993.

Wilkinson, Warren. *Mother, May You Never See the Sights I Have Seen: The Fifty Seventh Massachusetts Veteran Volunteers in the Last Year of the Civil War.* New York: Harper & Row, 1990.

Willard, George L. *Comparative Value of Rifled and Smooth Bored Arms.* Washington [n. p.] 1863.

Wyckoff, Mac. *A History of the 2nd South Carolina Infantry, 1861-1865,* Fredericksburg, VA: Sergeant Kirkland's, 1994.

_____. *A History of the 3rd South Carolina Infantry, 1861-1865,* Fredericksburg, VA: Sergeant Kirkland's, 1995.

Articles

Bilby, Joseph G., "Remember Fontenoy. The 69th New York and the Irish Brigade in the American Civil War," *Military Images Magazine,* Vol. IV, No. 5, March-April, 1983.

_____. "A Better Chance Ter Hit: The Story of Buck and Ball," *American Rifleman,* May, 1993.

Campbell, Eric, "Caldwell Takes the Wheatfield," *Gettysburg Magazine,* No. Three, July, 1990.

Garland, J. L., "Some Notes on the Irish During the First Month of the American Civil War," *Irish Sword,* Vol. V, Summer, 1961.

Lang, Wendall W. Jr., "Corps Badges, Pt. I: First through Fifth Army Corps," *Military Images Magazine,* Vol. VII, No. 6, May-June, 1986.

Lonergan, Thomas H., "Thomas Francis Meagher, "*American Irish Historical Society Journal,* Vol. XII, 1913.

Maryniak, Ben, "Their Faith Brings Them," *Civil War,* Vol. IX, No. 2, March-April, 1991.

McAfee, Michael, "69th Regiment, New York State Militia - The National Cadets - 1861,' *Military Images Magazine,* Vol. XI, No. 5, March-April, 1990.

McCormack, Jack, "A Touch of Green Among the Blue: Irish Troops in the Army of the Potomac," *Military Images Magazine,* Vol. XI, No 5, March-April, 1990.

_____. "Blue, Gray and Green: The Fighting Irish," *Civil War,* Vol. IX, No. 2, March-April, 1991.

Miller, Bismuth, "Fredericksburg's Dead Line," *The Sun* [New York] April 22, 1911. (Copy in Lt. Col. Kenneth H. Powers Collection)

New York State Archives & Records Administration, "Irish Immigrants in the Civil War Fighting for Acceptance," *For the Record,* Vol. VII, #4. Fall, 1989.

Nugent, Robert, "General Nugent's Description of the Sixty-Ninth Regiment at Fredericksburg." *Third Annual Report of the State Historian of the State of New York,* 1897.

O'Brien, Kevin E., "Commands -The Irish *Brigade,* "*America's Civil War,* May, 1994.

Purcell, Richard J., "Ireland and the American Civil War," *Catholic World,* Vol. CXV, 1922.

Rogers, Stephen, "A Bridge Too Many -- Or, How to Be *in* Two Places at Once," *Military Images Magazine,* Vol. XIII, No. 4, January-February, 1992.

"Unmarked Graves Give a Glimpse Into a Civil War Soldier's Life," *New York Times,* September, 16, 1994.

Other Studies

Conconnan, John J., "Colorful and Gallant General Michael Corcoran." Monograph to accompany memorial ceremony at Calvary Cemetery, Queens, New York, April 29, 1990.

Culleton, Edward, "John Kavanaugh, Young Irelander, 1847-1862." Typescript in the John Kavanaugh Papers, United States Army Military History Institute, Carlisle, PA

Kelly, Bernard B., "The Chaplains of the 69th Regiment of New York." Monograph to accompany Irish Brigade Association Encampment, 1990.

_____. "The Historic Civil War Irish Colors of the 69th Regiment." Unpublished Monograph, 1994.

Murphy, William A., "The Charge of tile Irish Brigade at Marye's Heights in the Battle of Fredericksburg, Virginia During the American Civil War." Unpublished Monograph, 1965. Possession of Veteran Corps, 69th Regt. Inc..

Pohanka, Brian, "James McKay Rorty: A Worthy Officer, A Gallant Soldier, An Estimable Man." Monograph to accompany memorial ceremony at Calvary cemetery, Queens, New York, 1993.

McAfee, Michael J., "69th New York State Militia, Company K (Irish Zouaves) 1861." Monograph to accompany Don Troiani print, 1988.

McLaughlin, James H., "James Haggerty of Tir Conaill, Irish Patriot - American Hero." Monograph to accompany memorial ceremony at Calvary Cemetery, Queens, New York, 1992.

Noonan, J. "69th New York History." Typescript, Kenneth H. Powers Collection, United States Army Military History Institute.

O' Grady, William L. D., "Lincoln and the Irish Flag." Letter to *New York Herald,* February 10, 1917. Copy of reprint in Lt. Col. Kenneth H. Powers Collection.

Powers, Lt. Col. Kenneth H., "Raise the Colors and Follow Me: The Irish Brigade at the Battle of Antietam." Monograph to accompany Mort Kunstler print, n.d.

_____. "The Fighting 69th − The Sixty-Ninth Regiment of New York, Its History, Heraldry, Tradition and Customs." Monograph to accompany the 1993 New York State Ancient Order of Hibemians Convention.

_____. "The Meagher Sword." Monograph detailing the History of the recovery of General Meagher's Sword, n.d.

Smith, Col. James J., "Address Delivered at the Armory of the 69th Regt. N. Y. N. G., Oct. 13, 1906, on the presentation of the Battle Flags of the Irish Brigade, by Col. James J. Smith, 69th Regt. N. Y. Vet. Vols.." Typescript in Lt. Col. Kenneth H. Powers collection.

Spink, Barry L., "From Cavan to Cold Harbor: The Life of Colonel Richard Bymes." Monograph to accompany memorial ceremony at Calvary Cemetery, Queens, New York, 1994.

Newspapers

Irish American, New York
The Pilot, Boston
Courier, Jersey City
Times, New York
Harper's Weekly

Manuscripts and Letters

Chipman, Charles, Letters. United States Army Military History Institute, Carlisle, PA. [129th Mass.]

Carman, Ezra A. Maps prepared for the Antietam Battlefield Board, Antietam National Battlefield Park.

Clancy, Thomas L. to author, August 23, 1994, with service and pension records of Thomas McGrath.

Corby, Rev. William, "Scene of a Religious Character on the Historic Battlefield of Gettysburg," Gettysburg National Military Park.

Corcoran, Michael, to W. B. Field, Esq., October 6, 1860. Lt. Col. Kenneth H. Powers collection.

Flint, Dayton. Letters copied and transcribed from Washington, NJ *Star.* John Kuhl collection.

Halsey, Edmund. Journal, United States Army Military History Institute, Carlisle, PA.

Holmes, Orrin D., Letters. Civil War Miscellaneous Collection, United States Army Military History Institute, Carlisle, PA. [29th Mass.]

Rafferty, Peter. "Experience of a private soldier during the Peninsula Campaign, 1862. Company B, 69th N. Y. Vol." New York State Archives.

Reid, William F. "Report of the Irish Brigade While Under General U. S. Grant." Possession of Veteran Corps, 69th Regiment Inc. [28th Mass.]

Registered State Papers, 1864, #16,765. National Archives, Republic of Ireland.

Index

A

Abolitionist · 71
Adger, Steamer · 192
Alabama · 85
Alabama, 3rd Inf. · 192
Alabama, 4th Inf. · 192
Albany, NY · 21, 28, 29, 98, 113, 187
Albuera · 69
Alexandria, VA · 41, 45, 128
Allen's Farm · 207
American Revolution · 6
Ancient Order of Hibernians · 184, 192
Anderson's North Carolina Brigade · 76
Anderson's Mill · 166
Andrew, John A. · 128, 173
Annapolis, MD · 21, 40, 192
Antietam, MD · 2, 7, 29, 54, 59, 66, 75, 77,
    83, 96, 98, 100, 126, 127, 178, 184, 197,
    199, 203, 207
Antietam Creek · 128
Antietam Iron Works · 130
Appomattox Court House · 56, 94, 112, 211
Aqueduct Bridge · 41, 43
Arlington Heights, VA · 22, 41, 192
Armory Square General Hospital,
    Washington, DC · 173
Army of Northern Virginia · 89, 95, 100,
    110
Army of the Potomac · 1-3, 9, 10, 59, 60, 74,
    77-79, 89, 90, 95, 97, 100, 102, 112, 116,
    125, 126, 133, 134, 146-148, 159, 163,
    164, 179, 180
Art Students' League · 185
Atoll, Makin · 193
Auburn · 82, 111, 155, 156
Australia · 71, 97
Averell, William W. · 129

B

Bachelder, John · 116
Bagley, James · 48, 52, 173
Ball's Crossroads · 44

Banks' Ford · 146, 147
Bardwell, George H. · 65
Barksdale's Mississippi Regiment · 61
Barlow, Francis C. · 84, 91, 170, 171
Barlow's First Division · 84
Bayard, George D. · 121
Beattie, George W. · 174
Bensonhurst · 175
Bentley, Richard C. · 76, 81, 98, 104, 112
Binney, Henry M. · 161
Bird, Patrick H. · 174
Black Horse Cavalry (VA) · 192
Black, Patrick W. · 161, 162, 174
Blackburn's Ford · 47
Bland, Elband · 106
Bland, Elbert · 80, 105
Bloody Angle · 2
Bloody Lane · 2, 75-77, 127
Blue Ridge · 47
Bolivar, Simon · 7
Bonaparte, Napoleon · 7
Boonsboro, MD · 126
Boston Massacre · 6
Boston, MA · 28, 71, 77, 82, 86, 96, 112,
    123, 128, 143, 159-164, 194, 198, 206
Bottom's Bridge · 123
Bowling Green, VA · 52
Brady, Matthew · 43
Brandy Station · 158
Brennan · 89
Breslin, John · 44, 54
Brian Boru Harp · 197
Bristoe Station · 82, 111, 112, 155, 156
British royal family · 19
Brock Road · 83, 84
Brooke, John R. · 90
Brooke's brigade · 107
Brooklyn · 175
Buffalo, NY · 185
Bull Run, 1st · 3, 22, 26, 35, 39, 47-49, 51,
    52-55, 71, 97-100, 119, 192, 194, 199
Bull Run, 2nd · 77, 128, 132, 139
Burke, B. H. · 51
Burke, Denis F. · 99
Burnside, Ambrose E. · 49, 59-61, 127, 200
Butler, Benjamin · 134, 170
Butler, James · 38, 41
Butler, William · 55

Bynes, Catherine · 173
Bynes, Ellen · 173
Bynes, Margaret · 173
Byrne, Alfred S. · 206
Byrnes · 89, 98, 120, 121, 125, 126, 129-
    131, 133, 134, 136, 138-141, 143-164,
    168, 169, 171, 172, 175, 176
Byrnes, Andrew · 98
Byrnes, Ellen T. · 123, 175
Byrnes, Mary L. · 175
Byrnes, Richard · 54, 69, 86, 88, 94, 95, 106,
    109, 112, 118, 119, 121, 123, 125, 133,
    135, 138, 165, 166, 168, 170, 171, 173,
    175, 203
Byron · 91

C

Caldwell, John C. · 77, 80, 102, 104, 108,
    109, 111, 151, 155
Calvary Cemetery, Long Island City, NY ·
    173
Canada · 188
Caraher, Andrew P. · 129, 131
Carl, Jeff · 81, 106
Carlisle Barracks · 184
Carlisle, PA · 184
Carrowkeel, Ireland · 13, 186
Cartwright, George W. · 128, 129, 132, 139,
    164, 173
Cass, Thomas · 205
Cassidy, John · 83
Castle Pinckney · 23
Castlehackett, County Galway · 97
Catholic · 1, 3, 5, 11, 36, 49, 61, 79, 103,
    117, 190, 199, 200, 205
Catholic Church · 186
Catholic School · 40
Catlett's Station · 156
Cavanagh, James · 54, 67, 202, 203
Cemetery Ridge · 79, 95, 99, 101, 104, 109,
    111
Centreville, VA · 31, 46-48, 51, 120, 155
Chancellorsville, VA · 78, 85, 96-99, 113,
    146-148, 207
Chapman, Samuel · 148
Charleston, SC · 21, 23
Chase, Albert A. · 174
Christ, Benjamin C. · 129

City of Dublin · 199
City Point, VA · 55
Clarke, Joseph I. C. · 210
Clear, Samuel · 83-86, 88, 90, 94, 114
Clinton, Henry, Sir · 6
Clontarf, battle of · 197
Clooney, Parick F. · 77
Cobb, Thomas R. R. · 65, 68
Cobb's Georgia Brigade · 65
Cochrane, William F. · 86
Colburn, A. V. · 119
Cold Harbor · 86, 88, 94, 111-113, 125, 169,
    170
Collins, Williams · 114
Columbia, SC · 25
Columbian Artillery · 205
Columbian Association · 205
Condon, Patrick · 136, 203
Confederacy · 5, 23, 60, 211
Congressional Medal of Honor · 82, 113
Connally, Richard · 187
Connecticut, 27th Inf. · 139
Connor, John · 174
Conyngham, David P. · 9, 99, 112
Cook, Philip St. G. · 124
Cook, Thomas · 174
Coonan, John · 55
Cooper Institute · 34
Corby, William, Rev. · 5, 7, 61, 79, 102,
    103, 111, 113, 116, 117, 150, 165, 173
Corcoran Legion · 55, 193
Corcoran, Elizabeth · 31
Corcoran, Heaney, Mrs. · 32
Corcoran, Mary M. · 17
Corcoran, Michael · 12-52, 54, 55, 71, 184,
    186-190, 192
Corcoran, Thomas · 13
Couch, Darius N. · 147
County Waterford, Ireland · 97
Court of Saint James · 188
Coveney, Jeremiah W. · 129, 144, 148
Crampton's Gap, MD · 153
Crawford, Dan · 84
Creeslough, Ireland · 14, 186
Crosbie, M. · 50
Culpepper, VA · 60
Culpepper Court House · 154
Curtin, Andrew G. · 121
Custer, George A. · 121, 125

D

Dale, Richard C. · 85
Daly, Charles P. · 38, 73
Daly, Maria L. · 38
Dana, Charles A. · 172
Danes · 7
Davis, Thomas · 46
Declaration of Independence · 6, 44
Deep Bottom · 91, 113
Delaware, 1st Inf. · 164
Delaware, 1st Volunteers · 83
Democrat · 15, 17, 19, 21, 40, 71, 97, 112, 187
Democratic State Convention · 187
Denio, Frank · 93
Deserters · 92
Devil's Den · 79, 102
Devlin, Daniel · 198, 199
Doheny, Michael · 187
Donahoe, Patrick · 128, 129, 161, 163
Donegal · 14
Donovan, Jack · 67
Donovan, John · 65
Dranesville, VA · 121
Driscoll · 74, 89
Dromahair · 186
Dublin, Ireland · 206
Duffy, Felix · 75, 77
Dwyer, John · 68

E

Earl of Lucan · 13
Edward, Albert, Prince · 19, 55, 188
Election, of 1860 · 71
Ellsworth, Ephraim E. · 41
Emmitsburg Pike · 102
Emmitsburg Road · 150, 152
Emory, William H. · 124
Engineers, U.S. · 41
England · 7, 14, 21, 39, 55, 71, 199
Esther, Margaret · 123
Evans' Georgia Brigade · 85

F

Fair Oaks · 3, 73, 197, 207
Fairfax Court House · 31
Fairfax railroad station · 32
Falmouth, VA · 60, 134, 148, 200, 204
Faneuil Hall · 161
Farmville · 94
Faugh A Ballagh · 62
Fenian convention, Chicago, IL · 32
Fenian Phoenix Brigade · 52
Fenians · 10, 21, 30, 94, 214
Fields, B. · 188
Fleming, James · 84, 88, 89, 174, 211
Foltz, Christain · 65
Fontenoy · 38, 50, 69, 211
Fontenoy, battle of · 46
Fort Benton, Montana · 4
Fort Corcoran · 22, 43, 44, 46, 51, 52, 192
Fort Leavenworth, KS · 140
Fort Riley, KS · 158
Fort Schulyer · 73
Fort Stedman · 89
Fort Sumter · 21, 71, 192
Fowler · 77
Fowler, Henry · 75, 76
Frailey, Peter F. · 84, 88
France · 7, 194
Fraser's Farm · 207
Frederick, MD · 100, 116
Fredericksburg, VA · 2, 5, 7, 59-61, 68, 69, 77, 96, 98-100, 105, 134, 135, 138, 145, 146, 157, 168, 169, 179, 180, 194, 200, 202, 204, 206, 207
Fredericksburg, VA (Map) · 63, 137
French · 6, 9, 46
French Canadian · 200
French's Division · 64

G

Gaine's Mill · 3, 73, 125, 207
Gallagher, Young · 81, 108
Galwey, Thomas F. · 76, 88
Gardner, Henry J. · 205
Garry Owen · 1
Georgetown · 40, 43
Georgetown College · 22, 40, 42, 192
Georgia · 6, 46, 84, 85, 108, 201

Germanna Ford · 157
Germans · 9, 77, 96
Germantown · 47
Gettysburg, PA · 2, 6, 7, 31, 55, 66, 79, 82, 83, 85, 89, 95, 96, 99-102, 110-112, 114, 116, 150, 152, 179, 207
Gettysburg National Military Park · 117
Gilbert Islands · 193
Gleason · 76
Glendale · 207
Goble, William C. · 180
Gordon, John B. · 85
Graniteville · 123
Grant, Ulysses S. · 56, 83, 84, 86, 89-93, 111, 112, 158, 165, 168-170, 172, 180
Great Britain · 17, 188, 193
Great Potato Famine of the 1840's · 71
Greeley, Horce · 22
Green Flag of Erin · 104
Green House, Falmouth, VA · 200
Griffin, Martin · 163
Griffith, Paddy · 178
Grogan, Robert J. · 88

H

Haggerty, James · 47, 48, 49
Halpine, Charles G. · 204
Hancock, Winfield S. · 60, 69, 80, 83, 95, 99-103, 111, 139, 141, 145, 150, 160
Hancock's Corps · 147
Hancock's Division · 64
Hancock's Second Corps · 84, 86
Hanover Court House · 123
Hanover Court House Road · 123, 169
Hanover Street · 62
Hanovertown Ferry Road · 124
Hare House · 89
Harling, Thomas · 106
Harpers Ferry · 44, 77, 154
Harper's Weekly · 190
Harrison's Landing · 123
Hartwood Church · 146
Haupauge, NY · 184
Hawkins' Zouaves · 30
Hayward, Wheeler L. · 157
Heaney, Elizabeth (Lizzie) · 31
Heaney, John H. · 15, 17, 31
Heaney, Mrs. · 17

Heenan, Dennis · 69
Heintzelman, Samuel P. · 120
Henry Hill · 49, 50, 54
Hibernian Hall · 15-18, 37, 187, 192
Hill, A. P. · 127
Hill's Third Corps · 84
Hodnett, John P. · 175
Hooker, Jospeh · 100, 146
Hosmer, Addison A. · 142
Howard's Mill · 123
Hudson River · 38
Hudson, T. W. · 149
Hughes, Archbishop · 73, 194
Hungarians · 9
Hunter, David · 119
Hunter's Brigade · 46
Hunter's Division · 49, 119

I

Ireland · 1, 2, 6, 7, 9, 10, 13, 14, 17, 21, 22, 29, 30, 35, 38, 39, 46, 50, 59, 79, 92, 94, 103, 114, 163, 186-188, 197, 203, 205, 206
Irish Brigade, 1st Division, 2nd Corps · 60
Irish Color, 1st · 185
Irish Color, 2nd · 185, 207, 208
Irish Legion · 7, 28, 29, 30, 31, 54, 55
Irish mythology · 197
Irish Republic · 199
Irish Revolution · 199
Irish Rifles · 16, 17
Italians · 9

J

Jackson, James T. · 41
Jackson, Thomas J. · 5, 50, 73, 147
Jackson's Brigade · 50
James Adger · 38
James River, VA · 25, 26
Jersey City, NJ · 173, 175
Jones, John P. · 7
Joyce, John C. · 77

K

Kansas · 140
Kavanagh, John · 76, 77
Kelly, James · 52, 77
Kelly, Patrick · 54, 69, 78, 79, 81, 89, 94, 95, 97, 98, 101, 102, 104-108, 110, 112, 146, 151, 203
Kelly's Ford · 146
Kelly's Irish Brigade · 80
Kennedy, John F. · 199, 206, 208
Kershaw, Joseph B. · 68, 81, 104, , 105 106, 107, 108, 111, 201
King Edward VII · 188
King George VI · 193
King James II · 13
Kirker, J. B. · 55
Knight, John · 174
Know Nothing Party · 186
Kunstler, Mort · 184

L

Landis, Allen · 100, 110
Lawler, Andrew J. · 86, 154, 166
Leddy · 203
Lee, Robert E. · 5, 56, 59-61, 69, 73, 75, 83, 85, 86, 89, 91-93, 96, 98, 100, 101, 112, 146, 155, 156, 170, 203, 211
Lee's Army of Northern Virginia · 84
Leinster House, Dublin · 199, 206, 208
Lieb, Frank R. · 171
Lincoln, Abraham · 2, 5, 21, 31, 52, 59, 71, 97, 112, 119, 148, 192, 194
Little Round Top · 104
Lockport, NY · 99
London · 6
London Times · 69
Long Island · 73
Long Island City · 173
Longstreet, James · 102
Longstreet's First Corps · 84
Lonsbury, Earl · 185
Loring, Amos A. · 172
Loudon & Hampton Railroad · 43
Louisiana Tigers · 73, 192
Louisiana Zouaves · 49
Lowe, Percival G. · 145
Lowe, Thaddeus · 145

Lynch, George · 76

M

Magner, James · 86, 87
Maguire, Robert T. · 65
Mahone, William · 91, 92, 187
Maine, 5th Battery · 78, 147
Maine, 5th Inf. · 148
Malin, Francis · 81, 106
Malvern Hill · 3, 7, 73, 74, 96, 126, 197, 207
Manassas, VA · 3
Manassas-Sudley Road · 49
Marshell House · 41
Martinsburg · 127
Marye's Heights, Fredericksburg, VA · 5, 64, 66, 67, 69, 105, 200
Maryland · 2, 7, 66, 100, 126, 130, 184, 203, 207
Mason, James · 54
Massachusetts · 27, 86, 112, 128, 130, 138, 155, 157, 159, 160, 163, 172
Massachusetts, 4th Cav. · 158, 160
Massachusetts, 9th Inf. · 73, 205, 206
Massachusetts, 19th Inf. · 61
Massachusetts, 20th Inf. · 61
Massachusetts, 28th Inf. · 2, 60-62, 64, 65, 69, 79, 80, 82, 84, 86-90, 92-94, 96, 98, 99, 105, 106, 109, 111, 114, 118, 120, 122, 128-130, 132, 134, 140, 144, 146-150, 153, 154, 157, 161, 170, 171, 173, 179-181, 194, 198, 200, 203
Massachusetts, 29th Inf. · 74, 77, 205
Mattapony River · 168
Matthew's Hill · 49
McAllister, Robert · 179
McCarter, William · 64, 67
McCarthy, William H. · 174
McCleland, William · 65
McClellan, George B. · 59, 73, 74, 77, 121, 123
McClelland, William · 81, 106
McDonagh family · 13
McDonagh, Mary · 13
McDonald, Miles · 89
McDonnell, John H. · 144
McDowell, Irwin · 41, 44, 48, 51
McGee, James · 75, 89, 90, 199
McGlim, John · 174

McIvor, James P. · 55
McParland, Mr. · 174
Meade, George G. · 100, 101, 116, 155, 156, 157, 166, 169
Meagher, Thomas F. · 3, 4, 9, 12, 16, 22, 26, 32, 34, 39, 41, 44, 45, 48, 51, 52, 54, 62, 64, 65, 71, 73-78, 93, 94, 96-99, 111, 112, 134-136, 145-148, 177-179, 184, 187, 200, 204, 205, 207
Meagher's Irish Zouaves · 41
Meagher's horse, KIA · 50
Mechanicsville · 125
Memoirs of Chaplain Life · 7
Memoirs of General Thomas F. Meagher · 183
Mexican War · 99
Mexico · 16
Michigan, 7th Inf. · 61
Miles, John · 171, 174
Miles, Nelson A. · 90
Mine Run · 82, 111, 112, 157, 158
Minor, John H. · 174
Mississippi, 16th Inf. · 76
Missouri River · 4, 78, 112
Mitchell, John · 187
Mitchell, W. G. · 165
Montana · 78, 112
Mooney, Thomas, Father · 43, 45
Moroney, Richard · 76, 82, 90, 98, 109, 113
Mozart Hall · 71
Mule Shoe · 84, 165
Mulholland, St. Clair A. · 62, 78-81, 83, 96, 99, 101, 103-105, 107-110, 113, 175, 200
Murphy · 89
Murphy, Matthew · 55
Murphy, Murtha · 91

N

Nagle, William J. · 66, 97
Nason, Hiram T. · 133, 147, 156
New Jersey, 11th Inf. · 179
New Orleans · 71
New York 5th Inf. · 40
New York City · 2, 13, 14, 16, 19, 21, 22, 23, 24, 25, 28-32, 36, 38, 40, 45, 46, 49, 54, 62, 71, 82, 90-92, 96, 97, 99, 108, 111-114, 153, 179, 180, 184-188, 192-194, 197, 199, 207, 211

New York City draft riots · 82
New York Harbor · 21
New York, 4th Heavy Artillery · 52, 93
New York, 7th Inf. · 52, 193
New York, 7th Heavy Artillery · 92, 93
New York, 9th Inf. · 30, 194
New York, 12th Inf. · 47
New York, 13th Inf. · 49
New York, 13th State Militia · 47
New York, 59th Inf. · 183
New York, 60th Inf. · 194
New York, 63rd Inf. · 2, 54, 60, 64, 68, 69, 73, 76, 79, 80, 82, 90, 92, 93, 96, 98, 102, 104, 105, 107, 110, 112, 136, 146, 171
New York, 69th Inf. · 2, 21, 44, 60, 64, 65, 67, 71, 73, 75, 79, 80, 82, 86, 89-93, 96-98, 101, 105, 106, 113, 146, 173, 177, 180, 183, 184, 186, 187, 196, 199, 206
New York, 69th National Guard Artillery · 55, 173
New York, 69th State Militia · 3, 12, 13, 35, 41, 42, 48, 49, 52, 53, 56, 97, 191
New York, 79th Inf. · 49-51
New York, 82nd Inf. · 149
New York, 88th Inf. · 2, 6, 54, 60-62, 64, 65, 73, 78-83, 89, 90, 92, 93, 96-99, 102, 103, 105, 112, 113, 135, 146, 147, 178, 179
New York, 125th Inf. · 178
New York, 170th Inf. · 55
New York, 182nd Inf. 55, 173 *as called New York, 69th National Guard Artillery*·
Nolan's Ferry, MD · 134
Normans · 7
North Anna · 86, 88, 111, 168, 169
North Carolina · 25, 54, 85, 194
North Carolina, 2nd Inf. · 76
North Carolina, 4th Inf. · 76
North Carolina, 14th Inf. · 76
North Carolina, 30th Inf. · 76
Notre Dame, Univ. of · 102, 113, 198, 206
Nowlen · 106
Nugent, Robert · 36, 48, 52, 54, 56, 67, 69, 73, 90, 92-94, 111, 173, 194, 200, 203
Ny River · 166

O

O'Brien, Edward F. · 155
O'Flaherty, Patrick D. · 206
O'Gorman, Richard · 187
O'Grady, William · 178
O'Mahony, John · 38, 39, 173
O'Neill, B. S. · 89
O'Neill, John · 65
O'Neill, Joseph · 69, 76
O'Reilly, Father · 45
O'Shea · 89
Oak Ridge · 101
Ohio · 44
Ohio, 8th Inf. · 64, 76
Order of the Holy Cross · 6
Ouellett (Willett), Thomas · 200
Own, Meager · 194

P

Palmer, Innis N. · 119, 120
Pamunkey River · 86, 88, 111, 169, 170
Parker House Hotel · 161, 163
Patterson · 44
Peach Orchard · 79, 81, 95, 102, 104, 107, 108
Pegram's Virginia · 85
Peninsula campaign · 73, 123, 205
Pennsylvania · 2, 6, 7, 31, 83, 95, 98, 99, 100, 108, 111, 150, 179, 180, 184, 185
Pennsylvania Avenue, Washington · 40
Pennsylvania, 1st Cav. · 121
Pennsylvania, 4th Inf. · 125
Pennsylvania, 69th Inf. · 55
Pennsylvania, 115th Inf. · 194
Pennsylvania, 116th Inf. · 2, 60, 62, 64-67, 69, 77-86, 88, 90, 93, 94, 96, 99, 100, 103, 105-107, 110, 114, 135, 146, 148, 150, 171, 172, 175, 179, 180, 200
Pennsylvania, 140th Inf. · 107
Perrin's Alabama Brigade · 85
Petersburg, VA · 55, 89, 90, 92-94, 111, 112
Philadelphia, PA · 1, 6, 71, 77, 82, 96, 99, 114, 194
Phoenix Zouaves · 38
Pickett, George · 66, 110
Pickett's charge · 55, 82, 110
Pilot, The · 123, 128, 161

Pleasant Valley, MD · 154
Pleasonton, Alfred · 127, 159
Plum Run · 79, 101, 104
Po River, VA · 164
Poles · 9
Port Royal · 194
Porter, Fitz-John · 123
Porter's brigade · 49
Portugal · 7
Posey's Mississippi Brigade · 75, 76
Potomac River · 127
Poughkeepsie, NY · 28
Powderly, Michael E. · 174
Power, John · 175
Prince of Wales · 12, 19, 35, 39, 50, 71, 184, 185, 188, 190, 193
Prince of Wales Ball · 189
Prince of Wales Color · 191, 193
Prince Street · 15, 17, 28, 34, 37, 187, 192
Prisoners · 23-25, 43, 81, 84, 92, 93, 101, 107, 108, 121, 127, 133, 151, 157
Protestant · 1, 6, 9, 200

Q

Quarantine Hospital · 18
Quarantine Riots · 187
Queen Victoria · 19, 35, 188
Quinlan, James · 54, 65, 66

R

Rand, Arnold A. · 160
Rapidan River, VA · 90, 111, 157, 158, 164
Rapidan Station · 154
Rappahannock River, VA · 59, 60, 61, 134, 146, 204
Reams Station · 91, 113, 162
Relly · 52
Renfrew, Baron · 188
Republican · 19, 71
Return of the Flags of the Irish Brigade · 8
Reynolds · 100
Rhode Island · 48, 49
Rhode Island, 12th Inf. · 179
Ribbonmen · 14, 186
Richardson's Division · 75
Richmond postal authorities · 23

Richmond Prison Association · 23
Richmond Road · 124, 125
Richmond, VA · 23, 25, 60, 168-170
Ripley, James W. · 177
Ritchie · 129, 159
Ritchie, Harrison · 128, 158
Robertson's Tavern · 157
Rochester, NY · 47
Rose Farm · 107
Royall, William B. · 123

S

Sacriste, Louis J. · 82
Salisbury prison, NC · 25
San Francisco · 21, 190
San Martin, de Jose · 7
Sanborn, Charles H. · 129, 144, 148
Sandy Hook, MD · 154
Sanitary Committee · 23
Sarsfield, Patrick · 13
Savage Station · 3, 73, 207
Savannah, GA · 6
Schenck · 44
Schenck's Brigade · 44
Schoales, Michael · 88
Schouler, William · 143
Scott, Winfield · 44
Scott's Mill · 147
Sedgwick, John · 159
Seminary Ridge · 101
Semme's Brigade · 81
Seven Days · 3, 73, 74, 197
Seven Pines · 98, 207
Sharpsburg, MD · 127, 128, 184
Sheedy, Joseph E. · 139
Shenandoah Valley · 44
Shepherdstown, WV · 127
Sheridan, Philip · 93
Sherman, William T. · 22, 46, 49, 51, 52, 71, 78, 112, 192
Sherman's brigade · 47-50
Shiloh · 98
Sickles' Third Corps · 102
Sickles, Daniel · 79, 95
Slaves · 71
Slidell, John · 54
Sligo, Ireland · 13
Smith, Cadwalder · 107

Smith, Charles V. · 153
Smith, James J. · 82, 106, 108, 111, 113
Smith, William A. · 60, 78, 100, 110, 114
Smyth, Thomas A. · 54, 82, 83, 86, 94, 160, 164
Smyth's Irish Brigade · 84, 85
South America · 7
South Bend, IN · 206
South Carolina · 21, 23, 77, 80, 134, 190, 205
South Carolina Brigade · 80, 81
South Carolina, 2nd Inf. · 201
South Carolina, 3rd Inf. · 80, 81, 104, 106
South Carolina, 7th Inf. · 80, 81, 104, 105, 106
South Carolina, 15th Inf. · 108
South Mountain, MD · 77, 126
South Side Railroad · 93
Spain · 7
Spaulding, Henry F. · 199
Spotsylvania, VA · 2, 7, 84, 86, 87, 88, 92, 111, 114, 154, 162, 164, 168
Sprague, Governor (RI) · 48
St. Louis · 119, 211
St. Mngely · 105
St. Patrick's Cathedral · 15, 32
St. Patrick's Day · 2, 77, 184
Stanton, Edwin M. · 26
Staten Island · 18, 29, 123, 187
States Rights · 40
Steuart, George H. · 120
Stevensburg, VA · 158, 159, 164
Stony Hill · 80
Stuart, James E. B. · 123, 147
Suffolk, VA · 29, 30, 32
Sullivan, John · 76
Sumner, Edwin V. · 60, 127, 134
Sutherland Station · 93
Swedes · 9
Sweeney, Peter · 187
Swift Creek · 169

T

Tammany Hall · 17, 19, 21, 28, 29, 187
Tammany Judiciary Committee · 187
Tammany organization · 29
Taneytown Road · 81, 108
Tasmania · 97

Tennessee · 25, 98
Thomas, George H. · 121
Thomas, Lorenzo · 143
Tiffany · 195, 207
Tilden, Samuel · 187
Todd's Tavern · 164
Totopotomoy · 86, 88, 169, 170
Touley, Thomas T. · 79, 96, 102, 104, 113, 107
Tribune · 22
Trostle House · 104
Tufts, Mr. · 173
Turner, Richard · 83
Turner's Gap, MD · 126
Tweed, William · 187
Two Taverns · 153
Tyler, Daniel · 45, 47
Tyler's Division · 47
Tyrell, William H. · 66

U

U.S. Army War College · 184
U.S. Ford · 146, 147, 148
U.S. Sanitary Commission · 94
U.S., 5th Cavalry · 98, 141
U.S., 17th Inf. · 98
U.S.S. Antietam · 196
Uniontown, PA · 83

V

Vienna, VA · 46
Virginia · 22, 41, 54, 98, 99, 105, 127, 128, 146, 153, 162, 177, 199, 207, 211
Virginia, 10th Cav. · 126
Virginia, 13th Cav. · 51

W

W.P.A. project · 185
Walker, Francis A. · 176
Walton · 69
Warren, Gouverneur K. · 156, 157, 183

Warrenton Turnpike · 50, 119
Warwick Court House · 123
Washington, DC · 141, 192
Washington, George · 6
Washington's Continental army · 6
Waterloo · 69
Webb, Alexander S. · 159
Welsh, Peter · 61, 65, 66, 80, 85, 94, 99, 106, 109, 111, 114, 133, 135, 138, 139, 144, 162, 203
West Virginia, 7th Inf. · 75, 76
Westover · 125
Wheatfield · 2, 6, 79, 80, 81, 95, 102, 104, 105, 108, 111
White House · 26
White House Landing · 172
White Oak Bridge · 207
White Oak Swamp · 73, 207
White Oak Swamp Bridge · 125
Wilderness · 83, 85, 88, 111, 113, 149, 158, 162, 164, 173
Willard, George L. · 178
William's Farm · 89
Williamsburg, VA · 123
Wind Watch Hotel · 184
Winslow, Reuben C. · 120
Wisconsin, 2nd Inf. · 49, 50
Wofford's Brigade · 81
Wood, Fernando · 71
Wood, Thomas W. · 8
Woodbury, Daniel P. · 41
Worcester, MA · 28
Wright's Georgia Brigade · 84
Wyckoff, Mac · 137

Y

York River · 169
Yorktown · 207

Z

Zook's Brigade · 64, 80, 104, 105